PRIVATE EYE ANNUAL 2023

EDITED BY IAN HISLOP

Published in Great Britain by
Private Eye Productions Ltd
6 Carlisle Street, London W1D 3BN
www.private-eye.co.uk

© 2023 Pressdram Ltd
ISBN 978-1-901784-73-2
Designed by Bridget Tisdall
Printed and bound in Italy
by L.E.G.O. S.p.A

2 4 6 8 10 9 7 5 3 1

PRIVATE EYE ANNUAL 2023

EDITED BY IAN HISLOP

*"What can you recommend to go
with Aperol Spritz?"*

POETRY CORNER

In Memoriam Queen Elizabeth II (1926-2022)

So. Farewell
Then Your Majesty.

You spent your life
Waving at us
And now it is us
Who must
Wave goodbye
To you.

> E.J. Thribbute
> (poet laureate-in-waiting)

GOD SAVE THE QUEUE!

How long did you have to wait?

Not as long as you!

DID MEGHAN KILL THE QUEEN?

Almost undoubtedly.

"I'm not really a mourning person"

THE TIME THE QUEEN SPOKE TO ME
by all MPs, Journalists and Celebrities

I WILL never forget the moment the Queen looked me in the eye and addressed me directly.

It was one Christmas, just after lunch, and I was in my living room. I will always remember what she said to me: "This has been a difficult year," she confided, and told me frankly that over the last twelve months she had visited various Commonwealth countries, including Canada and the Gilbert and Sullivan Islands.

Sadly, I fell asleep at this point. And when I awoke, she did not bat an eyelid, but gracefully and courteously continued, almost as if she hadn't noticed.

She was charm personified, and concluded by smiling and wishing me a very merry Christmas. *(You never met her, did you? Ed.)*

RADIO HIGHLIGHTS

Just an Hour
with Gyles Brandreth
(All channels)

Respectful funeral fun from the BBC, as Gyles Brandreth is set the task of speaking for 60 minutes about Her Majesty the Queen and the Duke of Edinburgh without hestitation, but with an enormous amount of repetition and deviation!

Enjoy no one interrupting him as he delivers an endless and seamless monologue containing all those familiar anecdotes, reminiscences and tall tales that have made Gyles a by-word for filling airtime.

Can he keep it going? Of course he can.

EYE RATING: *Buzzzzzzzzzzzzz*

That Westminster Abbey Funeral Procession in Full

(continued from page one)

On Foot

Gentlemen Herald Tribunes Pursuivant

The Knights of the Garter Who Say Ni

Regimental Band of the Coldplay Guards

Her Majesty's Brigade of Archers (led by Eddie Grundy and Linda Snell)

Midshipmen from HMS *BoatyMcBoatface*

Queen Consort's Own Beefeater and Tonics

The Royal Canadian Mounted Lumberjacks (dismounted)

Moderators of the Presbyterian Church of Twitter

1st Division of Chefs from the Household Carvery

Chaplains to the Bishops Move of London

First National Express Coach

His Royal Highness King Kong

The Emperor Ming of Merciless

Queen Daenerys, Mother of Dragons

King Burger of Whoppers

The Life President of the Gilbert and Sullivan Islands

First Replacement Bus

The Duke and Duchess of Potato

The Dowager Countess of Grantham

Count Binface

The late Count Dracula

First Black Maria

Prince Andrew

> *(That's enough procession. Ed.)*

Moving tributes paid to the queue

TRIBUTES from Britain and around the world poured in today as the Queue suddenly came to a sad and abrupt end.

The Queue had come to symbolise everything about Britain, so it was only natural that there would be an outpouring of grief at its passing.

"We will never see the Queue's like again," agreed everyone, "at least, not until Asda opens again at 5pm after the funeral."

With its quiet dignity, the Queue symbolised a devotion to proper British values without recourse to rioting, chuggers and dogging. It will long be missed.

Twitter users shocked at Twitter being Twitter

A famous person on Twitter has expressed outrage and disgust that during the period of mourning after the death of the Queen, Twitter users have continued behaving exactly as they always do on Twitter.

"I am shocked and sickened to see that rather than being obsequious in tone to our new King, people on Twitter are continuing to act as disrespectfully as they always have done and are posting the same distasteful jokes and memes they always do," said the famous Twitter user.

"Instead of maintaining a period of digital silence, they have posted endless tweets, even during the funeral," he tweeted.

"No one wants to read about the clergyman dropping the piece of paper, the candle placed in front of Meghan's face, or Harry singing 'God help us, Charles is King'.

"Why did no one tell me that Twitter was not *(cont. p94)*

Queue Jumpers

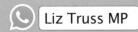

The Brand New Prime Minister's WhatsApp Group

> Hi! This is Prime Minister Truss's first message. Wow! I'm Prime Minister! I can't believe it!

Boris Johnson
Nor can I.

> Oh, I thought you'd been banned. Particularly after you finished off the Queen.

Boris Johnson
Now look here, Trusster. Her Maj was in fine fettle when I last saw her. When I told her I'd come to resign, she gave a big smile and danced a little jig, I've never seen her in a better mood. "My work here is done," she said, whatever she meant by that.

> Don't accuse me of getting rid of the Queen. I've always been in favour of the Royal Family, ever since I wasn't.

Jacob Rees-Mogg
Splendid and loyal sentiments, Elizabeth, if I may be so bold. Your ability to hold two contradictory opinions at once reminds me of our dear departed former great leader.

> Thanks, Business, Energy and Industrial Strategy Secretary.

Boris Johnson
Who says you don't have a sense of humour, Liz?! By the way, great tribute to Her Majesty. Shame it wasn't as good as the one I gave, which rather stole your thunder. Sorry about that. Utterly unintentional.

> Admit it, you're furious that I get to do the whole 10-Day Funereal Photo Op. Big black hat, little black dress, front row seat, on telly 24/7, hobnobbing with world leaders and reading the lesson. You'd have loved it!

The Administrator has removed Mr Johnson from the group.

> Now, let's get on with business – or should I say Lizness?

Jacob Rees-Mogg
Oh I say! What a capital start to your Premiership wordplay!

Thérèse Coffey
Listen, Poshboy, if anyone's going to blow smoke up Liz's arse, it's me. I've got the cigar and I'm raring to go.

> Thank you, Health Secretary. Now, first item on the agenda is to announce the details of our energy bill. It's a massive subsidy to the British public of £150 billion. It's great news.

Kwasi Kwarteng
Have we worked out how we're paying for this handout?

> It's not a handout, remember. We don't do those. It's a fiscal event.

Suella Braverman
You mean a Budget?

> No. The one thing it isn't is a Budget. If it was a Budget, the Office of Budget Responsibility would look at it closely and predict whether or not it was going to work. And we don't want that.

Kwasi Kwarteng
The important thing is, we're not like Labour. We don't tax and spend. We cut tax and spend more.

> It's called Trussonomics!

Jacob Rees-Mogg
Marvellous! As your Business, Energy and Whatnot Minister, may I say that the old-fashioned Treasury orthodoxy of balancing the books and making the sums add up is horribly out-of-date.

Thérèse Coffey
Just like you!

> Please, would everybody behave. This is going to be a unified Cabinet, where we treat each other respectfully and show loyalty to our colleagues.

Jacob Rees-Mogg
Most amusing, Prime Minister.

Kwasi Kwarteng
One small point. Now that we've given a handout to the poor, do you think we should level up, as it were, and give an extra handout to the rich? Let's cancel the cap on bankers' bonuses.

Jacob Rees-Mogg
I for one think it's an excellent idea! My objective view is that it's only just and fair for the very, very rich to be given the incentive to be even richer.

> That makes sense. More Trussonomics!

How is the Queen now?

THE GNOME'S ASTROLOGER **HORACE COPE** FINDS OUT

WELL, luvs, I've pierced the veil, and I can reveal to you now that our dear Maj is very happy. Very happy indeed. She's been reunited with her favourite corgis and she's having tea with her late father, Charles Darwin and Maureen from *Driving School*, who was a close personal friend of mine.

And I can tell you now that she and Princess Diana are getting on like a house on fire, would you believe it? Tonight they're doing karaoke with Elvis and Keith Flint from the Prodigy, and guess what? Diana has completely forgiven the newspapers for hounding her and she wishes Camilla well in supporting dear old Charles.

Is this respectful enough? *(Yes. More from the astral plane please. Ed.)*

"Stop comparing yourself to others, you're a better person than that"

IS GWYNETH PALTROW DESPERATE FOR MEDIA ATTENTION?

by **Phil Space**

As Gwyneth Paltrow hits fifty, the world is once again asking "Have we not seen enough of her naked ambition?"

Every year it's the same. Gwynnie poses in her birthday suit, leaving little to the imagination, in the belief that minimal clothing coverage will gain maximum press coverage.

Well, Ms Paltrow, we're just not falling for it! Nobody's interested in you and your perfectly toned physique any more. And no, we don't care if you're nude in a bath, aged 49, and we care even less if you're painted gold, aged 50. Nor will we be interested in seeing how you present that remarkably well-preserved starkers body of yours next year! We do NOT want to see it! Put some clothes on, for God's sake!

INSIDE
Gwynnie bares all, as she leaves her Phwoarties in style!
Pages 2-94

"Well, it'll just have to wait, won't it?!"

HEALTH SECRETARY – 'I'M NOT A ROLE MODEL'

by Our Health Staff **Monty Cristo** and **Dom Perignon**

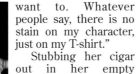

THE recently appointed Minister for Health, Thérèse Coffey, has acknowledged that her own personal life choices should not necessarily be followed by others.

"Okay," she said, in between sips and puffs, "I admit that I'm a Conservative. It's my vice. But just because I'm a Tory doesn't mean it's a good idea for everyone else."

She went on to say, "Some may say that it's a nasty habit, and it's really bad for everyone's wellbeing, but it's a free country and I'm just going to carry on living life the way I want to. Whatever people say, there is no stain on my character, just on my T-shirt."

Stubbing her cigar out in her empty flute, she concluded, "Yes, it can be harmful to others and there may be instances of suffering from passive Conservatism but, trust me, the more you drink and smoke, the less long you'll have to live under Tories like me."

LATE NEWS
■ Critics claim Health Secretary has already missed important target, ie her mouth, judging by wine stain on t-shirt **p3**

Working From the Pub – our reporter writes

by Our Workplace Correspondent
Lunchtime O'Boozer

I'VE been sent to Work From the Pub, which is going to be the new trend this year! It's too expensive to warm your house and the office has given away my desk, so I'm going to be spending the day here and reporting back for the paper.

This is a really brilliant development, because it keeps pubs in business and means hard-working freelancers get a bit of company, rather than sitting alone in their flats!

9.34am So far, so good. It's lovely and cosy, there's free tea all day, and I'm really getting on well with this article! Maybe I'll reward myself with a small drink in a bit!

10.16am I've plugged in my laptop, the music's nice and quiet, and I'm writing extremely fast. Not only that, I've decided to have my end of the day pint early, so I feel the benefit for longer. Great stuff.

10.44am End-of-day pint finished earlier than expected, so am having tomorrow's pint now too, meaning I'll be able to clear my head sooner and write more tomorrow. Feeling nice and warm and getting a surprising amount of writing done here too – think this could catch on!

11.22am Have had my lunch sandwich already – the sun's over the yardarm and I think it'll be a good idea to accompany it with a small glass of red! Whilst I'm at it, think I'll have my post-lunch Scotch now for added concentration! Have written down some brilliant ideas, although my writing's a bit hard to read for some reason. Also the table must be very wobbly, because I've just spillled my Irish coffee.

12.03pm Am having Friday's round of post-wrok shotsz becuse there's no problem with my work ethic nad the boss nca fog furek himself. Fi hre rings me I'sll tell him sotoe his facce.

12.39pm don't ettll mme wehat to do yo u bastreds I am RWEROKING FROERM THEPUBFN.

1.03pm bledfdsf.

THE ☙ TIMES

New editor for the Times announced

Old editor   New editor

Times NewsCorpse was today delighted to announce that the next editor of the prestigious London Times of London will be the promising, youthful, 98-year-old Rupert Murdoch, who takes over from the much-respected veteran, 98-year-old Rupert Murdoch.

Said the new editor, "It's a privilege to be taking over from such a great newspaperman. Rupert had an instinctive feel for news and a genuine desire to tell his employees what to write. I intend to follow in his footsteps to the best of my ability, but he's a hard act to follow. You, Gallagher, drop that story about Boris and the blow-job! And get me some tea while you're at it! Attaboy!"

A Doctor Writes

AS a doctor, I am often asked, "Doctor, what can I do? I'm suffering from severe stress." The simple answer is "You're a doctor too, aren't you?"

What happens is the patient, or rather the doctor in this case, experiences symptoms including exhaustion and depression, and finds it difficult to carry on working.

This syndrome is known by the acronym NHSGP or, to give it its full technical name, *medicalis sanitas nationalis servicium normalis*.

The only known cure is to quit, go private, go to Australia and find work there, either as a doctor or as something less stressful like a crocodile wrestler or shark patrol officer.

If you're worried about being a doctor and would like to see a doctor about it, there's a shorter wait if you just look in the mirror. © *A doctor*

POUND 'REACHES PARITY WITH THE TURNIP'

PRIME MINISTER Liz Truss has insisted that her economic plans, as laid out in the Chancellor's fiscal statement, will eventually work, despite the pound for the first time in its history reaching parity with the turnip.

"I'm not going to join the doom-mongers who see this as some sort of humiliation for Great Britain," a defiant Liz Truss told reporters. "It's easy to forget that the turnip was once the pre-eminent currency during the Dark Ages, and it feels that long ago that the pound was too.

"I believe that once my economic plan is fully implemented, the pound will regain its strength and by early 2023 will be on parity once more with the kumquat and even, possibly, the pineapple."

Notes&queries

Who or what is a Kwarteng?

A Kwarteng, as any physicist will tell you, is a sub-atomic particle released when a boson implodes after contact with a kwark. It is one of the smallest nucleoids to have been identified by the Large Hadron Collider. The best known quality of the Kwarteng is that it absorbs all known matter into a collapsing hole and is so dense that light cannot pass through it. Some scientists believe that there is an even denser sub-particle which imitates the behaviour of the Kwarteng. This is known as the Quasi Quarteng.
Professor Stephen Hawkwind, Department of Astro-Pysics, University of Brian May (formerly Queen's College)

Professor Hawkwind is looking through the wrong end of his electron microscope, I fear! *Kwarteng!*, as any student of British comedy will tell you, is the catchphrase of one of Lenny Henry characters from the show *Tiswiz!* Sir Leonard, as he is now, would appear in African costume and shout *Kwarteng!* before emptying a bucket of custard over Chris Tarrant. Of course, it wouldn't be allowed in today's woke media world, as health and safety would require a trigger warning alerting audiences to upsetting scenes of "violence involving dairy desserts"!
Professor Mike Rutherford, Department of Mechanics, University of Genesis (formerly Charterhouse School)

Oh dear, so much for the knowledge of some of our supposedly distinguished professors! Kwarteng is actually a type of tea grown mostly in China's Qua Zi province. Its pungent flavour is similar to Sajeeling and Lap Sap Suella Chong but very unlike the mild and watery David Camomile. Kwarteng was at one time highly prized by beverage importers, but sadly its price per pound has now plummeted and it is now virtually worthless. Hence the common expression, first coined by traders on the markets, "Kwarteng's not my cup of tea!"
Professor Van de Graff-Generator, Department of Rock Science, The Free University (formerly Amorous Poly)

TRUSS GOES FOR BROKE!

POUND CRASH

MORTGAGE DISASTER

CONFERENCE GLOOM

U-TURN FARCE

A Tank Driver writes

"Rumour has it you're a bit reckless"

Vlad 'Mad' Putin, Tank No: ZZZZ
Every week a well-known tank driver gives his opinion on a matter of topical importance. This week, the recent reverses in fortune of the special military operation, and the appearance of roadworks on the Kerch Bridge, leading to an irritating contraflow system and a tailback to Moscow…

YOU WANT to go to the Crimea, mate? I'm not going South this time of night. Or any other time, really. Cos they've only gone and blown the bridge up. We are going to have to go the loooong way round. Via Belarus. Sorry about that. Bloody terrorists, using explosives to attack military targets. I mean that's not how you do it, is it?! Look. There's a civilian. Whoops. Not anymore. Sorry mate, but they really wind me up. Like our state-of-the-art nuclear missiles. I mean I'm not racist, but those Ukrainians. What's their problem?! Well, I am, obviously. But why don't they want to be part of dear old Mother Russia? What's not to like? If them Ukrainians stopped fighting and became Russian, I could conscript them and they could start fighting again. Against the real enemy. Ukrainians. Stands to reason, doesn't it? And I'm a reasonable man. Anyone says I isn't and it'll be no more Mr Nice Guy. And no more them. Or their children. These problems need to be nuked on the head. Anyway, Happy Birthday to me, by the way. Guess how old I am. Nah, you bastard, I'm only 70! And in perfect health. Is that the earth shaking as the result of an explosion? Oh no – it's just me. And did I tell you I'm in perfect health? Got all my marbles. And some other people's as well. Some say I should retire. But I say – Nah! I like the job. Driving a tank, gets me out of the house. Away from all the Missuses. Moan. Moan. Moan. Why is money suddenly tight? Why aren't there any potatoes in the shops? Don't look at me. I said DON'T LOOK AT ME!! I'd shut that window in the back or else you might fall out of it. Oh whoops-a-daisy! I did warn you. And people think I'm bluffing! I had that General Armageddon in the back of my tank. Very clever and knowledgeable man. Told me to keep going. Put my foot on the gas. And stop it flowing!

© A tank driver.

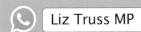
Kwasi Kwarteng
Hello? Hello? Anyone seen Liz?

Kwasi Kwarteng
HELLO?!!! Is there anyone here? Come on, guys, talk to me!

Rishi Sunak
Hi, Kwasi. How's it going? Sorry to hear about the financial crash and all that.

Kwasi Kwarteng
Everything's fine. Everything's going to plan. As I will explain on November the 23rd.

Rishi Sunak
If you're still there, mate ☝ . Sorry I can't be at the conference to help out. Very busy in my constituency. A lot of voters complaining about something. Better find out what it is 😕 .

Rishi Sunak has left the group.

Kwasi Kwarteng
At least he didn't say "I told you so".

Rishi Sunak has joined the group.

Rishi Sunak
By the way. Forgot to say. I told you so.

Sorry, Liz here, Prime Minister, remember? Been terribly busy facing the music. Well, it was the Bee Gees on Good Morning Derbyshire.

Rishi Sunak
Was the song "Tragedy"?

Thérèse Coffey
No, it was not, Rishi. I was having my breakfast. Cigar. Champagne. And appropriately the song was "Staying Alive".

Thank you, Health Secretary. The important thing is that I've spoken not only to Susan Smedley on Good Morning Derbyshire's popular "Top of The Peaks" slot, but I've also spoken to President Zelensky and I've confirmed my absolute support for the Ukraine.

Rishi Sunak
Has he asked for the UK contribution to be in roubles rather than pounds? 🙈

Haven't you got a constituency to go to?

Rishi Sunak
Unlike most Tory MPs in three weeks' time. Just saying. Bye!

Rishi Sunak has left the group.

Right, Chancellor – about your budget.

Kwasi Kwarteng
MY budget?!

Yes, YOUR budget.

Kwasi Kwarteng
It was OUR budget! It was Trussonomics in action.

No, it wasn't. it was Kwartenomics!

Kwasi Kwarteng
Would it help if I gave some more money to hedge-fund millionaires to really get the economy going?

Crispin Odious
Yes, please! Good thought, Kwarteng. You were always a promising lad when you worked for Odious Asset Management. That's why I bet so heavily against you! Kwasi Kerching!!! 💰

Kwasi Kwarteng
Thank you, sir. Will you promise me to trickle the money down and not just keep it all?

Crispin Odious
Yes. Absolutely. My word is my bond. So would you like to buy it at a very inflated rate? 💰💰

Kwasi Kwarteng
Sounds like a great deal to me!

Why's everyone ignoring me? I'm the Prime Minister, you know. This is my group. I want you to listen to me! I'm the one in charge here!!!

Kwasi Kwarteng
Oh, so it WAS your budget?

The International Monetary Fund has joined the group.

IMF
WTF?!

It's all going very well. Thank you for your concern but I know what I'm doing, as I told Radio Humberside only this morning. Weren't the IMF listening to that?

IMF
FFS!!

Thérèse Coffey
You were great, Liz! I heard you just between the traffic update and the School Run Shout Out when the Beatles were singing "Help"!

IMF
OMG!!

Ken from Radio Humberside was concerned about the Chancellor's budget.

IMF
UK RIP!!!

POETRY CORNER

In Memoriam Hilary Mantel, Booker Prize-winning author of the Wolf Hall trilogy

So. Farewell
Then Hilary Mantel.

Sadly, we have reached
The end of
Your story.

Many readers imagine
That now you will
Meet Thomas Cromwell,
Who you made the hero
Of your Tudor epic.

But perhaps, as my
History teacher said,
You were a bit
Too kind to him
And he's actually
Down below,
Where we hope
You aren't.

E.J. Thribb
(17½ pages read,
though I did watch the entire telly
series with Mark Rylance)

Mantelsplaining

"She was certainly one of our greatest female writers"

Russian tourists spotted near Nord Stream pipeline

by Our Travel Correspondent
Jason Bournholm

TWO entirely innocent Russian tourists, with an interest in deep-sea marine engineering, have been identified loitering several fathoms below the surface of the Baltic Sea.

The two tourists, who were enthusing about the marvellous 750-mile pipeline, had gone for a day trip to see the underwater sights.

"This is our best excursion since Salisbury Cathedral," said Colonel Cutgazov. "Yes, indeed," agreed his friend and fellow sub-aquatic architecture enthusiast, Major Blowitupski.

"It truly is a feat of energy-supply construction genius and it would be a great shame if anything ever happened to it, depriving the West of all energy forever.

"We were a bit disappointed not to find a café or a gift shop, as we were hoping to buy a fridge magnet saying 'I've blown up...' I mean, 'visited the Nord Stream Pipeline'."

"You won't believe it, but we met online"

ONLINE EXPERTS ON COVID AND WAR ALSO EXPERTS ON ECONOMICS

by Our Expertise Correspondent
Noah Itall

IN A shock development, all the people on the internet who have spent the last two years being massive experts on epidemiology and land wars in Europe have turned out to know enormous amounts about macroeconomics and how to ensure growth while carefully controlling tax and spending.

One person you follow online, who appears to have studied English Literature and doesn't even have an ISA, is now offering wise advice to anyone who will listen about how to stabilise the gilt market and why the Bank of England is economically illiterate to have intervened as it did last week. This person – who has lots of followers for a reason you can't understand – also knows huge amounts about both military procurement failures leading up to Russia's invasion of Ukraine and why it was perfectly obvious there was going to be a pandemic, despite them not even spelling "coronavirus" correctly until May 2020.

Another person, who has GCSE maths but no more, has done "a lot of my own research" into how to run one of the biggest economies on the planet and is fairly sure they know where Kwasi Kwarteng went wrong.

On other pages
■ Same people know what the weather will be like tomorrow, unless it isn't, in which case they will have already known that too

President Putin 'denies sabotage'

by Our Russian Correspondent
Perry Stroka

PRESIDENT Putin has rubbished EU claims that Russia sabotaged the Nord Stream 1 and 2 pipelines that run under the Baltic Sea to North-eastern Germany, insisting the two pipelines had voted in a referendum to blow themselves up.

"We respect the democratic right of these two gas pipelines to vote freely and fairly to blow themselves up," President Putin told the Russian people in an address from his bunker.

"Oh no, not more Scandi drama"

Royston

WORD CLOUD ABOUT WORD CLOUDS

Desperate Misleading
Meaningless Lighter font
Small font
Piss-poor Annoying Unread
Dull
Lazy Snooze
Formulaic Big font
Yawn Boring Unresearched
Page-filler Made-up

Open marriage

Top media couple **Phil** and **Philippa Space** talk frankly about the subject that's on every couple's minds.

A few years ago, as a happily married couple, we discussed having an open marriage.
Yes, we certainly did, dear.
It's all about trust and communication. And we both agreed it was a bad idea.
Oh...
What do you mean, "oh"?
Is that what we agreed?
Well, I thought we did. Are you telling me you had an affair?
I thought you said it was all right? Because you said you fancied Brad Pitt.
I didn't mean I was shagging him. He was just on telly.
Oh, I seem to have got the wrong end of the stick.
Who was it, you bastard?
I'm not saying I slept with Sandra from Design.
Sandra! That cow?
It meant nothing. It was after the Christmas party.
You bastard!
I was drunk.
In that case, I don't feel so bad about Trevor.
What! Trevor from Marketing? You never!
Might have. Three times. And sober.
Well, that's it, we're finished!
What, the marriage?
No, writing this article.
Oh, do you mind if I write another article about open marriage with someone else?
Of course.
Is that a yes or a no?
It's a definite... (continued p94)

DIARY

THE REV. RICHARD COLES

Richard Coles @RevRichardColes
Have you ever been for a ride in a sledge pulled by huskies?

Richard Coles @RevRichardColes
Me neither.

What goes up must come down, or so they say. But what if something doesn't go up? Surely it can't then go down, because down is where it already is. I was grappling with this great imponderable in the company of my good friend Professor Brian Cox the other day. It got me thinking about all the other things which go both up and down. Prices, for instance. Bouncy balls. Kites. And Spacehoppers. Now we're on the subject, whatever happened to Spacehoppers? As a novice vicar in a rural parish, I once successfully delivered a sermon on the miracle of the loaves and fishes while bouncing about on a Spacehopper. The congregation seemed to enjoy it, or at any rate those who were still there at the end. I told this to my new best friend TV news presenter Graeme Matlock and he found the notion of my Spacehopper homily really quite amusing.

Richard Coles @RevRichardColes
Anyone got a favourite husky story?

Richard Coles @RevRichardColes
Me neither.

Ho-hum. My eye was caught last week by an item about the best way to bake a quiche. Being partial to quiche of all, or at least most, varieties, I took an especial interest in the item. The trick seems to be to follow any given recipe, rather than improvise. Having set eyes on said item, my new friend Alan Titchmarsh, of horticultural renown, called to say that his own favourite was Quiche Lorraine. I asked Alan if there was a Lorraine in his family, and whether this might have biased him towards his choice. When he had stopped snorting with laughter, he assured me that his family contained no Lorraines, but

several Sarahs. "Sadly, there's no Quiche Sarah as yet, Alan!" I quipped, without pausing. "But if ever I hear of one, I'll be sure to let you know!"

Richard Coles @RevRichardColes
Absolutely nothing to tweet about today. Ho-hum. Anyone out there suffering from a similar problem?

Richard Coles @RevRichardColes
I just thought of something to write about, but then seconds later forgot what it was!

Richard Coles @RevRichardColes
Doh, as the incorrigible Homer Simpson might put it!

Recently, I've caught the bird-spotting bug off my new buddy Jim Moir, aka Vic Reeves of "Reeves and Mortimer" fame. Bird-spotting might not be something you would normally associate with gay men of the cloth, though of course I'm now talking about birds of the feathered variety. I've made some useful discoveries. At the seaside, one is more prone to finding seagulls, hence their name. In fact, now I come to think of it, the names of a great many birds hold the clue to their distinguishing characteristics. The blackbird, for instance, has exceptionally black feathers, while swifts fly very fast, woodpeckers peck at wood and auks can be embarrassing.

Richard Coles @RevRichardColes
Left a filtered milk out yesterday and it's gone off. That's never happened before.

Richard Coles @RevRichardColes
I tell a lie. It did once, but quite a while ago.

Richard Coles @RevRichardColes
We're talking well over a year ago, or possibly closer to eighteen months.

Market day, so I went to pick up a loaf for my neighbour and gazpacho ingredients for me. On the way back I stopped at the deli for a flat white and joined another neighbour and her friend for a flat white.

This got me thinking. It's not often you pick up a loaf for our neighbour, buy ingredients for gazpacho and join your neighbour and her friend for a flat white at the local deli, and all on the same morning. And on the way home, I spotted a navy-blue volvo, a fairly uncommon occurrence, given the way so many Volvos seem to be silver or white these days. What are the chances of all these things happening within the space of an hour or two? Very small, I would guess.

"I'll tell you what," I said, as we settled the bill, "I'm going to ask my new buddy Rachel Riley of Countdown fame what the odds are on all these things happening at once."

Gratifyingly, my neighbour and her friend agreed that this might be a very good idea indeed.

Richard Coles @RevRichardColes
Are eggs better scrambled or poached? The jury's out.

Richard Coles @RevRichardColes
Then again, if you feel like just one egg, then poached is probably the better option. (You may of course disagree).

Back to gazpacho. I've been a fan of this refreshing, chilled Spanish soup for many years, ever since I first encountered it in a much-visited cafe in Barcelona. I always make it with tomatoes, cucumber, garlic, red onions, green peppers, olive oil and leftover bread, though some friends, including my new buddy Richard Madeley, of Richard and Judy fame, always insists that sherry vinegar is also an essential ingredient. Moreover, Richard's gazpacho is a model of its kind. Ho-hum. It all goes to show that, in any human enterprise, there is neither a right way nor a wrong way of doing things. If we are able to draw advice from all sections of the community – young and old, gay and straight, rich and poor – then we should surely do so. Variety is, as they say, the spice of life.

Richard Coles @RevRichardColes
I am minded to add a portobello mushroom to the holy trinity of beans, fish-fingers and toast. Your thoughts?

Richard Coles @RevRichardColes
Are zebras black with white stripes, or white with black stripes? Well worth a ponder.

Richard Coles @RevRichardColes
One thing I've noticed. Once you've toasted bread, it's impossible to de-toast it, ie turn it back into bread. Or is it? Come on, all you aspiring inventors out there!

Richard Coles @RevRichardColes
No funny husky stories, unfortunately. Anyone got a funny story about a dachshund they'd like to share?

As told to
CRAIG BROWN

ALL HOMES TO BE RETRO-FITTED WITH 'DAD'

by Our Energy Correspondent A.R.P. Warden

DESPITE refusing to conduct a public information campaign to reduce energy consumption over the winter months, the government confirmed today that it would be retro-fitting every UK home with a "dad".

"These 'dads' are incredible devices for slashing energy consumption, spending their time walking around the house muttering 'I'm not made of money you know'.

"Their role will be to turn off lights in empty rooms, turn down radiators and thermostats, then switch off the heating after an hour, telling their children, 'It can go back on after I win the lottery'," said a government spokesman.

Downing Street says that by retro-fitting all UK homes with a "dad" for the winter months, we can slash the nation's energy usage by a third, thereby ensuring no rolling blackouts.

"Well, I'm sorry, dear, but you'll just have to play spaceships somewhere else"

Liz Truss MP | **The Caretaker Prime Minister's 'Looze with Liz' WhatsApp Group**

Before I say goodbye, I'd like to thank you all for the amazing job you did helping me achieve so much in my time as Prime Minister. Firstly, I am proud to say that under my leadership, the Queen died.

Jeremy Hunt
And then the economy did as well.

I wasn't going to mention that. You have to be bold. And I was. And decisive. And I was.

Jeremy Hunt
If by bold and decisive, you mean reckless and mad, then fair enough.

Thank you, Jeremy. That's very kind, but the global circumstances were wrong.

Thérèse Coffey
That's right, hun, we really should have asked the global circumstances to resign in disgrace. You did a great job.

Jeremy Hunt
Have you been drinking, Thérèse?

Thérèse Coffey
Of course, I'm Minister of Health. I'm self-medicating. 🍷🍷🍷

Before I go, I'd like to quote a Roman philosopher called Sennapod.

Thérèse Coffey
I think you mean Seneca, luv. Though I've got some old Sennapod in my handbag if you're a bit bunged up.

James Cleverly
Bunged up? The rest of us have got the shits! 💩💩💩

It was Sennapod who once said "a low tax economy based on unfunded borrowing guarantees growth".

Jeremy Hunt
No he didn't, Liz.

I also wanted to add, in my defence, that whoever takes over will inherit...

At this point, WhatsApp crashed, unable to cope with the unprecedented volume of political manoeuvring by Conservative leadership candidates and there was a nationwide outage lasting several hours.

Thank you for listening.

Jeremy Hunt
Gosh, that's an amazing achievement, Liz. You've managed to crash WhatsApp as well as the economy. 👏

Boris Johnson has joined the group.

Boris Johnson
Guess who's back, folks, to save the day! It's the Bozzter! It's Cincinnatus back from his sun-lounger by the pool! It's Sir Boris Churchill back from his tropical luxury wilderness to save a grateful nation once again!

Thérèse Coffey
I think we all need a drink now. 🍺🍸

Boris Johnson
It's King Arthur, the once and future World King, yanking his sword out of the missus to claim his birthright! Sorry, a big jet-lagged. History a bit all over the shop. Here's me rounding up the troops.

 Forget Party Gate, it's Party Great!

Jacob Rees-Mogg
Hurrah! It's the Second Coming! It's the Resurrection, He is with us! Exultamus et jubilamus!

Boris Johnson
Thanks, Creepie, now let's make this happen. I've got the numbers. Dudders assures me I've got 350 million MPs behind me, so I'll be in Downing Street by Friday. Put the wine back in the fridge and get the paper hats out, we're going to party like it's 1922! 🥳🎉

Sir James Duddridge MP
Um, about those numbers. It's less like 350 million and more like 54.

Boris Johnson
What?! Dudders by name, Dudders by nature! Still, never mind! The dear old dotty members won't listen to the MPs. They adore me!

Sir Graham Brady
Hm, perhaps we won't let the members have a say this time.

Boris Johnson
Pish and tosh, Brady Bunchster! The momentum's behind me. I've just got to do a deal with Rishi or get into bed with Penny.

Nadine Dorries
Boo-hoo-hoo, it's so unfair. 😢👎

Boris Johnson
Not literally, Mad Nad. Though those old swimsuit shots... Phwoar! Splash! I'm up for it! The leadership, that is. 😏🥒

Sir Graham Brady
Following a hasty overhauling of the system, we have decided that Boris has lost, Rishi Sunak has won, and there will be no need to send emails to the nursing homes of this great nation to get their view.

Rishi Sunak has joined the group.

Rishi Sunak
Hello, everyone. And goodbye, most of you. I've just won! This is MY WhatsApp group now. My ultra-cool media team have renamed it "Liz Out to Help Out".

I don't get it.

The administrator has removed Liz Truss from the group.

NEW FRONT DOOR INSTALLED AT No.10

ME AND MY SPOON

THIS WEEK

MIRIAM MARGOLYES

Do you have a favourite spoon?

Fuck off! Whoops! Silly me! Am I on air?

Yes. As a leading actress, have spoons played an important part in your career?

Fuck off, you bastard! Sorry, what am I like? Honestly! You can't take me anywhere – except up the jacksey! Whoops! Naughty old Miriam!

Has anything amusing ever happened to you in connection with a spoon?

Yes! I once bumped into Stephen Fry, who offered me his spoon to stir my tea. And instead, I put the spoon right up his...

Oh fuck! Get this woman off the fucking programme before I get fucking fired!

Me And My Spoon would like to apologise to any reader who may have been subjected to some bad language in the course of this interview.

NEXT WEEK: *Bob Geldof – Me and My Fucking Money.*

That Elon Musk Ukraine peace plan in full

- Referendum to be held on Twitter answering question *"Is Elon Musk the man to bring peace to Europe?"*

- Ukraine to lose Crimea and occupied provinces, subject to democratic ballots conducted by independent, heavily-armed Russian observers

- Russia to declare victory in return for promising not to nuke Tesla headquarters in Texas

- Ceasefire to be guaranteed by driverless miniature submarines, built by MuskSubs Inc, roaming

- Black Sea armed with peace-seeking Russian missiles

- Anyone who objects to Musk peace deal will be called a "pedo guy" and banned from Twitter before being zapped by new giant SpaceX death ray *(coming soon)*

- Musk to receive Nobel Peace Prize and moon, as soon as it is annexed by Russian peace delegation

(That's enough peace plan. Ed.)

"I'm taking you off the iron tablets"

Outrage as minister called the 'C' word

THERE was fury amidst Conservatives last night after the broadcaster Robert Peston referred to Jeremy Hunt MP by the "C" word.

Peston, in his acclaimed ITV show *Peston with Peston*, starring Robert Peston, was heard calling Jeremy Hunt "Chancellor".

Said one disgusted viewer, "I can't believe I just heard that live on television. It may have been an honest mistake, but there's no excuse for making the man who brought the Health Service to its knees the new Chancellor of the Exchequer. If Peston wants to call him a c*nt, then fair enough, but the rest of us do not want to hear that Hunt's got one of the highest offices in the country."

Jeremy Hunt commented, "This puts me on a par with Steve Baker, who was called the 'C' word on Channel 4 News."

Krishnan Guru-Murthy has been suspended for referring to Mr Baker as a "C*nservative", when we all know he's a raving far-right Euro-nutter.

(Rotters)

CHANNEL FOUR PROGRAMME IDEAS MEETING

"...and thousands have died in this latest disaster..."

"Doesn't he look a prat in that scarf"

JOHNSON NOT TO WITHDRAW FROM PUBLIC LIFE
by Our Political Staff **U. Biquitious**

RACHEL JOHNSON has dramatically announced that she will not retire, saying it is "in the national interest" for her to be on television or radio "at this time and, in fact, all the time".

Despite pressure from colleagues and friends to step down, the blonde former Prime Minister's sister was adamant that she would continue to talk about her brother on national media until "at least 2024 and maybe beyond".

This means that the contest to be the most annoying Johnson must go to another round, with Stanley Johnson declaring that he too is "still in it to win it" and claiming to have "hundreds of supporters".

Meanwhile, Lord Jo Johnson of *(cont. 2094)*

US satirist in UK racism row

by Our TV Correspondent **Tess Daly-Show**

TOP American TV satirist Trevor Noah-Idea has expressed his shock at the levels of racism in Britain, following the broadcast of a single nutter talking about Rishi Sunak on a LBC phone-in show.

Said Noah-Clue, "This is appalling! One bloke ranting on local radio constitutes a racist backlash on a scale unseen in... say, America... where we merely have occasional police victimisation of innocent black citizens, the odd KKK lynch mob terrorising communities and a few joggers shot by armed householders for daring to be black in possession of trainers."

Said a British spokesperson, "This really is the pot calling the kettle racist."

13

The New Prime Minister's Highly Confidential WhatsApp Group

> Right, everyone, let's get down to business. So my first job is to assemble a Cabinet of All the Talents.

Jacob Rees-Mogg
That won't take long. Hahaha. Quite amusing, if I say so myself.

The administrator has removed Jacob Rees-Mogg from the group.

Boris Johnson
Damn and blast you, Rishi! I could have been Prime Minister if I wanted to. But I didn't. I won, really. But in the national interest, I decided to lose. So now the result's been decided, I'm pulling out early.

Jeremy Hunt
That's a first!

The administrator has removed Boris Johnson from the group.

> When I say Cabinet of All the Talents, I mean All the Talents. Plus Dominic Raab. And James Cleverly. And Gavin Williamson, Nadhim Zahawi and Grant Shapps.

Matt Hancock
May I be the first to congratulate you, Prime Minister. You are an extraordinarily brilliant person and will make an incredible Prime Minister. Wise, imaginative and with the boldness of vision to give former Health Ministers a second chance.

Jeremy Hunt
I only screwed the NHS. Not a spad in the stationery cupboard.

Matt Hancock
Hey, that's unfair! My only mistake was to fall in love – just as I have with our amazing new leader! 🖤🖤🖤

Thérèse Coffey
I feel sick.

> I haven't even demoted you yet! You're going to be Minister for the Environment.

Thérèse Coffey
Environment? Who cares about that?

> This is what you've got to sort out.

Thérèse Coffey
What's the problem? They're all smoking. Looks good to me.

Matt Hancock
Ah-ha! I think I spot a sudden vacancy in the Health Department!

> Not for you, Matt. I've given the job to Steve Barclay.

Matt Hancock
Oh! Excellent choice! Displaying all the wisdom I'd expect from such a towering figure on the political scene, with so many jobs yet to hand out. You really are great!

The administrator has removed Matt Hancock from the group.

> Suella, despite my reservations, I'm telling you in confidence that you are back as Home Secretary.

Suella Braverman
Great. I'll just email It to everyone I know! Along with these cabinet minutes and your password. Anyone know the nuclear codes?

Ben Wallace
You clearly don't know the ministerial codes.

Suella Braverman
Butt out, Wallace, I can do what I like. I've done a grubby deal with Rishi.

James Cleverly
Wow! A deal ! What's that all about?

> Suella now holds one of the most important jobs in politics – keeping the far-right off my back.

Jeremy Hunt
What happened to your promise of this government having "integrity, professionalism and accountability"?

Suella Braverman
Well, nought out of three isn't bad.

> Come on, guys! This happened six whole days ago. Let's not argue about ancient history. Westminster is a completely different place now, compared to that distant time of last week. The days of backbiting and plotting are over!

Penny Mordaunt
Absolutely ! Though I should point out that I came second in the contest – and if you're anything to go by, I should be Prime Minister by Christmas! 🎄

Sir Graham Brady
Do you actually think Rishi is going to last till Christmas? Excellent news. Stability at last!

Keir Starmer
WRITES

HELLO! Well, what a week it's been! With the accession of Rishi Sunak to PM, I've finally got the Conservative party exactly where I want it!

It's a well-known fact that saddling yourselves with a boring, dry policy wonk who struggles to inspire anyone as leader is political death for any party – and I should know, because Angela Rayner tells me this about a dozen times a day!

I have a grudging sympathy for Rishi (one can't help but find empathy for a man who has to take over as leader from a swivel-eyed lunatic!), but one can't allow one's personal feelings to get in the way of opposing the government, and by "opposing" I mean, of course, agreeing with the government on everything that matters! From stiff sentences for climate protestors to not reversing Brexit, there's nothing they can't propose that we think should be broadly kept and slightly changed in tiny, fiddly ways!

But I do disagree with them on one major point: we should have a general election! It's pitiful that the Conservatives are just changing leaders to avoid the judgement of the voters and Rishi is showing wretched cowardice by hanging around without a mandate and running down the clock down!

It would have been a lot better if we had had a general election against Liz Truss, rather than Rishi Sunak, because she was a lot easier to defeat at Prime Minister's Questions – usually because she didn't turn up and was under a desk!
Never mind.
Sincerely, Keir

THE KING OF TROUBLES

A short story special by Dame Hedda Shoulders

"ONE DOES so worry that this awful Crown thingie on the TV will make people think that I am some sort of weirdo..." King Charles was in ruminative mood as he confided in his oldest and most trusted friend. "I mean, the viewers are bound to believe that it is a documentary and that the strange, eccentric and bad-tempered Charlie on the telly is the same as your actual old chum, Charles."

There was no reply from the aspidistra in the corner of the Royal Drawing Room in Buckingham Palace, where the Artist Formerly Known As Prince Charles kept his easel and watercolours, should the muse strike him at any time.

Charles was suddenly aware of the presence of Sir Alan Fitztightly, Royal Pen Poursuivant, Steward of the Stinkwell and Master of the MontBlanc.

"You're not talking to the plants again are you, Sire? I'm afraid the aspidistra doesn't have security clearance and the new Prime Minister has just arrived."

"Oh, not again. Dear oh dear. She really is..."

Charles stopped himself in mid-flow, expecting a reprimand from his ever vigilant aide-de-campion at the slightest indication that the new Monarch was about to express an unconstitutional opinion of the sort he was now sworn to abjure. But in this instance, like the aspidistra, Sir Alan said nothing, leaving the missing word hanging in the air like the pungent smoke from the Queen Consulate's Menthol Health Cigarillos.

"Your Majesty, may I present your Prime Minister, First Lord of the Treasuretrove, Amazon Primus Inter Pares and Leader of the Conswervative and Uturnist Party..."

"Hello, Mrs Truss!" But instead of the awkward curtseying automaton Charles had expected, in walked a small, dapper Asian-looking gentleman in a shiny suit whose trousers, to a layman's eye, seemed to have stopped short on the journey to his shoes.

Sir Alan then swiftly whispered in his master's ear, "This is Mr Rishi, Sire."

"Oh yes, of course," Charles blustered, whilst privately thinking who on earth was this Mr Rishi? Was he one of those Commonwealthy chaps... yes, that was probably it, he must have met him on his tour of the Subcontinent when he visited the Hendu Kushti and the... great temples of the Flujab. "So pleased to meet you again, Mr Rishi." And what was it Mama had taught him to do next as she had prepared him for the onerous duties of Kingship over the long decades of apprenticeship...? Of course... Now he remembered... "Have you come far?" he asked Mr Rishi, brightly.

"Indeed I have, Sire. As I said in my video, let me tell you a story of a young couple who arrived in a new country and made a life through hard work and sheer dedication to..."

"That's fascinating!" Charles hastily interrupted what looked like being a very long answer. "And which Commonwealth country are you head of again?"

"Britain, Sire."

Charles was somewhat flummoxed by this unexpected reply. "And how are things going there?"

The suave Mr Richi looked thoughtful and sincere.

"Mistakes have been made, Sire. But I promise you, I can fix them."

"Mr Rishi's family come originally from India, your Majesty," Sir Alan explained.

"What a coincidence!" replied the King. "We used to own India."

"It now belongs to my wife," said Mr Rishi.

Charles was impressed. "Well, that's handy – perhaps she could lend us some money? Apparently, the previous lot in charge here have made a terrific hash of things. It said in one of my Red Boxes that the UK has lost so much money that the economy looks like the Black Hole of Calcutta... but not in a good way."

Mr Rishi laughed and bowed nervously, his trousers riding up above his knees, as Sir Alan hurriedly ushered him out of the room.

"Thank you for coming in, Mr Rishi, I am sure we will see you here again. Or maybe not. Who knows? Ciao!"

Charles meanwhile turned towards his companion in the corner. "Well, that went rather well I thought," he declared to his reticent green friend.

(To be continued...)

Hi guys! Blah, blah, blah, bullshit, bullshit, bullshit, blah, blah, blah....etc.

POPE WARNS CLERGY ABOUT 'ONLINE EVILS'

What's black and white and red all over?

A nun caught watching porn

Exclusive to all newspapers

MY FORD FIESTA MEMORIES

by Our Motoring Correspondent
Phil Herup

YOU never forget your first Ford Fiesta – even if you've never owned one. When I heard the news that the Ford Fiesta had reached the end of the road, and that my editor required 1,000 words by lunchtime, I leapt into the driving seat and tried to get started. Three hours later my brain was still stuck in neutral and I was going nowhere. But then, after a helpful push from the editor, I was up and running. There was no stopping me!

I drove into paragraph two at full throttle. Now I was motoring. Going up through the gears, even though I wasn't too sure which way to steer it. There's nothing fancy about a Ford Fiesta piece, but you know it'll get you to your destination – the bottom of the page. And economical with it, doing 100 words to the pint. A smooth ride, nice and reliable, and... Hang on. I seem to be slowing down to a s – t – o – p. What to do? Like many journalists, I rang the AA, to ask if they could help me with my drink problem... *(That's enough – Ed. I think you may have taken the wrong turning.)*

DICTIONARY CORNER
Going AMOL
(broadcasting slang, believed to originate at the BBC)
Being everywhere all the time. Suffering from ubiquity. Experiencing omni-presence. The opposite of AWOL (Absent Without Leave).

HANCOCK ON 'I'M A CELEBRITY GET ME OUT OF HERE'

£400k!
It's money for
old grope

Who croaked?

Everybody's granny, actually

This protective equipment is useless

£35bn failure of Test and Trace

by Our Covid Correspondent
Pam Demic

THE Covid Inquiry has heard a strong condemnation of Test and Trace after it was revealed that, despite being given £35bn of public money, it had been unable to find any trace of humility in Matt Hancock.

"You would have thought that, given his multiple failures as health secretary, the huge death toll, the cronyism and the fact that he had to resign in disgrace for breaking the lockdown laws he created, it would be able to find some shame," insisted one panel member.

"But it found no trace of humility, shame or decency, as Matt Hancock pocketed £400,000 for a couple of weeks in the jungle, directly against the wishes of the bereaved families of Covid victims."

THOSE TOP MEDIA JOBS AWAITING MATT HANCOCK IN FULL

1 Happy Birthday messages on Cameo. £10 a time.
2 Back of panto horse at Rochdale Octagon.
3 Advert for Curry's CCTV hidden-camera set.
4 Matt Hancock lookalike.
5 LBC phone-in (as caller on line three).
6 Opening supermarket (as deputy branch manager).
7 Red carpet appearance (vacuuming carpet).
8 Mail online "You won't believe what they look like now" feature.
9 Er…
10 That's it.

THAT TRUMP FATHER OF THE BRIDE SPEECH IN FULL

My fellow Americans, on the occasion of Tiffany's wedding, it fills my heart with joy to see my daughter looking so gorgeous, so blonde, and wow, so hot! But enough of Ivanka. This is more than just a wedding to me – this is also an alibi for when the January 6th Committee subpoena me. Because if I'm here, then I'm not flushing top-secret documents down the gold-plated john.

And today, I am not so much losing a daughter... because the Donald doesn't lose. No way. She was stolen from me. Just like the midterms. And the previous election. This time, I had all my selected Maga Trumpians standing for the GOP across the nation, but sadly, because of irregularities such as women voting, Crooked Hillary, Sleepy Joe not being asleep and the votes being counted, they lost. These candidates were MY guys, and there comes a time when you just have to accept

responsibility. And I accept that the person responsible for this crapfest is my wife. It's not the first time Melania's made a catastrophic error of judgement! So don't blame it on the Donald, don't blame it on the sunshine, don't blame it on the moonlight, don't blame it on the New York Times, blame it on the boogey-man: Rudi Giuliani. Yes! It's all Rudi's fault, as well as Melania's!

But today is not the day to apportion blame to other people for my mistakes. I did that yesterday and I'll do it again tomorrow. This is a traditional wedding, so of course we had something old, something new, something borrowed and something blue – the Senate! And that is so not my fault! Fake lose!

So be upstanding and charge your glasses – to a shell company in Panama that the IRS will never find out about – and let's toast our great victory in the midterms, my even greater victory when I lose in 2024 – and let's show our love for the glamorous blonde whose big day this is. Me.

You may now kiss the bride and my arse.

Donald Trump
45th and 47th President of the United States

"Dad, this is Colin, my new boyfriend"

ATLANTIS HAILS PROGRESS AT COP2700 BC

by Our Man From Atlantis **AA Gills**

THE island state of Atlantis, host of this year's Cop2700 BC, reported excellent progress had been made in the fight against rising sea levels.

The President of Atlantis, Mr Kredulos, congratulated the conference for a really constructive dialogue with realistic target setting, and attainable goals.

He thanked the leaders of Ancient Greece, Minoa, Mesopotamia and Persia for their commitments to slowing the process of climate change due to the release of carbon emissions following the discovery of fire a few million years earlier (*Is this right? Ed.*)

"We are confident," said Mr Kredulos, "that smaller island nations like ours can avoid the dangers of excess flooding, thanks to the generous and considerate behaviour of the rest of the known world."

He continued, "I'm sure that with these sincere promises and pledges of long-term action, we can avoid glug, glug, glug."

"Er, actually, we're supposed to be throwing tomato soup at the sunflowers"

COP27 CLOSES WITH PLEA TO END WORLD'S RELIANCE ON FOSSILS

Failing school to be put under special measures

FOLLOWING a series of appalling results from its alumni, Ofsted is to investigate Eton College with a view to closing it down.

Said the Head of Ofsted, "There is now conclusive evidence that the education standards at the school are directly affecting national well-being.

"Successive old boys seem to have had no education at all in core subjects, such as economy, politics, reality and morality.

"Cameron D., Rees-Mogg J., Johnson B., and now Kwarteng K., have displayed complete ignorance of how the country, or indeed the world, works."

Ofsted is considering a number of options, including turning Eton into a centre for refugees, or possibly a prison, which a number of old boys will, of course, be welcome to attend, including: Guppy D., Aitken J. and notorious law-breaker Johnson B. *(Rotters)*

LATE NEWS

Oxford University to be put under special measures

■ Following a series of appalling results from its alumni, OfS (Office for Students) is to investigate Oxford University, in particular the PPE Faculty, after the latest Prime Minister, Ms Truss, demonstrated no grasp of Politics, Philosophy or Economics.

Ofsted is now considering turning the entire university into something more useful, such as a permanent theme park and hotel complex for the Harry Potter franchise "Fantastic B and B's and Where to Find Them". *(Potters)*

COP27 UPDATE

1.5% COMMITMENT FROM RICH COUNTRIES

IN WHAT is seen as a major breakthrough, rich countries at Cop27 have committed to keep 1.5% of the promises they made at the conference about limiting temperature rises in the next twelve months.

"This is a massive increase on the 0.1% of promises they kept after Cop26 in Glasgow last year," said a weeping Cop27 spokesman.

Asked what residents of low-lying countries threatened by climate change should do in the meantime, Cop27 delegates unanimously agreed that it should either be backstroke or front crawl.

....

THOSE ALTERNATIVE FUEL SOURCES TO GAS IN FULL

■ Offshore wind

■ Solar

■ Burning Cop climate change conference brochures

Climate protestors trying to save all life on earth really annoying, agrees everyone

by Our Protest Correspondent **Glue Edwards**

It has been universally agreed that the climate protestors, who are pointing out that if we carry on like this, our entire planet is toast, are very annoying. Aren't they infuriating?!

I mean, yeah, they're very young, so they can be forgiven for being a bit silly – unless you count all the old ones, of course, who are probably just exaggerating things, the old dears – and yeah, they're very posh, which is also annoying although admittedly everyone's got the right to an opinion, and admittedly they didn't actually do any damage to those paintings because they were covered in glass, but you know, they might have done if some of the soup had magically gone through the glass, and yes, individual tiny actions like these protests are a drop in the ocean compared with the very real prospect of species going extinct and the planet heating up and cooking us all and billions of people being driven from their homelands, sure, but…they are ANNOYING, aren't they?

Holding up traffic? So annoying! I mean, yeah, obviously travel is a huge part of it, but you know, let's just stick our fingers in our ears and agree how annoying they are, and maybe the problem will completely solve itself because we've agreed we are a bit irritated with these studenty types! Phew!

'Just Stop Oil' protestors' fury

'Just Stop Oil' protestors planning to bring the M25 to a standstill have reacted furiously after discovering the motorway was already permanently at a standstill.

"We were trapped for hours in a tailback by junction 9 trying to make our way along the M25 to junction 16 where were planning to bring the M25 to a standstill," said one.

"We will not allow the M25 to scupper our protests by being more at a standstill than we can make it," said another one *(cont. p94)*

QATAR WORLD CUP OPENING CEREMONY

"It'll be decided by very strict penalties"

"We're the group of death"

PREMIER LEAGUE CONDEMNATION

THE Premier League has condemned Qatar for its repressive and backward attitudes to homosexuality.

"Gay men in the kingdom being too scared to admit what they are, living a life of lies, is just horrible," said a Premier League spokesman. "It's hard to imagine a place where you are too scared to admit your sexuality for fears of a backlash.

"We're just lucky that, of the 557 strapping, young, super-fit, hunky male athletes playing in the Premier League, none are gay. Not even one! Such a stroke of luck, really."

"It's terrible – now I can remember watching the matches"

New Beckham 'One Love' armband

■ David Beckham says: "I love money, and it's important for me not to discriminate where it comes from. It's not up to me to tell people how they should show their financial feelings for me. I'm entirely behind the LTD and PLC community."

Great football chants to try out in Qatar

I can sing a rainbow *(Trad)*

Somewhere over the rainbow ♪ *(Judy Garland)*

Since you've been gone *(Rainbow)* ♪

Singing in the rainbow *(Gene Kelly)*

♫ It's raining bows! *(Weather Girls)*

I can't stand the rainbow *(Tina Turner)*

While my Qatar gently weeps *(Beatles)*

How gay conversion therapy works in Qatar

■ Invite foreign ministers to be lavishly wined and dined in Qatar for the World Cup.

■ Convert them into thinking gay fans are welcome, despite the fact they aren't.

■ Have them return home singing the praises of Qatar.

■ Er...

■ That's it.

EYE FOOTIE POLL
Man U fans

MANCHESTER UNITED

Who do you think is the most fit and proper new owner to return your team to its glory days?

☐ The Emir of Qatar   ☐ Elon Musk

☐ Vladimir Putin   ☐ Kim Jong Un

☐ Mr B. L. Zeebub of the Hades Corporation

QATAR BANS ENGLAND FAN OUTFITS

"What a medieval and backward-looking country!"

"Let's sack Southgate..."

"...and Constantinople on the way home"

ME AND MY SPOON

WORLD CUP EDITION

FIFA PRESIDENT GIANNI INFANTINO

Do you have favourite spoon?

No, there are no favourites, and I resent the suggestion that I have received any financial inducements from any national cutlery organisation whatsoever to promote their spoons.

But do you have a favourite?

Qatari spoons are great. But spoons are for everyone. Today I feel a spoon. Today I feel a fork. Today I feel a spork. Spoon? Fork? I don't care – that's how diverse I am. Today, I feel knives are out to get me.

Can you be trusted with the world's spoons?

Look, when I was a small boy I was bullied for only having a wooden spoon, so I know how it feels to be the victim of spoonist attitudes. To have your life ruined by spoonism. And I say to Europe and all its silver spoons – look in your own kitchen drawers before you start rifling through the golden cutlery of the poor Qataris.

Do you think people should be allowed to spoon with whoever they like?

Can't we just get on with the football?

Has anything amusing ever happened to you in connection with a spoon?

I once laughed all the way to the bank when Michel Platini came in to see me with a suitcase full of... *(This interview has been terminated on the advice of top libel lawyers, Carter-Fork, to save our spoon editor from ending up in the soup.)*

NEXT WEEK: *Sepp Platter, Me and My Platters.*

DIARY

GRAYSON PERRY'S FULL ENGLISH

GRAYSON PERRY: I'm Grayson Perry, an artist and an Englishman. But I'm not really sure what Englishness means. Is it Eng, or lish – or is it ness? Or is it a bit of all three? Have we forgotten what Englishness actually is? Or what it isn't? Or what it would be if it wasn't what it was? In this series, I'm travelling the length and breadth of England in a white van and meeting a huge variety of people in the hope of unearthing a wide range of views on all sorts of different things.

Today, we're paying a visit to Dover, legendary home of Vera Lynn, to meet a man called Derek who likes dressing up as a bluebird.

Grayson on a boat with a man dressed up as a bluebird

GRAYSON: So what I really want to know is this, Derek – why do you like dressing up as a bluebird?

DEREK: I just do!

GRAYSON: *(Throaty laugh)* Brilliant answer! I guess it must be something to do with the White Cliffs behind us!

Panorama shot of White Cliffs

And how long have you been dressing up like this, Derek?

DEREK: Ever since this morning when I heard you were coming.

GRAYSON: *(Throaty laugh)* Tremendous! And what do you think of foreigners?

DEREK: Don't much like 'em, to be honest.

Grayson looks concerned. Back in the van, driving along a motorway, Grayson talks to driver Kirk

GRAYSON: Listening to what Derek was saying has set me thinking about this and that. If we have this, can we also have that? So what is that, when it's at home? And, just as importantly, what exactly is this? Or are they two halves of the same thing?

Now I'm going to meet another odd person in an unusual setting to try to find some answers to whatever it is I'm meant to be asking.

Grayson sits round a table with two men and a woman with spoons in their hands

WOMAN IN FUNNY HAT: Porridge up!

She places bowls of porridge in front of them

GRAYSON: So here I am in a cafe in the heart of England with three people who just love porridge! They really can't get enough of it! Fabulous! So tell me, Ryan, what's so great about porridge?

RYAN: It tastes just tastes so lovely and well, sort of porridgey, Grayson!

GRAYSON: *(Throaty laugh)* In a funny sort of way, porridge tells us a lot about the nature of our national identity. Because what starts out as oats and water turns into something very different. Yet essentially the same. You're obviously a porridge fanatic, Bruce. So how often do you eat it?

BRUCE: At least once a week.

GRAYSON: Blimey! And has it changed what you think about the nature of our national identity at all, Daisy?

DAISY: There's no place like home, that's what I say.

GRAYSON: Well, that's given me plenty to chew on – a bit like your porridge! *(Throaty laugh)*.

Back in the van, Grayson muses to Kirk on what he has just heard

GRAYSON: It's easy to dismiss them as just three nutters who like porridge, but something Daisy said really struck an important chord. She said, "There's no place like home". And that made me wonder what exactly do we mean by home? And what do we mean when we say an Englishman's home is his castle? Well, you're not gonna believe this but now we're off to meet a real live Englishman in a real live castle! *(Throaty laugh)*

GRAYSON: I'm about to play out that English fantasy of taking afternoon tea with a real live Lord and Lady!

Grayson is served tea at Castle Snoots with Lord and Lady Cholmondondely

GRAYSON: This seems like a million miles away from the industrial heartlands of England – yet Birmingham City Centre with its mosques and Indian restaurants and amazing cultural diversity is only eighty miles away! Tell me, how long have you lived here?

LORD CHOLMONDONDELY: More than eight hundred years.

GRAYSON: And you've never thought of moving?

LADY CHOLMONDONDELY: We've grown to like it here very much indeed, thanks awfully.

GRAYSON: More tea, vicar? Only joking! *(Throaty laugh)*

Grayson, back in his van, muses to Kirk

GRAYSON: I felt a bit ashamed, if I'm honest, to be sitting there in that sumptuous castle taking afternoon tea with His Nibs when I knew deep down in my bones that millions of people in the Arctic were freezing to death in their igloos or whatever. And in this place the rest of us are content to call England there must be plenty of Eskimos who will never be able to afford their own castle. So why do we never hear about them? We're on our way to talk to a typical Eskimo family, the Akeeshoos, who have come to live in Bournemouth.

GRAYSON: How do you find living in Bournemouth?

MR AKEESHOO: The weather is clement, the educational opportunities excellent and the prices competitive.

GRAYSON: But you must miss putting on your furry anorak, cutting a hole in the ice and catching yourself some lovely fish for supper in your igloo, am I right?

MRS AKEESHOO: We have been delighted by the range of fishmongers in Bournemouth. They sell a wide variety of fresh fish, all responsibly sourced.

Grayson in his van

GRAYSON: Something tells me that the Akeeshoos, for all their bravado, will never feel quite at home in England So who are the English? Now we're out of Europe, with a new monarch on the throne, this is a question we'll have to confront wheresoever on these islands we live. And that's why I'm off to Shepton Mallet, to speak to a family who live in a yurt, have a pet mongoose and like walking around on stilts. Do they feel excluded? And, if not, why not? *(Throaty laugh)*

As told to

CRAIG BROWN

BRITAIN'S GOT TALENT SHOCK

by Our Britain's Got Talent Correspondent
Brendan Circuses

SIMON COWELL has expressed outrage as judge David Walliams was forced to quit after a recording came to light of him saying offensive things about the contestants.

"The Britain's Got Talent contestants, 'whatshisname who did the Opera', 'her, you know the one who could sing a bit but looked weird', 'the saddo teen with the dancing dog' and 'the fat bloke who jigged about', deserve to be treated with dignity and respect," said a clearly furious Cowell.

"These contestants have given the British public much entertainment and, more importantly, given me three superyachts, villas in Miami, Ibiza and the Seychelles, and a gold Bentley.

"When I was informed of what Walliams had said, I was stunned, though, given all the Botox I've had, that is pretty much my only expression these days.

"Will David Walliams be missed as judge? That's a no from me."

"...and Eileen will also be fondly remembered as a passionate and life-long advocate for the versatility and practicality of Tupperware"

Elon Musk ruining Twitter, users warn

by Our Twitter Correspondent
Rhea Tweet

TWITTER users have expressed their worry that the website known across the world as a forum for reasoned debate and calm, sensible exchange of accurate information and informed views, has overnight become the worst place on the internet.

"It's now toxic and unpleasant," tweeted one user, **@sadBoy97**, to his seventeen followers, "as opposed to how it was before Elon Musk, when it was a happy place full of nice people trying to make the world better."

"No it wasn't, you wanker," said another user, **@truthwarrior44**.

"We spent the whole day screaming at each other about Donald Trump and Piers Morgan and Katie Hopkins. It was great."

Another user, **@Contrarian Librarian**, added, "Actually, you stupid fascists, it was always a horrid place where disgusting people even gave spoilers to Game of Thrones and I had to tell them to stop or else they'd die of cancer."

A fourth user, **@elonmusk**, joined to say, "Shut up, you paedos, or give me $8 a month."

@sadBoy97 summed up the situation by threatening to leave Twitter for the thirty-seventh time: "I am going to join an exciting new website aimed at young men in their bedrooms, called MasturBate, instead." (*Surely Mastodon? Ed.*)

Twitter users 'urged to try alternative'

by Our Social Media Correspondent
Judge Tinder

TWITTER users angry at Elon Musk's purchase of the social media site have been urged to try an alternative called "going outside and having a walk".

"Going outside and having a walk involves stopping endless doomscrolling through your Twitter feed, switching off your laptop and your phone, walking up to the front door, opening it and going outside," said one former Twitter user out for a nice walk.

"The walk can then take you to 'the pub', a place where you can interact with people you barely know, just like on Twitter.

"You can also get into silly fights about politics here too… but, as there's booze, there's also the chance of a drunken sing-song and a snog with someone you fancy if they 'like' you in real life at the end of the evening."

Some tweeters are predicting that "the pub" could be the future of people being social, once they abandon Twitter doomscrolling and go get some fresh air.

Supermarket

"Don't worry – we all used to be nurses"

NHS sees 42% rise in demand for treatment linked to gambling addiction across England

Those odds in full

Gambling addiction continues to rise	**EVENS**
Gambling adverts continue to increase	**EVENS**
Gambling companies continue to tell gamblers to gamble responsibly	**EVENS**
Gambling companies continue to lobby MPs	**EVENS**
Government does something about it	**5000-1**

TV HIGHLIGHTS

Don't Carry On, Nurse!

Nurse: One out, all out!
Patient: Are you talking about my organs?!

■ Made-for-TV reboot of the black and white comedy classic, in which the nurses at St Innuendo's threaten to "down tools", "pull out" and "not take things lying down", only for management to laugh at them.

Things get worse when Health Secretary Sid James (played by an in-form Steve Barclay) makes an improper suggestion and is told "your package isn't big enough".

The strike begins, but can the nurses keep it up? Or will they just be given the clap again?

Don't miss the classic scene in which Nurse Bigguns asks hospital administrator Mr Weeny, "Is that a pay rise in your pocket or are you just pleased to see me?" To which he replies, "No, it's a gun. The army are being brought in to do your job," adding, "Carry on, Sergeant."

EYE RATING:
You won't be in stitches.

TRUMP ALLOWED BACK ON TWITTER

Let's make America hate again

DING DONG

R.I.P LESLIE PHILLIPS

POETRY CORNER

In Memoriam Leslie Phillips, actor and legendary screen Casanova

So. Farewell
Then Leslie Phillips,
Star of the 'Carry On' films.

Now, sadly, you
Will no longer be
Carrying On.

You were Mr Bell
In 'Carry On Nurse'
In 1959, which is
When you first uttered
Your immortal catchphrase
"Ding Dong!"
Which served you
So well for the next
63 years.

But now, alas,
The bell
Is tolling
For thee.

E.J. Thribb
(Certificate 17½)

Keir Starmer WRITES

HELLO!

Welcome to my new column – that is, if you like columns. If not, it can easily be a think-piece, a lifestyle article or an op-ed featurette! Whatever floats your boat. And if you're not keen on boats, whatever floats your pedalo, dinghy or catamaran. And if floating's not your thing, then sinking is absolutely fine with me!

Now that's out the way, and I've made my position crystal clear, I'd like to get on to my main point – which is my utter disdain for Rishi Sunak half-heartedly tying himself in knots in a desperate attempt to please all of the people, all of the time.

Just look at his stance on immigration. He has a ludicrous position of being ANTI immigration whilst at the same time being PRO job-filling from overseas! I, on the other hand, have a completely contrary and more credible stance of being somewhat PRO job-filling from overseas whilst remaining somewhat ANTI immigration.

So you can see the clear difference between us. Rishi is wishy-washy, sitting on the fence and trying to be all things to all men – whereas I am quite clearly resolute and steadfast about my desire to appeal to one and all. I'm sorry, but if you don't like that, then there's nothing I can do. Other than modify everything I've just said into something you'd rather I had said. Like strikes. Of course, I'm fervently in favour of the right to strike. But at the same time, I'd rather you didn't strike, if that's all right with you.

So, whether you're aboard a pedalo, dinghy or catamaran, you can see the clear blue water that lies between me and wishy-washy Rishi. And if you prefer dry land, then who am I to disagree? The important thing is we're all singing from the same hymn sheet – unless you're Hindu, of course, or Muslim, or Buddhist, or Wiccan, or Satanist, or Corbynite, or *(cont. until 2024)*

Sincerely,
Keir.

The Eye's Controversial New Columnist

The columnist who has been to the crèche of real life and the nursery of hard knocks

This week, I am very angry at all this fuss and attention given to the eight billionth person born in the world. Yet again, we see it just happens to be a baby, which is of course sinister messaging by the globalist mainstream media to blame babies for world overpopulation. Speaking as a baby *(see photo)*, I have to ask why is it always us who are chosen to represent how many people exist on Earth? Why couldn't it be, for example, a 40-year-old photocopier repairman named Keith? This sinister attempt to blame a single section of the community for everything is demagoguery of the worst kind, and I think I smell the day-old nappy stench of wokeist remainer liberal elites behind it. If anything, I am a leading proponent in the war against over-population. I have many solutions that I implement on a daily basis, like leaving toy cars at the top of a flight of stairs, and keeping my parents up all night so they are more inclined to murder one another at the drop of a *(cont. p94)*

The Big Ronaldo TalkTV Interview

CRISTIANO RONALDO meets PIERS MORON

Ronaldo: Great to have you on the show, Piers.

Moron: Thanks very much.

Ronaldo: Now, let's be frank, Piers, you're paid an awful lot of money and you're simply not delivering.

Moron: Yeah, it is a waste of my talent. I'm used to performing in front of big crowds and being the centre of attention. Now, I'm just watching from the sidelines and I don't like it.

Ronaldo: Are you fed up with the management? Do you think Rupert's useless? Go on – get yourself into trouble.

Moron: Look, I owe Rupert a lot, from the beginning of my career, but now it's just not working.

Ronaldo: Would you like to move on?

Moron: Of course, but I'm tied by this contract.

Ronaldo: How would you feel if Rupert sacked you tomorrow and then sold News Corp to the highest bidder?

Moron: I think that would be best for all concerned.

THOSE GOVERNMENT TIPS FOR SAVING ENERGY IN FULL

- **Don't** put the heating on
- **Wear** lots of clothes
- **Don't** wash your clothes
- **Don't** have baths
- **Don't** take showers
- **Don't** use your oven
- **Turn off** your freezer
- **Don't** live in a house
- **Live** on the streets
- **Don't** ask us for money
- **Ask** other people for money
- **Er…** That's it.

CAMILLA TO HAVE 'COMPANIONS' INSTEAD OF LADIES-IN-WAITING

> So they'll have lighter duties?

> Every time I have a fag

"This is going to be a great murder podcast"

Royal airforce denies preparing new display team

FOLLOWING the allegations of abuse and inappropriate behaviour, an RAF spokesman has denied that a new team has been formed called the Black Arrows, named after their uniform and operating out of HMP Wandsworth.

"This is complete non-sense," he said. "There is no truth at all in the rumour that the Black Arrows will be putting on a dazzling display at His Majesty's Pleasure for nine months, with time off for good behaviour, in which they move up and down the exercise yard of Cell Block H in perfect formation."

He continued, "They are definitely not working on a dazzling display where they all get their lunch at precisely the same time from the prison canteen, then sit at exactly the same table by themselves and don't make eye contact with the other inmates."

He concluded, "There are no criminal charges, so the Red Arrows will remain as the Red-Faced Arrows and these silly rumours should be shot down immediately in a plume of coloured smoke."

THE KING OF TROUBLES

A short story special by Dame Hedda Shoulders

THE STORY SO FAR: The unfortunate row over Lady Marmalade Sandwich and the offended Charity Worker continued. Now read on…

CHARLES was deeply perplexed as he listened to Sir Alan Fitztightly explain the lasting damage that Lady Marmalade's clumsy attempt at small talk had wrought on the House of Windsor.

"Surely it's just a storm in a tea party, Sir Alan. The whole thing will blow over. Poor old Lady Marmers is toast. What more can one do?"

"I fear the matter is far from resolved," advised the Monarch's trusted Counsellor of the Privy, and newly promoted Serjeant of the Stinkyink and Marshal of the Mont Blanc. "We are going to have to revise the basic Royal Guide to Conversing with the Public."

Charles drew in a deep breath.

"But Mama laid it down that there are only two questions that a Royal personage should ask." The King quoted them from memory, so etched into his monarch's mind were they from early days of tutelage in the Royal Nursery under the strict eye of the constitutional historian, Sir Funkwell Gibbon. "One – what do you do? And two – have you come far?"

Sir Alan looked stern. "You must never utter either of those two sentences ever again!"

Charles's blood rose to the top of his ears as his exasperation manifested itself.

"But why?"

"Both questions are very rude. You should already *know* what a person does, and not to know is patronising, misogynistic, racist and imperialist."

"But, but…" stammered Charles.

"No buts! And inquiring how far a personage has come is offensive to anyone whose heritage is located further away than Windsor, and is also condescending, sexist, bigoted and colonialist.

"Trust me, Sire, the Air Vice Marshal and I went on a course of Sensitivity Training for Senior Officers and their partners. It was a hoot, actually. I won the karaoke night with my rendition of 'It's raining men, women and those who define themselves as…'"

"I get the idea, Sir Alan," Charles remonstrated. "This is all so unfair. I've always defined myself as a thoroughly modern monarch. I'm the *last* person you accuse of being a racialistic… the Prince's Trust, the Commonwealth… Inner City Skateboarding… I've devoted my life to wearing diverse national costumes and watching people dancing."

At that moment, the Queen Consulate entered the Victorian Vaping Room. Charles reached out to her for support.

"I'm not colour prejudiced, am I, darling?" he implored.

"Not at all," rasped Camilla. "Some of your best friends are green." She winked at Sir Alan and glanced conspiratorially at the aspidistra in the passage that led from the Ante Room to the Dec Room.

"This is no laughing matter," said the new forward-looking monarch, conscious of his status as Sir Alan's liege-lord, Chief Thane and Commander in Chief of the ancient order of the Knights Barron. "Sir Alan, tell me straight. Is this seemingly trivial matter going to bring down the monarchy?"

"Oh, no, Sire," soothed Sir Alan, the last of the Fitztightlys. "That's the Netflix documentary…"

Charles groaned. He had briefly forgotten about the tale of woe and blame that his younger son and his Californian wife were dishing up for the hungry public's consumption.

"But worry not, Sire," said the loyal factotum quickly. "I shall watch it on your behalf, assess the damage and weather the blow – as if it were an incoming egg from an ungrateful subject."

(To be continued… forever)

School news

St Cakes

St Cakes was delighted to host the former UKIP leader Mr Nigel Farrago to address the Sixth Form Very Conservative Soc last week. The Secretary, Mosley Minor, welcomed Mr Farrago to the Enoch Powell room, where he was greeted with a traditional rousing rendition of the school's 1930s anthem (since banned), *Küchen Uber Alles*. Pupils were delighted by Mr Farrago's views on such varied topics as immigration, immigration and immigration, and showed their appreciation for his talk by raising their right hands to ask him questions and shouting enthusiastically at pupils from the local state school who had *(cont. p94)*

"No, but where do you really come from?"

Film highlights

They Flew To Beijing
End of History Channel, 9pm

■ REMAKE of the legendary wartime classic *They Flew To Bruges*, with the action updated to 2022. Ex-Wing Commander Chalky Chalkington (played by Harry Styles) must lead a small band of former RAF pilots in a daring mission to get paid huge amounts of money to train the Chinese Air Force. Will they succeed before the Ministry of Defence finds out and starts complaining about conflicts of interest? Or will they save the free world by helping China invade Taiwan, as ordered by President Xi (an in-form Timothée Chalamet)? Thrilling aerial sequences over Taipei by the Extremely Red Arrows make this a must-see film or else you're arrested.

EYE VIEW: Never in the history of aviation has so much money been given to so few for such a terrible reason.

WILL THIS WEEK'S MASS SHOOTINGS IN A WALMART IN VIRGINIA AND A COLORADO GAY CLUB MEAN THAT FINALLY, DESPITE NOTHING HAPPENING AFTER THE LAST MASS SHOOTING AND THE ONE BEFORE THAT AND THE ONE BEFORE THAT AND THE ONE BEFORE THAT AND THE ONE BEFORE THAT AND THE ONE BEFORE THAT AND THE ONE BEFORE THAT AND THE ONE BEFORE THAT, THIS TIME SOMETHING WILL BE DONE TO CURB GUN USE IN AMERICA?

No.

TRAIN TICKET PRICE RISE 'WON'T FUEL INFLATION', GOVERNMENT SAYS

THE government has said that the biggest increase in train ticket prices in a decade will not fuel inflation in any way, "unlike demands from various public sector workers for percentage hikes in their pay".

A Department for Transport spokesman said the 5.9 percent rise, which comes into force on the 5th of March, will invariably encourage people to work from home or return to their cars to get to work, school or medical appointments, and definitely won't increase inflation.

He added, "It's quite simple: one rise is aimed at filling the pockets of greedy nurses, postal staff, border staff and rail workers, whereas the other is aimed at providing non-inflationary dividend payments to shareholders and increasing senior management pay packages, whilst they continue their asset stripping before they are bailed out by the taxpayer."

Companies will mitigate rail price rises

TRAIN companies, such as Avanti West Coast, say they will mitigate the pain of the 5.9 percent rise in rail fares in 2023 by continuing to cancel every train they operate.

"In 2022, we strived to give the public a service so wretched that in the end they had no choice but to abandon the railways and drive to work," said an Avanti spokesman.

"So in 2023, we're committed to going even further, by cancelling so many trains, our passengers won't be able to tell if it's a strike day or not."

"There are three of us in this marriage"

The Daily Torygraph

Stop striking from home!

AS we move into 2023, can we finally stop this insidious practice of SFH – or Striking From Home. In recent months, this refusal to go into work to withdraw your labour has become endemic in British industry, to the detriment of traditional small business. This is disastrous for the economy.

With strikers manning the sofa, rather than barricades, many firms have been left on the verge of ruin. Brazier manufacturers are shutting down. Donkey-jacket makers are going bust. Placard producers are claiming that "the writing is on the wall" rather than on a piece of cardboard bearing the legendary words "HONK IF YOU SUPPORT US".

These selfish, lazy Strikers From Home will no doubt claim that they cannot get to the picket lines because everyone else is on strike. But, in reality, they are just reluctant to stop watching *Bargain Hunt*, get off their backsides and turn up at their place of work in order to refuse to work there.

Michelle Mone denies having any involvement with her family

by Our Mone Correspondent
Fred U. Lent

ANNOUNCING that she was taking a leave of absence from the House of Lords to clear her name, Baroness Michelle

My story is full of holes

Just like Medpro's PPE equipment!

Mone strenuously denied having any involvement with her family.

"I have seen wild claims that my husband, Doug Barrowman, transferred £29m to an offshore trust, from the £65m he made from the Medpro PPE deal, for the benefit of my children and myself," Mone said in a statement.

"But I can assure you that I have never met my husband nor my children and have never had any involvement with any of them.

"Any suggestion otherwise will be handed on to my lawyers... whom I also have never met and have had nothing to do with."

Dictionary Corner

Philanthropy *(n.)*

1 *(archaic 19th century)*
The giving of money to charitable causes in order to improve the conditions of those worse off than oneself, eg "George Peabody and Angela Burdett-Coutts were well know for their philanthropy"

2 *(modern 21st century)*
The receiving of very large amounts of money in order to improve one's own conditions while talking about charitable causes, eg "The Duke and Duchess of Sussex were presented with a major award for their philanthropy."

The Eye's Controversial New Columnist

The columnist whose first words were 'woke leftie'

This week I am very angry about so-called "nepo babies". I am extremely against this type of thing. My grandfather (the owner of this paper) and my uncle (editor of this newspaper) and my aunt (major shareholder) have advised me to go big on this issue for the next few weeks, so write in and let us shame these *(cont. p94)*

The Prime Minister's Highly Confidential WhatsApp Group

Happy New Year, guys!

Penny Mordaunt
Why? Are you resigning? After all, you've been Prime Minister for over two months. Surely it's my turn now.

Great New Year bants, Penny. But seriously we've got so much stuff to be excited about. Like Sunakism!

Thérèse Coffey
What's that when it's at home? Or at second home? Or is it fourth home?

Everyone knows what Sunakism is. It's peace of mind, lower taxes and a genuine pride in Britain. 😊 🎖️🇬🇧

Jeremy Hunt
Well, nought out of three isn't bad. Did I mention I'm taxing the middle classes pretty heavily? But don't worry, it's not for long. Because they'll be lower class soon. 😔

Oh yes, I met one of them at a homeless shelter. Here's a pic

I asked the guy some really interesting questions about what section of the finance industry he wanted to get into. It turned out he was very interested in raising some capital and asked me to invest 10p in a cup of tea start-up. I was all-in on his investment strategy and promised I'd get back to him after doing due diligence. You can't just hand out money to people with no track record.

Steve Barclay
Unless it's PPE and the person in question is a fruity blonde who runs a lingerie business. 🤍

I can't comment on that, Steve, because it would reflect badly on whoever was Chancellor of the Exchequer at the time.

Dominic Raab
What fuckwit came up with the idea of putting a multi-millionaire PM in a photo-op with a down-and-out? Was it the same moron who thought you'd connect with the proles by having your billionaire missus opening up about how down-to-earth she is in posh-bible Tatler? 💩

Steady on, Dom, it was about interior design, which is what most people are interested in during a cost of living crisis.

Thérèse Coffey
Yeah, like mould on their walls. 🙉 You need some new advice.

Funny you should mention that. But I've been searching high and low for a new advisor and, would you believe it, I've found this brilliant guy called James Forsyth. And guess what – it turns out he went to school with me, I was best man at his wedding and we're godfathers to each other's children!

Michael Gove
Good to see the levelling-up meritocratic agenda is alive – though not very well.

And here's another coincidence. He's married to Boris's former spokeswoman, Allegra Stratton.

Dominic Raab
That was a shitshow, as I recall. 💩

Hey, you're being very negative, guys. Give him a chance.

James Forsyth has joined the group.

James Forsyth
Breaking news, Prime Minister... I've got us a table at the Old Wykehamists Ball, everyone's going! Hugo Snotterton-Ffinche, Jimmy Goldman-Sacks, Morgan Stanley, Ollie Garkski, and the life President of the Democratic Republic of Murdistan, aka Bingo, former captain of Fives! It'll be a hoot!

Thérèse Coffey
Am I the only one who thinks the optics on this won't look too good?

Dominic Raab
Yeah, well, you know all about optics! 🔫🥃

It's a fresh start with a new team and a new broom!

James Forsyth
Yes, with my Murdoch-honed communication skills helping Rishi to define Sunakism, Britain's going places.

Mark Harper
Not at the moment, it isn't. I've just advised everyone not to travel for two weeks, because of the rail strikes. And best to give airports a miss.

Suella Braverman
Rubbish. The army are doing a great job, driving trains, stamping passports and carrying out routine heart surgery. It makes you proud to be British. Which is what Sunakism is all about. 🇬🇧🇬🇧🇬🇧

Thanks, Suella. You can keep your job for another week.

Suella Braverman
And so can you.

POETRY CORNER

In Memoriam
Squadron Leader
Johnny Johnson,
Second World War flying hero

So. Farewell
Then Johnny Johnson,
The last of the
Dambusters.

You have died
Just before Christmas,
But you will live on
Every Boxing Day
Around lunchtime
On BBC2.

You may not
Have been a pilot,
But now you have
Your wings.

All together now:
"Der Der Der
Dum Diddy Dum Dum
Der Der Der
Dum Diddy Dum Dum
Dum De Dum Dum Dum
De Dum Dum Dum Dum
Diddy Dee Dum."

E.J. Thribb
(617½ Squadron)

GRAYSON PERRY MADE A KNIGHT

They should have made him a Dame

2022 WAS THE WARMEST YEAR ON RECORD

IN news that will shock nobody at all, which is why we've buried it on page 30 of this newspaper, 2022 was the warmest year on record in human history, which is part of a trend that will completely change the entire way life on earth functions before the century is over.

Yes, we have decided to mark this story, which is unbelievably significant and which has enormous ramifications for every future generation of life on the planet, on page 38 of the newspaper, below stories about a) interviews with celebrities on subjects they aren't experts on, b) single random events, c) people having to pay slightly more for their bills, and d) anything else we can think of.

We would have put it on page 39, but that's where we keep letters to the editor from readers who are annoyed about misuse of the word "whom".

The good news is you haven't read it either, have you? You can't bear to think about it and so you naturally have gone to the sports section, or the fashion supplement, which we have filled with pieces literally five times the length of this article about the future of life on earth in a feature about "The party dress trends of 2023".

To be fair, I haven't read it either; I'm writing it because a new report has come out and we needed a brief piece to go in between the advert for party food and the advert for Caribbean cruises.

On other pages
● Literally nothing as important as this story

SEX WORKER FINDS MP IN HOTEL ROOM

by IVOR FREEBIE
Our Foreign Affairs Staff

A HORRIFIED foreign prostitute has told reporters how she turned up to a local hotel room only to find a member of Britain's All-Party Parliamentary Group waiting for her.

"I was appalled," she said. "I mean, how sleazy can you get? There he was, a backbench MP, sitting on the bed, drinking from the mini-bar and loosening his Garrick club tie. I cannot begin to describe to you how shocked I was."

She continued, "These MPs have clearly been laid on by a discredited regime as some sort of blackmail and to compromise our reputations. I cannot afford to be associated with British Members of Parliament. If it got out, I would never work again."

FLU OUTBREAK

As Health Secretary, I'm the only one not coughing up

New Year Honours
(continued from page 1)

■ **Sir Tom Scholar** becomes Knight Grand Very Cross of the Order of the Early Bath for services to the Government for being fired from the Treasury by Liz Truss and Kwasi Kwarteng because he was completely right about their bonkers budget.

■ **Jason Knauf** becomes Lieutenant of the Royal Victoryovermeghan Order for services to the Monarchy for calling out the Duchess of Sussex on her bullying and making her look like a terrific humbug.

■ **Brian May** now becomes CBE, Commander of the Badger Empire, for services to making the Honours list respectable and not just an exercise in score settling.

■ The band **Queen** now becomes King *(That's enough honours, particularly because I didn't get one. Ed.)*

"Oh, for Heaven's sake, Mother. Haven't you been watching the news? We've been told not to do anything risky during the healthcare strikes"

TRIUMPH FOR FOOTBALLER IN SPARTS PERSONALITY OF THE YEAR

by Our Sparts Staff **Ian Wright-Onn**

AT A glittering, champagne-fuelled ceremony, held in the prestigious RMT canteen behind sidings at Crewe Junction, top Sparts personalities vied for the coveted trophy.

"It's been an amazing year for Sparts," said one of the judges, the Grauniad's Owen Goal, "culminating in a spectacular winter of discontent, which saw Sparts stars shining in the UK firmament."

But who would win? The bookies' favourite was top Spartsman, Mick Lynch, who sadly couldn't make the ceremony, as his train had been cancelled, but he joined the ceremony by Zoom link to make an impassioned speech, where he accused awards host Gary Salt'n'Lineker of being an idiot and said that he wanted 19% more airtime or else he was walking out.

The audience of dedicated Sparts fans were hugely disappointed when Mick, true to his word, stopped not working from home and left the Zoom call.

This left the field wide open and, at this point, judge Owen Goal tried to award the trophy to Sparting legend Jeremy Corbyn on the grounds that he had won the contest by coming second in 2019 and deserved to be awarded it in perpetuity.

But this controversial decision was rejected by the other judges when they consulted the VAR (Voting Assistant Referee), which proved conclusively that Corbyn had not been onside for a while and had definitely missed an open goal.

It was then that a dark horse emerged and, after a postal vote which saw only three envelopes arrive, the footballer Gary Neville was unanimously voted Sparts Personality of the Year for his performance in the Qatari World Cup, most notably in the half-time chat when he denounced the Tory government for being just as bad as the human rights abusers who had cruelly employed him and forced him to work on the maximum wage, for the entire tournament.

In his acceptance speech, the former Man United defender said, "This award is not for me, it's totally and basically for all the striking nurses in Britain who've been sickeningly treated, even worse than immigrant workers in Qatar, ie shamefully locked up and then personally flogged by notorious autocrat dictator Rishi Sunak, resulting, er, er, in the death of thousands of innocent pounds in my bank account, er, er, back to Roy Keane and Graeme Souness for their analysis of the state of the gilt market, vis à vis the pensions crisis, er, er…"

Other awards included the Sparts Team award which went to the Just Stop Oil team who had already glued themselves to the trophy, ensuring they had to take it home.

"Are you OK? You're looking a bit grassrootsy"

NEW MEMOIR: HARRY, HARRY, HARRY, WHILE SHOCKS LAST!

There is nothing worse than a frosty willy

I'm not frosty, Harold... I'm furious

Harry snorted cocaine!

But he disapproved of Camilla doing Charlie!

Your book's a bestseller!

I blame the press

It's all going Spare-shaped

ROYAL IRONYOMETER BROKEN

by Our Irony Correspondent
Br-Irony Gordon

ONE OF Britain's best-loved artefacts, which has been kept, along with the Crown Jewels, in the Tower of London, may finally be beyond repair.

The much-admired 15th century Royal Ironyometer has finally blown up.

Said the Keeper of the Royal Ironyometer, "It's taken such a pummelling in the last week, that I fear it's now beyond repair."

When asked what broke the Ironyometer, the Master of the Silver Humbug Detector went on to say it could have been any of the following:

● *When Harry said that he left the Royal Family in order to escape the media attention on his private life.*

● *When Harry said that he hopes that any talks about the contents of the book with his family will take place in private.*

● *When Harry accused Diana's former butler Paul Burrell of "milking" his mother's death in a tell-all book.*

● *When Harry said that the family didn't like his choice of wife and added that his father should never have married Camilla, whom he didn't like because she cynically* leaked *stories about him to make herself look better.*

● *When Harry said he moved to America to make his children safer, whilst drawing attention to the number of Taliban fighters he had killed.*

● *When Harry said he had never accused his family of racism, despite having happily accepted a human rights award from the Kennedy Foundation for speaking out against racism in the Royal Family.*

At this point, the Keeper of the Ironyometer also blew up.

Prince Harry, however, has given twelve interviews on five continents to make it clear that it was in fact the British Press who were to blame for the destruction of the Ironyometer by constantly writing about this book called *Spart. (Shome mishtake shurely? Ed.)*

LATE NEWS

■ Prince Harry hit back at critics of his philanthropic efforts, saying that charities will benefit from his book. He said, "Oxfam, in particular, will be grateful because in six months' time, they will have large numbers of second-hand copies of *Spare* in all of their shops, all over the country."

Nursery Times

············ Friday, Once-upon-a-time ············

WHO WAS THE OLDER WOMAN WHO SEDUCED PRINCE CHARMING AND TOOK HIS VIRGINITY?

by Our Royal Correspondent **Little Bo Peeping**

THE whole of Nurseryland is trying to guess the identity of the mystery older woman who dragged Prince Charmless into a field behind an alehouse and had her wicked witch way with him.

The encounter recorded in a fairytale by one of the Grim brothers is coy about exactly who the sexy siren was, but tongues are wagging throughout the land.

First to come under suspicion is Old Mother Hubbard, who shares the prince's love of dogs, but she has been quick to deny the rumours, saying, "The only thing bare that I have had my hands on is my cupboard!"

Next up is the Old Woman Who Lives in a Shoe, but she dismissed the allegations, exclaiming, "I have already got more children than I know what to do with! I am hardly likely to risk any more by having a chance sexual encounter with young Prince Harming!"

Others in the frame include Mother Goose, who has been known to goose young men in the past and may have grabbed him "by the rumplestiltskin". But most people now believe that the seductress in question was probably The Fine Lady who rode to Banbury "on a cock horse" and may well have treated the prince "like a stallion".

Prince Charmless, however, refuses to name names, but did confide to the Nurseryland Times, "I expect my Wicked Stepmother will leak the whole story to the Mirror Mirror on the Wall because that is the kind of indiscreet, scheming Snow-White-murdering evil Queen Consort that I wish all happiness ever after."

GLENDA SLAGG

■ JENNIFER COOLIDGE – dontcha-loveher????!!!! Who?????? What planet are you on, Mister??!? She's the gal with the Golden Globes!!?! Geddit!!!??! The Star of Amazon Hulu's smash hit new streaming sensation White Potus!!!?! And isn't it great to see a gal of a certain age and a certain weight appearing on screen as sexy and sassy. It gives all of us in the senior sisterhood hope!!!?! Ok, her character Kanya McWest *(subs, please check)* drinks a bit. Ok, she drinks a lot!!??! Who doesn't???! The main thing is she has FUN!!!!! (And then dies. Ooops!?!! Spoiler alert!!!)

■ JENNIFER COOLIDGE – arent-chasickofher???!!!! She's the supersized soak in Disney +'s White Flotus who's giving all of us gals of a certain age and weight a bad name!!??! Isn't it DEPRESSING to watch her a-snortin' and a-cavortin' around the Mediterranean???!!! And as for drink – she deserves all the boos she gets (Geddit!!!!!????) And no wonder she ends up drowning – and I don't mean her sorrows!!!?! Double ooops!!! There I go again!!!! At least I didn't tell you it was the Hawaiian guys whodunnit!!!!

Byeee!!

Doolally Mail

Sarah Vain

Writing exclusively on every page and on only one subject

I SAID it yesterday and I will say it again tomorrow. We have had enough of Harry. Can't he just leave us alone and give it a rest? He is obsessed! Doesn't Harry have anything else to write about? One does wonder!

* * *

OH NO! He's at it again. Harry, I mean. Today he has decided to go on and on and on about himself. Just for a change. He's like a cracked record. Harry Harry Harry. Put a sock in it Harry and stop boring us with the same old story.

* * *

PUT a sock in it Harry and stop boring us with the same old story! You are like a cracked record! Doesn't Harry have anything else to write about? One does wonder! He's obsessed. *(This is marvellous. Have some more money. Ed.)*

Avatar sequel 'The Way of the Water' reaches a billion in just 14 days

by Our Avatar Correspondent
Ava Tarr

Hollywood sources say the box-office smash *Avatar* sequel is already outpacing the first movie, with a billion people worldwide now unable to remember anything about the movie after just its first two weeks on release.

"With the first *Avatar* movie in 2009, it took nearly two months before the first billion people couldn't remember anything about that movie, apart from it being very pretty to look at, as it broke box-office records," said a Hollywood insider, puffing on a huge clichéd cigar.

"James Cameron has done it again! Delivering a box office goliath that no one can remember a single thing about. The man is a movie legend! He will go down in the annals of cinema history as the bloke who directed that Pocahontas rip-off about the Smurf-creatures."

Avatar: The Way of Southern Water

– PILBROW –

Keir Starmer WRITES

HELLO! It has come to my attention that there have been some serious questions relating to women and bullying in the Labour Party. Let me make myself clear. There is NO PLACE for women bullying ANYONE in the Labour Party!

Whenever I go into the House of Commons and sit down at my seat, I can't help but notice a woman sitting aggressively near me. Sometimes she shouts right in my ear and, to be honest, I find it quite intimidating, Angela!

At the moment, she is invading my personal space over striking teachers – twisting my arm (ouch!) to say something, or indeed anything. She seems to think I should take a more aggressive stance on things – but if school taught me one thing, it was that it's best to sit at the back and keep quiet. And I'm not afraid to shout it from the rooftops – that keeping quiet is the right thing to do!

Another lesson I learned was that the ones who keep quiet are the ones who avoid getting into trouble – and looking at the likes of shouty Nicola Sturgeon and gobby Nadine Dorries, I think you'll all agree that I'm right!

Now Angela's bending my ear that I've actually got the WRONG end of the stick about bullying – and that it's vulnerable women like Rosie Duffield who are being bullied by their male colleagues.

My message to Rosie is clear – the party has changed. Whereas BEFORE, this behaviour was encouraged, NOW it is ignored – which it always will be under my strong and decisive leadership. 10/10 to me! Well done, Starmer, top of the class!
Sincerely, Keir.

School news

St Cakes

The headmaster of St Cakes has signed a letter, along with 398 other headmasters of leading independent fee-paying day/boarding schools, to protest at plans to abolish the charitable status of their educational establishments.

Mr Kipling said that if St Cakes had to charge VAT, it would mean a huge loss of income for himself, and would furthermore lead to irreparable damage to the vital educational work conducted by the St Cakes Charitable Outreach Initiative, which has transformed the lives of so many underprivileged children in the local communities outside St Cakes' grounds.

He drew particular attention to the success of the access programme for local comprehensive school, Polly Toynbee Hall, whose pupils, he said, were granted "extraordinary levelling-up benefits".

When asked to name any, Mr Kipling quoted the school's policy of allowing comprehensive students to use the St Cakes' school pool on alternate Tuesdays from 7-7.30am in winter, involving some light ice-breaking duties.

When asked to name any more, Mr Kipling said, "Er, that's it", before leaving via the school helipad to attend an independent headmasters' conference in Mustique.

POETRY CORNER

In Memoriam
Astrud Gilberto, singer

So. Farewell
Then Astrud Gilberto.

You sang *The Girl*
From Ipanema,
But now it is you who
Has passed and we
Who say "Aah".

Altogether now:
Tall and tan and
Young and something,
The girl from Ipanema
Does something,
Doot do do doo,
Doot do do doo.
Doot da do da do.
Aaaaaaaah.

E.J. Thribb
(17½ million copies sold)

In Memoriam
Coolio

So. Farewell
Then Coolio.

You were a rapper
And won a Grammy
For *Gangsta's Paradise*.

You were not yourself
A Gangsta, but you
May be in Paradise,
As opposed to
The other place
Where people are
Not Coolio,
But too hot.

E.J. Thribb (17½ BPM)

In Memoriam
Jean-Luc Godard

So. Farewell
Then Jean-Luc Godard.
You were the captain
Of the Starship Enterprise.
Oh no – hang on...
Wikipedia says you
Were actually a
Legendary film director
Of the French
Nouvelle Vague.

So. Adieu
Then Jean-Luc Godard.
Your most famous
Film was *Breathless*,
And now, sadly,
So are you.

FIN.

E.J. Thribb
(Poet/Auteur, aged 17½)

THE KING OF TROUBLES

A short story special by Dame Hedda Shoulders

THE STORY SO FAR: Charles is feeling positive and optimistic, having survived the fall-out from his son's incendiary memoir 'Spart' attacking the monarchy. Now read on...

"YOU see, silence is golden. I learnt that from you, old friend," Charles thanked his wise and trusted confidant, the Aspidistra, who, as ever, kept his own counsel.

"Like you, we royals just say nothing and get on with the job of growing and being green and events take their course. Never complain, never explain and keep waving. That's the motto of the House of Windfarm and it seems to be working."

He smiled fondly at his leguminous companion and allowed himself the luxury of humming a merry tune – in this case, the Coronation anthem *Dixit Domino's Pizzas*. His reverie was interrupted by the arrival of the Queen Consulate, Duchess of Dunhill and future Menthol Monarch.

"Are you secretly briefing the vegetation again?" She rasped. "I told you that one is a plant!" Camilla laughed heartily at her own joke, which her soul-mate failed to find quite as amusing as she did. "Suit yourself," she added. "I'll give it to Jezza Clarkson for his Megbashing column. If he still has one. Ha ha ha!"

Charles's mood somehow did not match that of the Merry Second Wife of Windsor, who was searching the Emirates Conservatory (formerly the Mountbatten-burger Annexe) for a bottle of Shipsmithsh she had hidden there for emergencies. "It's Dry Ginuary!" she explained. "I'm only drinking G and T. Gin and Treble Gin!"

She retrieved her morning pick-me-up from underneath the rare but wilting Desert Orchid and headed for the Brandreth Library (so called because it was now entirely full of books about the royal family by the fabled raconteur and novelty-jumper aficionado). On her way, she passed Sir Alan Fitztightly wafting in, clutching a monogrammed clipboard.

"There are a few things I want to check about the plans for your forthcoming Coronation, Sire," he announced.

"Keep it short, Chazza, for God's sake – no one wants a three-hour bum number," Camilla counselled. "In and out... crown on your bonce, the Archbish squirts on the anointing oil, couple of hymns we can all belt out – *Amazing Grace and Favour House* – and then out onto the balcony for a gargle and a gasper!"

"Er... quite so, old thing... but I was thinking more of a multi-faith celebration of community and national dedication thingie, with a sort of all-embracing inclusivitiness, but still retaining a sense of majesty and awe..."

"Sounds awe-ful!" quipped the much maligned Unwicked Stepmother. "One hour tops or I'll borrow the Golliwog brooch from Princess Michael Von Kent!"

There were times, Charles thought, when banterous bonhomie really crossed the line of lèse-majesté.

Sir Alan coughed. "There are a number of details regarding Operation Coronation Chicken that we need to clarify."

"Yes, of course," replied Charles, "though I thought I had made most of it pretty clear."

"You wanted a choir that was LGBTQ+ and my partner the Air Vice-Marshal has got an old naval friend who runs the Portsmouth Pride Old Sailors Queer Choir who are huge fun and would really be up for some sea shanties or songs from *Mamma Mia*..."

"THANK YOU, Sir Alan. But I was thinking more of some younger people who maybe work for the NHS, perhaps singing *Za-Junior-Doc the Priest*...

"HRH Picky!" said the clearly offended royal factotum, who was doing his best to multi-task in his many roles, including Lord of the Listerine, Serjeant of the StinkyInk and now newly appointed Eggquerry in Chief with responsibility for defending the Monarch from incoming ovoid assault. "OK. Whatever. But you are going to have to deal with this one: invitations."

"Of course. We must have a representative of multi-faithful Britain... er... the Welsh Rabbi, the Mullah Lites, the Druid-in Chief, the Jedi Master, of course, the Wicca Men and those of no faith whatsoever."

"You mean the Church of England?" quipped Sir Alan, still smarting from the refusal of the Bishop of Finga's refusal to conduct a marriage ceremony for him and the Vice-Marshal in the Chapel of St Seven Brides.

"I meant the Agnostics, and the Atheists and the er... er..."

"Whilst we are on the matter of invitations, Sire, I do think we have to address the elephant in the room..."

"Excellent! An elephant. Emphasising our historic ties to the subcontinent and our attachment to the Commonwealthy..."

"No, Sire, the metaphorical elephant. Namely, what to do about Wills and Harry. The Prince of Wallops and the Count of Montecito."

Charles's noble brow furrowed.

"Ah, yes. Separate pews? Separate Cathedrals? Two coronations with one of them at each?"

Sir Alan was prepared.

"Prince Edward has a suggestion, Sire."

Prince Charles was relieved and delighted that the Wessexes were having an input. He had grown increasingly dependent on their calm and sensible judgement, as the rest of his family's behaviour became increasingly more outlandish.

"Eddie thought that you could solve their differences with a bit of showbiz fun and games."

Charles looked confused.

"*It's a Royal Knockout – the Sequel*. Wills and Harry in the aisle of the Abbey fight it out dressed as medieval knights with inflatable plastic sceptres, all staged on a wobbly drawbridge over a giant dog-bowl-shaped tank of Brown Windsor soup. Netfakes have apparently bought the rights already."

"I hope this is one of your unamusing jokes, Sir Alan," spluttered Charles.

"I will take that as a light pencil then?"

"Noooooooooo! That idea is simply... what is the word that I am not allowed to use anymore? And the fact that I am not allowed to use it is itself... what is that word?"

(To be continued...)

GOD. WHAT DID WE DO BEFORE THE INTERNET?

HANG ON I'LL LOOK IT UP

WARNER.

CHINA INSTIGATES MOVE FROM ZERO-COVID TO 100%-COVID POLICY

by Our China Correspondent
Yu Coffin Tuu

HOSPITALS and morgues began to fill today with people celebrating the news that China has abandoned its Zero Covid policy and switched to a new national policy of total Covid infection.

This stunning new initiative by President Xi has been undertaken in order to combat a deadly new outbreak of democracy across the country.

Said a Communist Party spokesman, "The situation was looking dangerous, but by stopping this deadly strain of democracy in its tracks, President Xi has given the public the freedom it craved to travel freely from overcrowded emergency ward to overcrowded ward with their sick elderly relatives, in joyous celebration of the end of Covid."

Senior party sources, however, did say that Xi's 'Zero Reporting How Many People Are Dying' Covid policy would remain in force for a short time, expected to be forever.

Lines on the historic passing of the Gender Recognition Act in the Scottish Parliament at Holyrood

'Twas in the year two thousand and twenty-two

That Scotland decreed men could use the ladies' loo.

At least, I think that was the gist of the Gender Recognition Act,

Though, forgive me, that may not be completely exact.

But I gather that in twenty twenty-three

A laddie can be a lassie if that's their chosen identity.

Which is, of course, all fair and fine and dandy,

Tho many folk thought a bit more caution might come in handy.

I hesitate, of course, to approach this topic in verse,

For fear that I could be Twitter-shamed or worse.

This issue has, sadly, led to much nasty online trolling

Of the controversial Harry Potter author, JK Rowling.

But Ms Sturgeon is adamant and keen to make a stand,

As culture wars might well boost the lookalike Krankie brand.

I now realise that by alluding to that young woman dressed as a boy,

I may have hit upon a whole new way both sides to annoy.

So, I apologise to everyone of all views in advance,

Hoping not to be cancelled and made a "forgot auld acquaintance".

May I therefore wish you all a Happy New Year,

Whether lesbian, gay, bisexual, trans or queer.

(Or straight.)

© *William McGonagall 1867*

"With the exorbitant price of school uniforms now, his new outfit has got to last him until he leaves"

MCLACHLAN

CHINA RECORDS FIRST COVID DEATH

The truth

Biden stunned by documents discovery

by Our Washington Staff
Miss Laid

Joe Biden was shocked to hear that classified documents in his garage clearly stated that he was President of the United States.

"Jeepers," said Biden, "Why am I always the last to know?" He continued, trying to play down the importance of the discovery, "I had forgotten that I was President of the United States, and I'd also forgotten why I didn't know that. But I'm sure that after a nap it will all come back to me."

Meanwhile, Republicans supporting Trump said that seeing a man so confused and utterly unsuitable in the Oval Office gave them great hope for the future.

BANX

"We like to think we're ready for the next pandemic"

Best Old Films

A Bridgen Too Far

Classic British drama about a doomed mission that goes horribly wrong. Andrew Bridgen is parachuted into a Tory safe seat and proceeds to wreak havoc with his scattergun approach to the truth. First, he fights a grim battle in court with his own family over a potato farm and is wounded when the judge shoots down his case and points out that he's a liar. Then he takes on the real enemy – the British Heart Foundation – and launches a full-frontal attack on their chief executive, accusing him of covering up evidence of a fiendish plot by the British government, Bill Gates, Big Pharma and Uncle Tom Cobley, to murder everyone by vaccinating them.

The Matrix

Neocon (Andrew Tate) takes a red pill and discovers an actual "real world" outside his carefully constructed alternate reality of life as an incel internet influencer. In this real world Neocon finds that he gets arrested by actual "real police" on charges of sex trafficking. He then complains about the Matrix, despite having bragged about his behaviour to millions of teenage boy followers in countless misogynistic YouTube videos. *(That's enough Tate. Ed.)*

EXCLUSIVE TO ALL NEWSPAPERS
WHY THE TEACHERS MUST GO BACK TO SCHOOL

OF COURSE, one sympathises with the plight of the unfortunate teachers, given the cost of living crisis and historic underpayment for their vital and hugely important work educating the nation's young.

But now is absolutely the wrong time to strike, for one simple reason – I have no childcare and I'm not going through home-schooling hell again, you uncaring bastards!

Perhaps you should think less about how you'll pay the rent and more about my marriage!!! Get back to work, you lazy sods. Please!!!!!!!!!

(© All newspapers)

ZAHAWI SACKED OVER TAX AVOIDANCE SCHEME

We can't have ex-chancellors with dodgy family finances

I accept your resignation

That Zahawi letter of resignation in full

Dear Prime Minister,

Thank you for your kind letter, accepting my honourable decision to be sacked. I accept your point that this is a matter of trust – which is excellent, as I have an offshore family trust in Gibraltar.

Your letter said that "carelessness" was not an excuse. This is, of course, quite right, and it is astonishing that you made such an error of judgement in appointing me Party Chairman.

When you gave me the job I told you everything was fine – which was true. The fine was £1 million. Your suggestion that I behaved in some way unethically means that you will, of course, be hearing from my lawyers. Your Ethics Advisor seems to have the wrong idea about what his job entails – namely, releasing a woolly report in three years' time, when everyone has forgotten about the issue and it can be safely ignored by the Prime Minister. Sir Magnum Scandalum will also be hearing from my lawyers – as will anyone who suggests that I am overly litigious.

And never forget, I arrived in this country fleeing persecution and speaking no English – and I still face persecution today, because I sadly never learned the English word for "tax". The Press are trying to have me lynched after a long campaign of racist vilification based solely on the fact that I am a Krook (surely Kurd?).

My parents arrived here with nothing and, according to my tax returns, they still have nothing. Educated in a run-down London public school, I pulled myself up by my boot-straps, and then filled my boots! I love this country, which nobly upholds the principle that you are innocent until proven guilty, and then you're still innocent. In no other country on earth would my unbelievable story be believed.

There are those who will say that you shut the stable door after the horse has bolted – but I would point out that the stable was very well heated at the taxpayers' expense, so any temperature drop while the stable door was open was thankfully minimal.

It has been an honour for you to have me in your government and I shall loyally support you on the backbenches (unless this turns out not to be true, through no fault of my own). Many people will no doubt say that there should be an apology in this letter – and I agree. I demand an apology from the Press, HMRC, the government and yourself.

As for my future, I shall expect a speedy return, which is admittedly not what I submitted to HMRC.

Your fiend,

N. Zahawi

Nadhim Zahawi

Where The Wild Things Are...n't

America hails equal rights progress

by **Liberty Bell**

AMERICAN civil rights campaigners hailed a turning point in race relations at the news that a young black man had been beaten to death by black police officers.

"It has taken a long time," said one spokesman for Black Lives Don't Matter, "but at last we now have a country in which black policemen have equal rights to murder innocent black men for minor traffic offences."

He continued, "I have a dream, a dream in which the colour of your skin will no longer determine whether you brutalise people indiscriminately."

He concluded, "As a sign of how far the US has come, these black police officers will have the right to be prosecuted – unlike all the white officers who got away with it."

FEWER BRITISH CARS BEING MADE THAN EVER BEFORE

We're going to go from 60-0 in the next five years!

A Tank Driver writes

Vlad 'Mad' Putin, Tank No: ZZZZ

Every week a well-known tank driver gives his opinion on a matter of topical importance. This week, the imminent deployment of British tanks in Ukraine…

Blimeyski! Heard the news?! Not what a Russian tank driver wants to hear. The bloody British are sending tanks over here. Not the new armoured vehicles, obviously, because they don't work. But the old tanks. Don't want to see one of them Challengers coming up the road, parping their horn, pointing their barrel at you and telling you to get out the way. Talk about road rage! I was thinking of getting a new tank, myself. One of the state-of-the-art Russian ones with all the bells and whistles and latest gizmos. Turns out they're quite hard to get hold of, on the grounds that they're in a bit of short supply, due to the fact they haven't been built yet. They are calling them stealth tanks. You see – very funny. Unless you're in charge of the tank programme and then you find yourself suddenly in a different vehicle altogether – a hearse. You gotta laugh. I SAID, YOU GOTTA LAUGH! Hang on – there's something wrong with this tank. It seems stuck in reverse gear! Hang on – I'm meant to be heading South of the River, but I seem to be going back to Moscow! I'll drop you here – out the window!

© A tank driver 2023.

PRINCE HARRY: A-Z OF PEOPLE WHO BETRAYED ME

A is for ABBA. Meghan and I were married in 2018. There was so much love. The whole world rejoiced. But the four members of Abba – I'm not going to name them – refused to reach out. They didn't say a word, and refused to sing at our reception. Sadly, they'd been silenced.

B is for BRIAN MAY. I was all ready with my guitar on the roof of the palace and I'd been practising for ages, but then Brian May barged past and started to play. My father's silence was deafening.

C is for CORGIS. It's basically the corgis who rule the palace. Nothing goes on without their say-so. When I was six, a corgi barked at me. No, I can't say which one, because there was this massive cover-up orchestrated by a special committee chaired by a senior family corgi. They ended up briefing the press that I had barked at the corgi. It's so unfair.

D is for DUMPTY, HUMPTY. Believe me, the palace was behind it, 100 percent. Their silence was deafening.

E is for EDINBURGH, DUKE OF. I'll never forget the day of Grandpa's funeral. William wouldn't let me have a sherbet lemon. I said give it. He said shan't. I said give it. He said shan't. I said give it. He said shan't. I said, I'll put it in my book. He said, you'll never. So I did. But they took it out of context.

F is for FROSTBITE ON MY PENIS. How did it get into my book? Just think about it. Too right. My penis leaked it to the tabloid press.

G is for PRINCE GEORGE. I genuinely believe and hope that there will be reconciliation between my family and myself that will have a ripple effect across the entire world but not until Prince George makes a full public apology for breaking a Mr Wobbly toy I gave him for his second birthday. I had put so much love into selecting that present and then wrapping it up, and to see it destroyed was... well, I really don't want to go there. Let's just say it left me in a very dark place.

H is for HITLER. Adolf suffered from unconscious bias, just like some others I could name.

I is for IPANEMA, THE GIRL FROM. Tall and tan and young and lovely, the girl from Ipanema took my virginity in a pub forecourt without asking. Yes, I may have put this in my book, but under direct orders from the palace, the press took it totally out of context, and conspired to make it look as though she took my virginity in a pub forecourt without asking.

J is for JACK AND JILL. Sure, Jack and Jill went up the hill to fetch a pail of water, and I have a lot of compassion for that. Then Jack fell down and broke his crown and Jill came tumbling after. Or that was the distorted narrative the rest of the world was offered. The truth is that Jack had said some very hurtful things to me and Jill had refused to lend Meghan her lipgloss.

K is for KATE. See under de Vil, Cruella.

M is for MIDGES. Staying at Balmoral, I had just taken a few shots of tequila and smoked a few joints when I saw a cloud of midges coming towards me. They looked as though they had something really important to tell me about, like, the universe. I truly believed I could form a bond with them. "Hey, guys!" I said. "You look like you're in a good place. Any wisdom to share with a young traveller just setting out on his own journey of healing?" But they didn't say anything. They just bit me all over. I've since learnt that it was an orchestrated campaign.

O is for OBAMA. Meghan and I asked Barack and Michelle to a pot-roast in Montecito last week, with Barry Manilow and Lionel Ritchie. Their people said they couldn't make it. Forgiveness is 100 percent a possibility, but first they need to acknowledge the hurt they've caused.

P is for THE PRINCESS ROYAL. How are we gonna make this world a better place? That's something Meghan and I are striving for, 24/7. There's so much pain and suffering in the world, and it's up to each and every one of us to do something about it. But when I suggested to my Aunt Anne that she should move out of Gatcombe Park to somewhere smaller and more in line with her status as a minor royal and let Meg and me use it as our own home and World Wellness Centre, she said something very hurtful.

Q is for QUEEN ELIZABETH II. She had such deep, deep respect for me, and that's what I admire about her. The last time I saw her, she said it was her dying wish to fast-track me to the throne. "Let's face it, Harry," she said, "your mental health is so much better than your papa's or your brother's, and Meghan will make a very caring, very loving Queen. So what are we waiting for, guys?" Then just as she was asking me for a pen and paper so she could change the line of succession, she passed away. But it was a private conversation, so I do not propose to discuss it here.

T is for TALIBAN. What I still can't quite believe is that the palace did absolutely nothing to stop the Taliban from shooting at me. In fact, their silence was deafening. Were they in league with senior Taliban leaders to stop me spreading my message of hope for the planet by blowing my head off? I honestly don't know, but if there's going to be any chance of reconciliation, then let's have that conversation, guys.

W is for WILLIAM. And another thing. He still owes me for that apple I gave him 26 years, five months, two weeks and one day ago. I asked for it back at Granny's funeral, but he just said "What apple?" and looked straight through me. So I fled the country.

X is for XI JINPING. We asked Xi over for a barbecue with James Corden and Serena Williams the other day, but his people said he was busy. You guessed it. The palace had been getting to him.

Y is for YO-YO. I was a child of six. I kept throwing that yo-yo away. But it kept coming back. Throwing away. Coming back. Throwing away. Coming back. I thought, if you want to do that, then do it. But don't ask me to join in. That's not who I am.

Z is for ZEBEDEE. All the figures in the so-called Magic Roundabout were acting under direct orders from my stepmother. But the worst was Zebedee. Whatever I did, he kept bouncing back.

As told to

CRAIG BROWN

Doolally Mail

BRAVE BORIS RETURNS TO THE FRONT

BRITAIN's Boris Johnson has spectacularly returned to the front page by risking everything to demonstrate his commitment to himself.

Boris flew to Kyiv to meet a number of photographers and pledge to do everything he could to win the war with Rishi Sunak.

While he was there, he was welcomed by the president, Volodymyr Zelensky, who said it was great to see him back on the front page.

The former and next prime minister gave a harrowing eye-witness account to the Daily Mail of what he saw during his visit.

"It is a shocking scene of a once great career now bombed and in ruins. Wherever I look there are weeping women and children without a father. And the devastation is appalling to behold. Over there, peeling gold wallpaper... and there in the garden, a broken swing and a smashed bottle by a stained sofa. And on the street someone has thrown out an old suitcase full of wine."

He continued, "I don't know how much it's going to cost to rebuild all this, but maybe £800,000 would be a good start." He then wiped away a tear. "You'd have to have a heart of stone not to laugh at my predicament."

LATE NEWS

■ Boris claims Putin threatened to kill him with cheat-seeking missile.

LATE LATE NEWS

■ Kremllin denies Boris missile threat: "He's desperate, he'll say anything!" claims Putin.

TORY BARONESS IN ONGOING PPE SCANDAL

There's no cover-up here

'Time to tidy away all your old opinions' says Marie Kondo

by Our Lifestyle Correspondent
JOY SPARK

THE Queen of Clean is back – and this time she's de-cluttering all her old opinions.

"Having made a tidy profit and cleaned up by telling you to chuck everything away, I'm now telling you to dispense with everything I've said before," she announced.

She continued, "Look, I've had a third child, and I've suddenly realised why everyone's homes are so messy. Who would have thought it? Kids create chaos! And the Pope is Catholic! And bears need potty training in the woods! Who knew? Apart from everyone, except me."

Said Ms Kondo, "Please read all about it in my new book, *'How to throw out all my old books to make room for my next books'.*"

Daily Mail   COMMENT

Hurrah for Germany sending tanks to fight against Russia

IT can't have been an easy decision for the Chancellor to make, but in the end it was the right decision for Germany and for the world.

Herr Hitler has shown great moral character, and one can sympathise with his initial hesitation. He was worried about escalating the local conflict into a world war that might last for years, but now he has seen that it is imperative that the forces of evil should be met with an allied response.

Supported by Mr Mussolini and General Franco, there can now be no doubt that the dictator Stalin will be defeated and toppled, thanks to the superior firepower of German tanks.

The Panzers that are now cruising through Ukraine to engage with the Russians on the Eastern front can only be considered a force for good, and will guarantee peace in this region for all time.

© Lord Rothermere 1941

"We had hoped to summit, but Toby hypothermed and Clive hamstringed"

THE OSCARS 2023

Academy acclaim for Ava Tár

Ava Tár leads the way with eleven Oscar nominations. The spellbinding story of a bright blue conductor with a long tail who flies around the oceans on a fish monster has delighted audiences and critics alike.

The totally CGI-constructed film about the predatory lesbian Smurf, swimming from concert hall to concert hall, seducing young cello-playing mermaids to the sound of Schubert's Trout Quintet, has left audiences leaving cinemas, stunned and delighted to have got out after only three and a half hours.

An amazing performance by Skate Blanchett playing conductress Ava Tár should secure her the Best Non-Human Digitally-Enhanced Virtual Actor in a Blue Movie Award.

THE BANSHEES OF INISHERIN UP FOR MANY OSCARS

How many do you think we'll win?

I can count them on the fingers of one hand

Now, on with the important work of winning the next election. Let me introduce my secret weapon: Deputy Chairman of the Party. The guy who's going to deliver us the Red Wall seats single-handed. Welcome, Lee.

Lee Anderson
Fooock off, you southern twats!

Dominic Raab
I like the sound of him. 👍

Lee Anderson
You can fooock off too, you limp-wristed nonce. Call yourself a bully?

James Forsyth
I say, Rishi, what a capital idea. Getting in someone even more unpleasant than Dominic. And he's actually working class! How marvellous!

Lee Anderson
'Oo the fooock are you, posh boy?

James Forsyth
He really is authentically ghastly. And he's even called Lee. The oiky voters are going to love him.

Yes. And in the interests of balance, I've also brought in a conventional safe pair of hands, viz Greg Hands, call-sign "Safe Pair of". 🤲

Greg Hands
Delighted to be brought in to replace someone who's just been sacked. Again. Call me the Minister Without Scandal.

Dominic Raab
Yet. ☝️

Now, everyone up to speed with the exciting Whitehall reordering and renaming of Departments? The Ministry for Paperclips becomes the Ministry for Stationery Requisites, but responsibility for staplers has been moved to the Department for Office Supplies (formerly Department of Supplies for Offices), which has now been merged with the Post-It Note Directorate.

Lee Anderson
Fooock me.

Grant Shapps
Rishi, just wanted to check, what's my new job?

You're in charge of Net Zero.

Grant Shapps
So I'm sacked then? That's very disloyal.

You're not sacked, Grant. I've given you the most important job in the Cabinet. It's your job to save the planet.

Thérèse Coffey
Hang on, I thought I was in charge of the environment. What am I meant to do?

Dominic Raab
Carry on pumping shit everywhere, fatso.

James Forsyth
Strictly, as Head of Comms, that's my job. 💩

Michelle Donelan
Talking of jobs, am I still in mine?

Who are you?

Michelle Donelan
Michelle Donelan. Culture Secretary.

Oh yes, but now you're doing Science, Innovation and Technology. You're going to create a Silicon Valley for British tech geniuses.

Jeremy Hunt
There already is one. It's in Silicon Valley. It's where all the bright Brits go when they can't get a job here. No offence, Rishi. 😊

Lee Anderson
The only business that's booming in Britain is the second-hand rubber boats industry. When are we going to send them all home to Rwanda? Or better still, hang the lot of them. That'll get us the swing voters! Call-sign "Hang Man".

Suella Braverman
Lee, you're talking my language.

Lee Anderson
That's lucky, cos it's English, not Hindustani, luv.

Great broad-church banter. There's room in this party for all sorts, from the ghastly to the very ghastly. The next election's as good as won.

Jeremy Hunt
By Keir. 😔

The administrator has removed Mr Hunt from the group for failing to display a delusional lack of self-knowledge.

"My name is Maximus Decimus Meridius, commander of the armies of the north, general of the Felix Legions and loyal servant to the true emperor, Marcus Aurelius. Father to a murdered son, husband to a murdered wife... but enough about me, tell me a little about you..."

BBC NEWS

Why are so many people leaving the BBC?

EXCLUSIVE Report by... er... Sorry, no one is currently available to write this page – as they have resigned or been made redundant.

This report will be filed as soon as we have someone available to write it.

■ **READ MORE** just as soon as we have someone new in position.

POETRY CORNER

Lines on the marriage of Buzz Aldrin, astronaut and second man on the moon

So. Congratulations
Then Buzz Aldrin.

Marriage is a small
Step for man,
But a giant leap
Of faith for a
93-year-old.

You have landed on
Another heavenly body,
The 63-year-old
Anca Faur.

Who is, coincidentally,
Wife number four.
I guess you always
Were good at the
Separation stage.

But now you must be
Hoping to live
To infinity and beyond.

(Is this the right Buzz? Ed.)

E.J. Thribb
(17½ orbits per second)

The Sunday Telegram

Sunday 19 February 2023

FOR the first time, the captain of the *Titanic* breaks her silence, in a 4,000-word essay explaining why she sailed into an iceberg and sank her ship

TWENTY-four hours ago I was the proud captain of the RMS *Titanic*, steaming across the ocean with a mandate to break international records for a transatlantic crossing.

Who would have thought that just a day later I would be sitting here in Davy Jones' locker after the worst disaster in maritime history?

After a period of reflection and soul-searching on the sea bed, I have come to a number of conclusions.

There was nothing wrong with the direction I was going in, ie straight towards the iceberg, but I admit that I was going too fast, particularly at the moment of collision. But this was not my fault, since no one had told me that it would be dangerous to hit an iceberg in the middle of the ocean.

I was trying to do something radical, something different and the only reason I failed was that the nautical establishment tried to prevent me. I thought that, as captain, I had the authority to do whatever I liked. How wrong I was!

Instead, as soon as I announced "Full Steam ahead into the iceberg", the bureaucratic blob swung into action.

"Stop, for God's sake, woman. Are you mad?" shouted one old-school officer on watch and that timid cry was echoed by all the so-called establishment experts on board.

This included the navigator, the first officer, the chief engineer and the entire crew, as well as everyone in the world, calling me on the radio telling me to "Change course before you kill everyone!"

But I still maintain that I was right and that the course I set was correct. But for the weakness of the ship at the point of impact, coupled with the unexpected strength of the iceberg and the unforeseen quantity of water in the ocean, which nobody could have predicted, the voyage would have been a huge success.

That is why I believe that my career as a captain is far from over. Given another chance, which would only be fair, given my blameless previous record, I believe that I could once again navigate the great ship of state into an iceberg even more successfully and with even greater loss of life and I would deliver the vessel in record time to its ultimate destination at the bottom of the sea.

© *Captain Liz Truss*

■ THERE will be an exclusive interview with Captain Truss on Specsaver TV, in which she will explain how she could not possibly have seen what was coming. She will also be quizzed about her decision to throw First Mate Kwarteng overboard just before the ship sank, even though he followed her instructions to the letter.

'NO MORE RETURNS' SAY RAIL FIRMS

by Our Transport Correspondent
Dee Lay

BRITAIN's rail firms have this week agreed to scrap the longstanding "return ticket" scheme.

For decades, passengers in Britain have been able to purchase both "day return" and "open return" tickets, which allowed travellers to go to their destinations and then come back again.

A spokesman for the railways said, "We are addressing the reality of modern-day rail travel and these tickets are completely outmoded.

"In the present conditions, passengers are extremely unlikely to reach their destination, so what is the point of having a ticket to come back again?"

He argued that most trains now only operate subject to industrial action, staff shortages, technical malfunctions and "the wrong kind of inclement weather on the line", which all contribute to the non-departure or non-arrival of the service.

He added, "This is a breakthrough and should decrease customer dissatisfaction with an under-performing rail network.

"Our next move will be to phase out 'single tickets' as well, so that there is no possibility of delays or cancellations – as there will be no trains scheduled at all."

LATE NEWS

New destination for HS2 planned

■ DOWNING Street has refused to confirm press reports that the final destination for the HS2 project could now be diverted from the long grass into the bin.

"Given the huge cost overruns surrounding the project, it makes sense for HS2 to end up in the bin," said a No10 insider.

"We believe we can cut the time it takes to divert the project from the long grass into the bin by as much as 17 minutes."

The government refused to confirm reports that, in order to save even more money, it would not be running trains along the line when HS2 was completed on the twelfth of never *(cont. p94)*

That historic Zelensky speech on visit to UK

Hold your nerve, Britain. I know things are tough, but you will make it through. I know it may seem hopeless, but we are all with you. When I walk around your ruined and empty streets and I see the pain on the faces of your citizens, I know what you are going through. But under your inspired leader, whichever one it is today, I am sure that you will triumph over adversity and rebuild your great country once again. Now give me the fucking planes.

Lines Written on the Historic Struggle to Create an Independent Scottish Prison Policy

'Twas in the year of our Lord two thousand and twenty-three
That the vexed issue of trans rights continued to vex the SNP.
Some of their MSPs joined in a controversial demonstration
To support Ms Sturgeon's bold stance on gender self-identification.
Unfortunately, placards there read "Terfs should be decapitated",
Which is not exactly language that is polite or understated.
(It is very tricky for me writing poems about Terfs
Because the only feasible rhyme for such persons is Smurfs,
Who are very blue and very small and live in toadstools
And do not worry overmuch about the use of pronouns in schools.)
But I digress – these slogans were illustrated by a guillotine,
Which you'd have thought everyone there would have seen.
The MSPs' claim that "we saw nothing" did them no favours
And folk commented that "they should have gone to Specsavers".
The First Minister said feminists had criticised her too in the past,
Though the difference in unpleasantness was clearly vast.
But Nicola's discomfort was not helped by the embarrassing news
That a trans woman prisoner was formerly a male rapist in troos.
In the uproar, the Justice Secretary said he would not intervene,
But this was before Sturgeon noticed how this farce was being seen,
So suddenly the self-defined woman was sent to a man's prison,
Which was the case of objections that had previously arisen.
So how would Sturgeon escape from her U-turn so screeching
To stop all the auld Scots voters whose support was now leeching?
She decided that it was necessary to change her position
And from her previous policy she would have to transition.
"This prisoner was creating a risk to other women," said she,
"Particularly one poor wee woman I know – ME!"

© William McGonagall 1867

"We've had reports about a smell of money"

BRITISH GAS 'SHOCKED BY DEBT COLLECTORS'

BRITISH GAS says it was shocked to learn that the debt collection company it employed to break into poor people's homes to fit expensive pre-payment meters wasn't the sweet, lovely, considerate company they thought it was.

"We could never have guessed that the debt collection company we employed, Absolute Total Bastards Inc, was actually a cold, soulless organisation, driven by money and staffed by absolute total bastards who revelled in breaking into desperate people's homes to drive them even further into poverty," said a wide-eyed, naïve British Gas spokesman.

"In future, we'll only employ lovely debt collection companies, staffed by kindly old grannies, kittens and unicorns."

(Rotters)

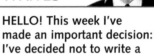
Keir Starmer WRITES

HELLO! This week I've made an important decision: I've decided not to write a column!

There will be no column from me this week because I've got together with my comms team and we've realised that the less I do, the further ahead the party is in the polls.

Currently, I'm at 50% in the polls this week – and I've done literally nothing. Have you seen me anywhere, doing anything? I certainly haven't. I even looked in the bathroom mirror this morning and I wasn't there!

That's how effective my new policy of non-appearance is – and I intend to do even less in future, if that's what it takes. I'll stop at nothing to do nothing.

Oh no!

I've now been told by the comms team not to mention that I'm not writing this column any more – because the optics are that it looks like I'm doing something.

Be assured, I'm NOT!
Sincerely,
Not Keir Starmer.

EX-LABOUR MP JAILED FOR COCAINE FRAUD

by Our Political Staff **Charlie Upnose**

THE Conservative Party was quick to condemn ex-Labour MP Jared O'Mara last night, as he was given four years for abusing his position as a Member of Parliament to commit multiple frauds and spending public money on cocaine and alcohol.

Said a Tory spokesman, "Yet again, the Labour Party have shown they've got no ideas of their own and are just copying Conservative policies. We've had dozens of cokehead, pissed-up fraudsters, yet, as soon as someone in Labour comes along doing the same thing, they get all the attention."

He continued, "It's very irritating for us to see this kind of theft, ie of our ideas. We in the Conservative Party are going to be talking about this, very loud and very fast, before moving on to a nightclub where we've been assured they have some really good stuff."

Said another, "O'Mara made sexist and homophobic comments, and gave his friend a job funded by public money. This is the most amazing rip-off and we'll be offering Mr O'Mara a safe seat and a cabinet position as soon as he's out of prison."

Turkey Earthquake Scandal

1) WAS YOUR REACTION TO THIS DISASTER ABYSMALLY SLOW MR PRESIDENT?...
2)
3)
4)
5)
6) NO.

WHY I DON'T THINK DOMINIC RAAB IS A BULLY

SO Dominic Raab's behaviour is under scrutiny because a handful of 94 complainants have suggested he humiliated them in the workplace.

Boo hoo hoo! Honestly, call that bullying? I'd like to see some of those lily-livered Whitehall civil snowflakes try to survive five minutes in the newsroom of the Daily Bullygraph.

Honestly, all of us in Fleet Street have suffered a lot worse than being told it's not good enough. Bullying is when your editor rings you up and says "I want a piece on bullying in three minutes, you worthless piece of shit, or you're fired and your children will starve," and that's when he's in a good mood.

Catch him after lunch, and he's more likely to say "Oi, fuckbrain! The bullying copy is crap, a five-year-old could do

better. Tell you what, why don't you fuck off home and catch your other half shagging the Foreign Editor, while I do your job for you! You pathetic, lame-brained retard!"

But do I complain? Do I call it "bullying"? No, I'm far too frightened to. As far as I'm concerned, it's just good-natured newsroom banter.

And, as my editor always says, "If you end up sobbing in the toilet, then why don't you save me a job and flush your head down the crapper while you're there!"

On other pages

■ Join our mental health awareness week **p7**

■ Mindfulness – why it's good for you **p8**

■ Charles Moore's top yoga tips **p94**

Nursery Times

Friday, Once-upon-a-time

SPY BALLOON SHOT DOWN OVER HUNDRED ACRE WOOD

by Our Espionage Staff **Bo Peep**

IN an incident which threatened to destabilise all of Nurseryland, alarm was raised over a balloon that was reportedly sent to spy on a colony of bees.

Beneath the balloon dangled a highly suspicious bear, codenamed Pooh, whose intention was clearly hostile.

A spokesman for the F Bee I said, "We knew that the bear's plan was to hover over our nest, disguised as a raincloud, and evaluate the honey, with a view to possible seizure at a later point."

He continued, "We decided we had no alternative but to take out the so-called weather balloon with all force necessary. Hence

the stinger missile we sent to disable the spying device."

Local resident, Piglet, reported hearing a "loud buzzing followed by a massive pop" before the wreckage of the balloon fell to earth, rapidly followed by a bear clutching a piece of string.

However, the bear, Xingie the Pooh, said, "I categorically deny spying on the honey tree, as I sang to everyone at the time, *I'm just a little black rain cloud, hovering under the honey tree. I'm only a little black rain cloud, pay no attention to little me.*"

Eeyore sighed and said, "So I guess it's a Third World War, then."

TOAD IDENTIFIES AS WASHERWOMAN, IN ORDER TO GET OUT OF JAIL

IT's been called the most disgraceful travesty of justice in Nurseryland history, as a criminal amphibian was allowed to define himself as a female laundry operative, purely in order to escape from a male prison.

Toad, a known reprobate from Toad Hall and convicted dangerous driver, denied cynically gaming the system by changing gender and exploiting Nurseryland's recently changed

Gender Recognition Act. Said Toad, "Poop! Poop!" as he *(surely "she"?)* hopped onto a barge and made his *(surely "her"?)* escape. This massive embarrassment for the Nurseryland judiciary was followed by a shocking new scandal, where a wolf identified as a grandmother, in order to try and eat an innocent young girl in a red hood.

AMOL RAJAN IN AGONY AUNT PHOTO CASEBOOK

Hey, look – I'm in your bed

Of course you are... you're in bloody everything!

Han-z-z-zard
Select Committees today

2:15pm Committee of MPs to decide whether MPs who lose their seats at elections should be given big pay-offs to tide them over before landing new jobs, and also be awarded a medal for their important contribution to national life. On a unanimous show of hands, the committee of MPs decided to recommend all the above.

3:15pm Committee of bears to decide whether bears should be allowed to use forested locations for defecation purposes, and also be awarded a medal for their important contribution to wood life. On a unanimous show of paws, the committee of bears decided to recommend all the above.

4:15pm Committee of Popes to decide whether or not they should be recognised as members of the Holy Catholic and Apostolic Church, and also be awarded big hats for their important contribution to Vatican life. On a unanimous show of white smoke, the committee of Popes decided to recommend all the above.

"Looks like we've got a potential jumper"

POLICE LOG
Neasden Central Police Station

08.24 Morning briefing (Thought for the Day: "There must be SOME good apples left in the barrel"). Reports that two officers from the Neasden service will be appearing in court every week for crimes, including violence against women, until 2027 are greeted as good news by service chiefs: this is a substantial improvement on previous statistics, in which no officers were being arrested or charged; the more officers who are prosecuted, the more the public will come to trust the Neasden service once again.

13.43 New hotline for public to report police brutality as part of the 'NEWsden' campaign for civic reform is unveiled by assistant chief constable. The hotline number will be available to any members of the public who consider themselves to have just been assaulted by uniformed Neasden officers, provided they report the officer who just allegedly attacked them within five minutes of the alleged incident.

16.27 Ceremony at central station takes place for unveiling of new station motto: "You Can't Beat Neasden Bobbies, But They Can Beat You." Officers take to streets armed with tasers to spread message, led by Sergeant 'Psycho' Smith and Constable 'Pervert' Perkins. The NEWsden hotline has received no calls whatsoever, due to successful operational security, ie not giving anyone the number, and station records are updated accordingly.

"How can we be sure you're NOT a real policeman?"

The Financial Times Friday 20 January 2023

New bank to open

by Our Financial Staff
Ivor Noverdraft

There was good news for borrowers last night at the announcement of a new bank that will be only too happy to lend to those with a proven track record of profligacy and incompetence.

"Forget the Bank of Mum and Dad," said one happy borrower. "This is the Bank of Mum and Dad's Distant Cousin. It's brilliant. It will lend you unlimited money, provided that you have no way or intention of paying it back."

The bank is based in Canada, and does not insist on a face-to-face meeting for the application to take out a loan.

It prefers never to have met you, and only needs two forms of identification – one showing that you're called Boris, and the other an envelope with your address on it – 10 Downing Street.

Said a spokesman for the bank, Mr Sam Blyth-Spirit, "It's the bank that likes to say, 'Yes, I would like to be Chairman of the British Council.'" *(Is this right? Ed.)*

Clerihew-the-hell-is-he?

Andrew Tate
Spreads misogyny and hate,
But the Romanian police acted on intel
And now, like his teenage fans, he is 'incel'!

ROYAL MINT UNVEILS NEW NHS 50p COIN

It's the pay offer to the nurses

News in brief

Cockroaches to sue

■ A group of Romanian cockroaches are to issue writs for defamation after YouTube influencer Andrew Tate claimed that they were his only friends in his vermin-infested prison cell.

"My clients have their good name as cockroaches to consider and they will not have their reputation sullied by being associated with this ludicrous and unpleasant creature," said the cockroaches' lawyer, Saul Goodman.

RICHARD SHARP'S NEW-LOOK BBC SCHEDULES

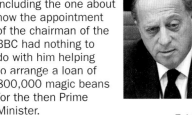

Jackatory

Fairy tales for children, including the one about how the appointment of the chairman of the BBC had nothing to do with him helping to arrange a loan of 800,000 magic beans for the then Prime Minister.

The Repair Shop

This week, the Repair Shop team face their biggest challenge yet. Boris Johnson is "broke". Can BBC expert Richard "Blades" Sharp fix it? No – it was all a coincidence!

Gone Fishy

Top comedian Boris Johnson, with lugubrious sidekick Dicky Shark, tries to net a huge 800,000-pounds catch. Gentle comedy as the two sit by a bank over dinner and humorously fail to chat about anything they are doing.

The Traitors

New reality show in which the Tory party finds out who are the Faithfuls and who are the Traitors. The Faithfuls support Boris and are rewarded. Who will win the cash prize of £800,000? Will it be Boris? Yes.

Pointless

Alexander Armstrong and Richard Osman lead a Pointless investigation into the BBC chairman's appointment, where two teams must try and guess how many people out of 100 think the whole sorry business stinks to high heaven.*

*It's 100.

The Daily Toffgraph

Friday, 3 February, 2023

Prince Andrew *Why I think Charles Moore might be innocent*

I know this is controversial, but I think we should at least concede the possibility that Charles Moore is innocent.

Yes, many see him as a subject of ridicule with his top hat, his sense of entitlement and his lack of engagement with the modern world. But I say, no. He has the right to be considered innocent, even if all the evidence would suggest otherwise.

Yes, that picture of him at the top of the column doesn't look good, but I think it's a fake. Nobody in their right mind would be caught posing like that. And many of his public pronouncements seem ill-judged, but they're just clumsy.

His choice of friends has been unfortunate, with his misplaced loyalty to the disgraced MP Owen Paterson making him look at best foolish and, at worst, in thrall to darker forces – the Carlton Club.

It is here that gullible girls, some as young as 50, are allegedly enticed to perform unseemly acts, such as massaging the egos of elderly grandees, in return for a steak and kidney pudding and a glass of claret.

But I refuse to think badly of Moore, an essentially well-meaning public figure, who has been unfortunately led astray by his own naivety, and whose only crime is his instinctive belief that nobby people such as myself must be beyond reproach.

© *Prince Andrew*

Open letter to Sarah Vain from Madonna

Sarah,

I love you to bits. You've been part of my life for so long. But now, as you reach 64 (thousand words), I have to tell you that I think you've lost it.

To be honest, your appearance in the Daily Mail is just sad and embarrassing. Your pieces are puffy and use a lot of filler. They've clearly had a lot of work done on them, but the result is still disappointing.

They're trying not to look old and tired and to hide the fact that you've written this piece a hundred times before. There are just too many lines. Everything looks stretched. And you can't tell what those expressions are meant to be saying.

Surely you sometimes see your photograph at the top of the column and think – that's not the real me. I'm just trying to look how I looked 20 years ago.

So, let me offer you some friendly advice, sister to sister. Just leave well alone, retire gracefully and stop making yourself a laughing stock.

Love you,

Madonna

x x

POETRY CORNER

Lines on the attempt to stop Welsh rugby fans from singing Delilah during matches

So. Farewell
Then Delilah.
Or not, as
It happened.

They tried to
Ban you
Why? Why? Why?

Well, because the lyric
Can be seen as
An apology for
Misogynistic murder.

But, apart from that,
It's a cracking tune.
Altogether now,
*"I felt the knife
In my hand
And she da da da...
Dee dee dee Delilah...
Da da da..."* etc.

E.J. Thribb
(17½ - 0 to Ireland)

FAWLTY TOWERS REBOOTED

Your favourite scenes as they will appear in the new, exciting, modern take on the classic series

And many, many more!

DIARY
THE GOLD (BBC 1)

INT. SECURITY GUARDS LOUNGING AROUND IN ARMCHAIRS, MAKING TEA.

Guard 1: There you go, mate.

Guard 2: Thanks, mate. Mmm. Lovely cuppa.

Guard 1: There you go, mate.

Guard 3: Thanks, mate. Mmm. Lovely –

(Men in balaclavas with sawn-off shotguns burst in. Tense music plays)

Man in Balaclava: GIT DAN! GIT ON THE FACKIN FLOOR! FICE TO THE FACKIN FLOOR! IT'S THE POSH WOT'S GOT THE MONEY BUT IT'S NOW 1983 AND THE TIDE OF PRIVILEGE AND ENTITLEMENT IS FACKIN TURNIN! OI SID GIT DAN!

INT: POSH COUNTRY HOUSE

Posh Lady: One's tennis court needs a good sweeping. It's most frightfleh leafeh! If only the common people weren't so workshy!

Dodgy solicitor husband with Rolex *(slapping on the Brut VIP aftershave)*: This country's changing, Isabelle. It's the eighties, and the noo money has the power. The old rules and traditions are being swept away. Your lot are on the way out. 'bout time too.

Posh Lady: Quate frenkleh, Edwyn, it's so dreadfleh vulgar, this thirst you hev for manneh! Deddeh warned me you were common! I should hev listened!

Radio Announcer: News just in. Six thugs in balaclavas have just stolen three tons of gold bars worth £26 million or £90 million in today's money. Police are on the look-out for cockneys.

Posh Lady: Nothing more oikish then a bellerclahvah!

INT: KENNETH NOYE'S COUNTRY MANSION

(Kenneth Noye unpacks 1,000 shiny gold bars from his hold-all)

Mrs Noye: Wossat, Kenny?

Kenneth Noye: Nuffink, love.

Mrs Noye: Looks like gold bars to me. I 'ope you ain't one of those – what do they call em, that's it – Brink's-Mat blokes, Kenny!

Kenneth Noye: Brink's-Mat? Wossat when it's at 'ome?

(Sound of kettle boiling)

Mrs Noye: Kettaw's boilin'!

(She leaves the room)

Kenneth Noye: *(whispering urgently down phone to John Palmer)*: I got three tons of gold 'ere, Johnny boy – and I wan' you to melt it down for me in your little garden shed!

INT: SCOTLAND YARD

DCI Hugh Bonneville: Evenin' all. I'm as 'onest as the day is long. Now listen up. Six villains. With three tons of gold. It's our job to nab 'em – and fast.

DC Nicki Jennings: I may be a woman, guv, but I've got what it takes! Let's Go! Go! Go!

DCI Bonneville: But first I want to tell you a little bit about myself. After highly distinguished service in the last war, involving a fair amount of tragic deaths for which I'll never forgive myself, the Establishment decided I could be an officer, only I wasn't the right class. They said I had the ability but not the breeding. I told 'em I was Lord Grantham, but would they bloody listen?

DC Jennings: Not a second to spare, guv – let's nab 'em villains before they scarper!

DCI Bonneville: But first let me tell you a little bit more about myself...

INT: PALMER'S COUNTRY MANSION.

Palmer *(to girlfriend)*: I'm gonna make a noo life for us, babe. After this job, there'll be no lookin' back. When I was a lad, I didn't wear shoes.

(Sympathetic music plays)

Nah. The Establishment didn't want poor kids like us to have shoes, 'cos then we might run away. But it's the eighties now and fings are different. After this job, we won't just be wearing shoes on our feet – we'll be wearing 'em on our hands and on our knees and on our heads!

(A tear comes into Palmer's eye. They snog)

Girlfriend: Just so long as you don't do nuffink illegal, babe! I so admire the way you bought this eight-bedroom country mansion from your paper round, just like you told the police, Yeah, you're not afraid of hard work, John, and that's for sure!

(Doorbell goes)

Girlfriend: Wossat?

DCI Jennings: Freeze! It's the working class police!

Palmer: I'm outta here!

(Palmer exits through catflap)

INT: MODERN FLAT IN CHELSEA HARBOUR

Dodgy solicitor: I'll take it! Do you accept gold bullion?

Female estate agent: Society's changin'. For too long the rich have had all the money. Now it's the eighties and it's all about ambition. Potential. Social equality. Fancy a shag?

INT. SCOTLAND YARD.

DCI Bonneville *(writing on white board with felt tip)*: We're lookin' for three robbers, four names and six tons of god. No. Six robbers, three names and four tons of gold. Sorry. Right first time. Four robbers, six names and three tons of gold. They'd have given me the arithmetic lessons if only I'd been born posh. Where's Carson when you need 'im?

DCI Jennings: Just had a call come in from Kent CID, guvnor! They say 7 percent of the population owns 84 percent of the land.

DCI Bonneville: You'll need eight of my finest men, Jennings, and three vehicles. Arrest the 7 percent. And make that sharpish.

INT. OLD BAILEY.

Kenneth Noye: I niver brutally stabbed that copper to death. It's an Establishment set up! He was runnin' with a knife and fell over on it fifteen times in a row. That'll learn 'im!

(Jury laugh sympathetically)

Foreman of the Jury: Not guilty!

INT: KENNETH NOYE'S COUNTRY MANSION

Radio Announcer: Football result just in. Snooty Chelsea have beaten good old working-class Millwall 2-1. Social justice still has a long way to go.

Kenneth Noye *(boiling down a couple of gold bars on his fancy new Aga)*: You know what, love? I spends me time in the ashes and smoke, but in this ole wide world, there's no 'appier bloke. Nowhere is there a more 'appier crew, than them wot sings chim chim cher-ee chim-cheroooooo!

As told to
CRAIG BROWN

ECO CHAMBER

30% of the planet will be protected by 2030

That'll be about all that's left of it

CEO BIG ENERGY PLC

We're very much focused on the green stuff

TIPPING POINTS

Amazon

Arctic

Aldershot

That Church Compromise On Gay Marriage In Full

The Reverend J.C. Flannel explains

"The Church of England has decided, in a real sense, to celebrate same-sex love as a gift from God, but simultaneously to register the limits of non-traditional sexual teaching in the modern world.

The new system will be simple, clear and compassionate. Same-sex couples will be permitted to have a formal blessing on their union and they will be publicly, unreservedly and joyfully welcome.

There are some reservations, of course: they must have already got married elsewhere, and they will not be permitted to have a marriage ceremony in church, and the definition of marriage remains between a man and a woman.

On the one hand, this is a terrific advance for the church, bringing it firmly into the 21st century and, on the other hand, this preserves the status quo, keeping the church firmly in the 17th century.

This may disappoint some of those with strong and sincere views in the Anglican Communion: including some of our African colleagues who wanted to reintroduce stoning and excommunication for homosexuality, and the passionate liberals who want to abolish heterosexual marriage and make homosexuality compulsory for members of the clergy.

This compromise ensures we can continue the most important work of the church, which is to argue with each other about sex."

The Church of England's latest bold decision

Bless you, my sons.

BIRCH

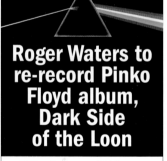
EYE GAME OF THE WEEK

Hogwash Legacy

by Our Gaming Correspondent
Phil Lonely-Hours

Return to the magical world of Hogwarts, where you play a young video-gamer who has been caught playing a game made by a firm in association with an author who has a political view that lots of people disagree with!

Can YOU survive the mob of other video-game fans tracking you down and posting your details online? Will YOU be strong enough to cope with the wave of Hogwash coming your way? Some may think this game is a bit complex, but don't worry, it's completely black and white. Just ask anyone who's threatening to kill you online!

There's no need to consider any possible nuances as you take on the forces of pure evil, ie "She Who Must Not Be Named", J.K. Rowling!

BONFIRE OF EU HEALTH AND SAFETY REGULATIONS

We don't need any of them... aaaargh!!!

GLENDA SLAGG

She's Fleet Street's Al Chatbot-tomofthebarrel

■ **AT LAST**, a Harry we can all go crazy about – not the Ginger Whinger Mr Meghan aka Shirty Harry (geddit??? Like Dirty Harry!!? You know, the Clint Eastwood movie from yesteryear!!! No!??) but the other Harry, who's got style(s) by the bucketload. Who am I talking about???!? Why, Harry Styles, of course, the ex-X Factor Brit star who wowed them all at the Brits?!!! Talk about X-appeal!!!!

■ **HARRY STYLES!!??!** Arentcha-sickofhim? Not content with hogging the headlines at the Grammys, now the X Factory(!) warbler has bagged all the Brits – not to mention all the front pages and every gorgeous lovely from Taylor Swift to most recent squeeze Olivia Wilde, or whoever it is now!!??! Talk about Flirty Harry (geddit??? Like **Dirty** Harry? **Surely** you millennials must've heard of it!!?? It starred Clint Eastwood, for Gawd's sake!!!!! Honestly, subs today!!!!)

■ **WHATEVER** happened to Harry Styles? We don't seem to hear much about Hazza these days??? Not so long ago my column was full of him. But now – just one mention in this paragraph!!! Could it be that his star is waning?!!?? Has he got the 'Ex' Factor (geddit???) Not so much Hazza, as Hazza-been!!!!???? Geddddit????!!!!

■ **HARRY STYLES??!?!** Dontcha-luvhim????!!!!! Talk about the comeback kid??!?! He's everywhere again!! It's Harry this, Harry that – it's 'As It Was' (Glenda referencing his bestselling single, millennial subs – perhaps this is one reference you won't have to check!!!!!?????) Harry, you're my all-male shortlist of one!!! Geddditt??!!!!!!!

Byeeeeee!!!!!!!

BRIT AWARDS *Sam Smith makes political statement*

I blame inflation

Augmented reality

"Darling! You've come back! And you've tidied up!"

RSJ

41

Lookalikes

Grandpa Munster   **King Charles III**

Sir,

I can't help noticing the incredible resemblance between King Charles III upon his recent visit to the Old Lands, and Grandpa Munster as played by Al Lewis in "The Munsters".

One resides in a creepy old house and is the senior member of a family of oddballs and misfits, and the other is a much-loved character from a hit 1960s US sitcom.

RAY MACFADYEN.

Gerry Adams   **James Bond**

Sir,

Should readers be concerned about MI6 agents impersonating people to infiltrate organisations?

MARK SOLON.

Brains   **Munchetty**

Sir,

Would it be possible for you to ascertain the truth behind the rumour that Naga Munchetty was recently auditioned for the part of Brains in the remake of Thunderbirds?

BRIAN DUCKWORTH.

Gollum   **Yevgeny Prigozhin**

Sir,

One threatened his enemies, saying he hoped they would "burn in Hell, eating their guts" – the other burnt in Mordor and ate raw baby rabbits.

ENA B. MARWOOD.

Jazz Club guy   **Bridgen**

Sir,

Andrew Bridgen, suspended Tory MP for NM Leics, and a suave Jazz Club lothario – separated at birth? Nice.

DR D. PURNELL.

Seagal   **Wright**

Sir,

I wonder is there any connection between Steve Wright recently signing off from his radio show, and the decision by Vladimir Putin to draft Russian passport holders with military experience?

I think we should be told.

DARREN HUNTER.

Mr Toad   **Mr Geldof**

Sir,

Is that the great Mr Toad of Toad Hall I see at the memorial service to Vivienne Westwood, or a certain lead singer of the Boomtown Ratties?

PHILIP THOMAS.

McIntyre   **Mum from Bao**

Sir,

Has anyone noticed, as I have, the extraordinary resemblance between the star of the animated short film Bao and the star of the highly animated Michael McIntyre's Big Show?

Are they, by any chance, related?

MATTHEW IVES.

Mr Potato Head   **Rishi Sunak**

Sir,

I wonder, now the chips are down, if our PM is able to spend less time entertaining children and more time giving public sector workers, a fair and decent deal?

PETER JONES (no, not that one).

Marais   **May**

Sir,

Listening to Classical Focus this evening on BBC Sounds I was intrigued to hear a piece by Marin Marais. I couldn't help but notice how much he resembles Brian May, of Queen.

ROBBIE G.

Freud's immigrant   **Putin**

Sir,

I spotted this in Lucien Freud's painting "Immigrants" in the recent exhibition at the National Gallery. The blurb said that he painted men in power.

It also said that he had a wide circle of friends from the aristocracy to the criminal underworld.

ANDREW JAY.

Rimmer   **Hunt**

Sir,

Has anyone noticed the striking resemblance between the smug and inept Red-Dwarfer, Arnold J Rimmer (Technician 2nd Class), and the similarly smug and inept Red-Waller, Arnold J. Hunt (Chancellor 2nd Class)?

Are they perhaps related?

ARNOLD J. McSLOY.

Cartoon captain

Lebedev

Sir,

During a recent journey with Brittany Ferries I was surprised to discover that our captain was none other than Evgeny Lebedev. Who knew that he had the time, given his frequent attendance in the House of Lords?
ABIGAIL TANN.

Munsters

Monsters

Sir,

Fans of the '60s show The Munsters will have been pleased to see GB News recent attempt to reintroduce the comic-horror genre to TV screens. This time the main participants appear to be Dan Wootton and Priti Patel.

PETER KENDALL.

Keir Starmer

Errol Flynn

Sir,

Imagine my surprise when, on opening the 25 February 1939 issue of Picture Show, I came across a photograph of a young Sir Keir Starmer.
TIMMY KILMINSTER.

Talos

Witchell

Sir,

Are your readers aware of the striking similarity between an ancient mind-control being of Talos IV from the pilot episode of Star Trek and Royals rune-reader Nicholas Witchell?

Live long and prosper,
DONALD McDONALD.

Q

Musk

Sir,

Has anyone noticed, as I have, the similarity between the overdressed megalomaniac-alien 'Q' on Star Trek and the new owner of Twitter?
Are they by any chance related?
ENA B. SHARP-REES.

Sloth

Infantino

Sir,

Have any of your other readers spotted the striking familial resemblance between character 'Sloth' in the cult 80s movie The Goonies, and the upstanding President of FIFA, Gianni Infantino?

PAUL BANDALL.

Mummy

Tate

Sir,

Has anyone noticed the resemblance of the infamous TikToker Andrew Tate and this mummy from the reign of Emperor Hadrian (AD 117-138), currently on display at the Manchester Museum?
I wonder which has the most outdated views? Tough to call!
ISAAC STRONGE.

Clarke

Coffey

Sir,

I must be the last one to point out the worrying, wanton disregard for health by Conservative health secretaries.
NICK TOLSON.

Renoir's dancer

David Blunkett

Sir

Has anyone noticed David Blunkett having a nice time in Renoir's Dance at Le Moulin de la Galette?
RICHARD SEAHOLME.

Lily

Camilla

Sir,

Has anyone noticed the similarity between the recently and tragically deceased Paul O'Grady and the Queen Consort? I understand they were great fans of each other.
TREVOR HOPKINS.

Wood

Condor

Sir,

Whilst watching a programme about whales, the California Condor made an appearance, making me wonder if he was related to a member of the Rolling Stones.
JOHN DAVIES.

Neanderthal

Roger Waters

Sir,

Has anyone noticed, as I have, the extraordinary similarity between Roger Waters of Pink Floyd fame and the latex model of a Neanderthal at the Natural History Museum? Are they by any chance related?
ENA B. GARTENBERG.

Pitch hero

Patch hero

Sir,

Did Erling Haaland learn his boyhood footballing skills in the cabbage patch?
LES SMITH.

HISTORIC JOKES REVISITED

There's a shortage of vegetables

Not in my government

Bag for life?

HOSPICE SHOP

Dictionary Corner

Salad days

[sa-luhd dayz] (*n.*)

1 (*Obsolete*) Happy days of one's youth (*see play of same name by J. Slade*)

2 (*Modern*) Days on which vegetables are rationed at Tesco, Aldi, Asda, Morrisons, and all good supermarkets (*see policy of same name by T. Coffey*)

Nursery Times

·········· Friday, Once-upon-a-time ··········

NURSERYLAND HIT BY FRUIT AND VEG SHORTAGE

by Our Agricultural Staff **Old Macdonald**

SHOPS in Nurseryland were this week stripped of their usual goods, as a nationwide shortage of fruit and vegetables hit supplies. Everywhere you looked there was chaos:

● An idle boy called Jack exchanged an entire cow for five beans, causing his mother to congratulate him on this brilliant deal: "These beans are magic, Jack," she said, "and much better than that over-valued meat."

● Meanwhile, in another corner of Nurseryland, another boy called Little Jack (Horner) stuck his thumb in a pie and pulled out no plum at all. He then said "What a malnourished child am I."

● In another incident, a Fairy Godmother was lambasted by Cinderella for turning a perfectly good pumpkin into a golden carriage. Said Cinders, "I was looking forward to eating that pumpkin and now all I've got is a useless, and frankly inedible, carriage."

● Meanwhile, children have been forbidden from repeating the popular counting rhyme: "One potato, two potato, three potato, four," on the grounds there aren't that many potatoes left.

Terrible scenes across Nurseryland

● A Wicked Stepmother defended her actions in giving her stepdaughter a poisoned apple. She said, "I thought I was doing her a favour, I had no idea the apple was past its sell-by date and therefore poisoned. I blame Brexit and the wicked politicians behind it."

Late news

■ The fruit and veg crisis comes on the back of a Nurserylandwide egg shortage. The only egg left was tragically broken last night after a suspicious fall from a wall and, due to lengthy ambulance waiting times, had to be treated by medically inexperienced military staff from the 2137th King's Horses and Men brigade.

"Ignore Colin – he's just having a señor moment"

44

Good morning, ladies and gentlemen.

James Forsyth
And may I remind everybody that no matter how confidential a WhatsApp group may appear to be, there remains the remote possibility that every single word will reappear in the Daily Telegraph tomorrow.

Dominic Raab
May I be the first to say that it's a privilege to serve this great country of ours and how much I respect and esteem all of my colleagues, of whatever rank.

Suella Braverman
And may I say that I am driven entirely by empathy and compassion for those poor souls trying to enter this great country of ours.

Grant Shapps
Integrity, Honesty, Transparency, Democracy, Accountability. They are all my middle names.

Lee Anderson
May I echo the excellent sentiments of my esteemed colleagues, particularly those from the South of England, and remind us all that we are here as representatives of the entire country, not just those who agree with us.

Well, this is an excellent level of debate. Much more collegiate. Well done, team!

James Forsyth
Hey, great news everyone. I've found an encryption bolt-on that doubles the security levels, so we definitely won't be in the Telegraph.

Dominic Raab
Thank fuck for that! I can't keep up this level of bollocks for much longer. Why did you scare us, Forsyth, you fuckwit? 😡😡😡

Lee Anderson
Cos he's a fookin' Soothern tosser and Rishi's public school bumchum, that's why. 😏

Actually, I was a dayboy.

Lee Anderson
Gayboy, more like. 🎓

Dominic Raab
You're good, Lee. From now on, I'm calling you Lee Anderthal.

Lee Anderson
You're too kind. Though that's not what all those 24 people you bullied are saying. Hahaha!

Dominic Raab
They're just ganging up on me, it's not fair.

Can we just focus on Northern Ireland, the world's most exciting economic zone. It's in a totally unique position. Access to both European and UK markets! Wow!

Jeremy Hunt
A bit like us before Brexit?

Steve Baker
May I just intervene here to weep?

Dominic Raab
I didn't touch him! I didn't even say anything to the blubbing nancy boy. 😢

Steve Baker
No, I'm weeping at Rishi's brilliant deal. You've no idea how tough it's been for me, making it tough for everyone else. The stress of ruining the country has been unbelievable and my mental health has been badly affected by everyone calling me a right-wing nutter.

Steve Baker
*running the country.

Steve Baker
Look, the beard, the jewellery – it's all part of my recovery from the awful populism that I stoked up. Honestly, since Brexit I've been anxious and depressed.

Jeremy Hunt
You and the rest of the country. ✋ 🎤

Matt Hancock
Hey, everyo Sorry about all that Torygraph stuff!

Jeremy Hunt
Don't talk to Matt, anyone. He's leakier than all the useless PPE equipment he ordered!

Matt Hancock
Come on, guys, don't be mean. I was betrayed!

Lee Anderson
Like your wife, you dirty little shagger. Look at that arse…

…with Gina Whatsherface.

Matt Hancock
That's unfair! You can trust me.

The entire WhatsApp group has left the WhatsApp group.

SHOCK RESULTS FROM THE EYE'S INCREDIBLE FOUR-DAY WORKING WEEK SURVEY

PRIVATE EYE, in collaboration with the think tank AutoGnomey, has spent the last year conducting a rigorous, scientific study of a four-day working week on 60 British firms. These are the extraordinary results:

11% agreed it was a great innovation

23% told us they would respond to the survey the next time they were in the office

31% said they were too busy doing the school run

32% said they were unavailable, as they had an Amazon package coming

45% were just making a quick snack but would get right back to us

53% asked if they could possibly try a three-day week instead

75% said they were too stressed to reply, as none of their colleagues were doing any work

100% said they'd like a new laptop

FASHION NEWS

YES!

The Seventies are back!
Trends making a comeback in 2023 include:

■ Flares
■ Glitter balls
■ Disco décor
■ The attempted murder of policemen by the IRA in Omagh

(That's enough 1970s. Ed.)

"Oh, come on, Derek – read the room"

New Putin Health Scare

■ Following Putin's state-of-the-nation address, Kremlinologists today gave an update on the worrying state of the Russian President's health.

After studying film footage of Vladimir Putin speaking for two hours to a crowd of thousands, the grim reality is that he is, to use the medical term, "perfectly healthy".

Following months of speculation that he was suffering from cancer, Parkinson's disease, or possible early-onset dementia, the terrible truth is that there is probably nothing wrong with him whatsoever.

Said one top Putin watcher, "He wasn't shaking, sweating, or slurring his words – he simply accused Ukraine of invading Ukraine and then ranted on like a perfectly healthy madman."

(Rotters)

Keir Starmer WRITES

MY HISTORIC MISSION-DRIVEN SPEECH IN FULL – WHAT YOU PROBABLY MISSED

HELLO. Now, these mission statements may seem incredibly controversial – but I make no apology for that.

You have to be bold when setting out your radical vision for the future. So here are my five mission statements:

Crime – make the streets safer!

Growth – it's good!

NHS – I like it!

Green energy – I'm for it!

Opportunity – yes, please!

Ok, now I know a lot of people are going to find this kind of ground-breaking agenda a bit too extreme, but that's the kind of Britain I'm going to create.

Now, for the other big issue – namely, war and peace. There are those voices calling for a cessation of hostilities, for compromise and, let's face it, appeasement. But I say no. We cannot stop until the last vestiges of Corbynism are removed from the small amount of territory that they still hold.

"War war, not jaw jaw," as the great Labour leader once put it.

You may now applaud.
Sincerely, Keir.

NEW SHORTAGE HITS BRITAIN

by Our Supply Chain Staff **Camilla Short**

DOWNING STREET was under pressure to comment last night on the latest shortage to rock the government. A shortage of trouser material has had worrying results, with the prime minister embarrassed to walk around in public, on account of his "seriously curtailed legware".

One worried pundit commented, "When Rishi sits down, we can see his socks quite clearly. What sort of country have we become when there isn't enough trouser material for the prime minister to have trousers that reach his shoes? It sends a terrible signal to the rest of the world. Britain can no longer hold its head up, or indeed its trousers down."

A government spokesman denied that there have been scenes of panic-buying, with the public believing that a shortage of trouser material necessitates the immediate stock-piling of properly fitted trousers. Queues at Marks and Spencer are feared, as desperate trouser-wearers fight for the last pair of men's slacks (regular) in the store.

"It's nothing to do with Brexit," said Grant Shopps as he *(cont. size 94)*

News in brief

Chatbot exam fears

■ As Artificial Intelligence programmes become more and more popular, and able to mimic any writing style, there are increasing concerns about the impact they will have on the educational sector.

Said one pupil, Archie (11), "I really hope my mum doesn't use one to do my coursework. That would be cheating and I might get marked down."

Jeremy (16) agreed, "Over the past couple of terms, my father has maintained an A grade with some highly impressive essays. It would be a great shame if he ruined my prospects by being busted for using AI, when he should be doing it himself."

A Tank Driver writes

Vlad 'Mad' Putin, Tank No: ZZZZ

Every week a well-known tank driver gives his opinion on a matter of topical importance. This week, the Anniversary of the Special Military Operation...

"Blimeski! Been in this traffic for a whole year now. Who'd have thought! I know I said I'd get you to Kiev within three days, but I thought the roads would be clear. Yes, of course the meter's still running. Someone's got to pay for this fuel. You seen the price of it these days?! Look at that bloke I've just driven into. Wasn't he looking?! It's all his fault. If he'd got out of the way, there wouldn't have been trouble. Fascist! See that old geezer, Joe Biden? What's he doing in Kiev, American tourist having his picture taken with the President of Ukraine? That should have been me! Although obviously Zelensky wouldn't have been alive. Only joking – I'm a peaceful man. If those Ukrainians would only stop fighting, we'd have peace tomorrow. They're the aggressive ones. Oi! Fuckwitski!! Get off my road!! Mind if I put on the radio? It's got me making a speech on all the channels. It's only a couple of hours. You'll enjoy it – or else! Anyway, Happy Birthday to the War! And Many Happy Returns – to all our troops who are trying to get back to Moscow after deserting. Ha ha ha! I had that Wagner bloke in the back of my tank once. I had to pay HIM! I mean, how mercenary can you get?! I know he is a mercenary, but honestly, the bloke's a money-grabbing psychopath. My kind of guy, really. Cheers! Be lucky!"

© A tank driver 2023

"We're living through a cost of lying crisis"

Daily Telegraph Friday 17 March 2023

Letters to the Editor

Drag shows for children totally inappropriate

SIR – May I add my voice to those of your many readers who have been asking why on earth we are allowing these revolting, depraved "drag shows" to be offered to our children?

In the old days, youngsters were taken to the pantomime, where they were treated to wholesome, traditional entertainment, where men dressed up as women, women dressed up as men and nobody mentioned it.

I fondly remember seeing Widow Twankey (played by a middle-aged man) and Dick Whittington (played by a girl) exchange delightfully innocent quips such as "Midnight and still no dick!" to the delight of the toddlers in the crowd.

I shall also never forget Christopher Biggins playing Aladdin's mother and saying, "Give it a rub, son, and see what happens!" The laughter echoed around the walls of the Worthing Hippodrome.

This was, and should remain, the classic way British children learn about life, not some tacky so-called drag show where transvestites make a mockery of all that we hold dear.

This Christmas, I shall be taking my grandchildren out of school and taking them instead to the Weston-Super-Mare Palladium to see Mother Goose (Patrick Stewart) saying "Come and goose me, ducky!" to the delightful young man, Buttons (Bonnie Langford). Surely this is the way forward for Britain in the 21st century. Oh, yes, it is! Oh, no, it isn't!

Sir Herbert Gussett
*The Old Inn-uendo,
Great Throbbing, Somerset*

JUNIOR DOCTORS' STRIKE THREATENS LIVES

How do you sleep at night?

In a corridor, on a trolley

PUBLIC DISGUSTED BY ONLINE GHOULS

THE public have expressed their outrage at the online ghouls who descended on St Michael on the Wyre during the three weeks Nicola Bulley was missing.

"I spent seven hours the other day being totally disgusted watching one of those TikTok ghouls broadcasting live from the village," said one horrified subscriber to the ghouls' TikTok channel.

"It's disgusting that I was forced to watch hours of another TikTok sleuth livestreaming his search of an abandoned house near the river. It makes me sick, thinking about watching it all afternoon," said another.

"Why do these ghouls do this? I didn't agree with a single theory dreamt up by the eleven TikTok sleuths I followed for the three weeks Nicola was missing," said another disgusted member of the public.

"I blame the mainstream media for being constrained by libel laws and not being nearly exciting enough throughout this whole tragic event," agreed everyone. *(Rotters)*

EYE 94-PAGE SUPPLEMENT ON THE MYSTERY THAT'S GRIPPED THE NATION

INCLUDING:

■ Lancashire police continue to search for excuse. "We're not giving up until we've found one," says police chief. "You may think it's all very murky and unclear, but we are confident that the excuse for our inept behaviour is in there somewhere."

■ Did the police have specific vulnerabilities – issues with alcohol or struggling with the menopause – that may have led to their erratic brain fog? "There were too many amateur detectives on the scene", says police chief, "including us."

■ Was the specialist diver too busy being on television to do any diving? "Just because I said the missing person definitely wasn't in the river when she was, doesn't mean I'm in any way wrong," he told Sky TV, ITV, BBC, Looks North, Looks South, Looks Everywhere Except in the River.

■ Why didn't the police call in Elon Musk? tweets @ElonMusk. "My minisub would have found the body, unlike the paedo diver," says Twitter boss.

■ Were Sky TV and ITV guilty of intrusion? We go round to the journalists' parents' houses, climb over the fence and shout through the letterbox.

■ What will happen to the armchair detectives? Speculation mounts. Will they move on to the next mystery and get in the way of that investigation as well? What were their motives? Who knows, but we'll just make it up anyway.

■ Are there any missing articles in the newspapers? No, we put them all in on every page, irrespective of merit or accuracy.

■ Are there any questions left to answer, and if not, why not?

Daily Telegraph

FRIDAY, MARCH , 2023

KEEP OUT OF BREXIT, YOUR MAJESTY!

THE spectacle of our woke, left-wing monarch sticking his big royal nose into political matters with his so-called Windsor Framework has sent shock waves throughout the nation.

Entertaining the self-confessed Euro-nut, Ursula von der Liar, to tea and being polite is a flagrant snub to all those of the decent hard-working majority who exercised their democratic right to exit Europe.

Doesn't he know how dangerous it is to have an unelected figurehead meddling in British politics – like Ms von der Leybensraum.

Why can't he follow the example of his mother, our beloved late queen, who always made one thing clear: that as regards politics, the Crown should only ever say, "I support Brexit", as she so memorably did in 2016 on the front page of that respected journal of record, *The Sun*.

Ok, so the Palace said she never said anything of the sort, but that's just typical of the loony left-wing Palace establishment who were trying to undermine our much-missed great Queen Elizabeth Truss.

So with all due respect, jug ears, bog off and go talk to a tulip!

EU-phemisms

"It's a victory for both sides"

Both sides lost

THAT NEW BREXIT DEAL
HOW IT WILL WORK

THE revised Northern Ireland protocol means a radical change to the way goods arriving from the UK are treated. There will now be a system of lanes to process imports.

Green Lane	Red Lane	Orange Lane
Goods destined for Northern Ireland will be fast-tracked with minimal checks	Goods destined for the Republic of Ireland will be subject to EU checks	All goods will be subjected to large man in bowler hat shouting "Nooooooooooooo!!!"

"This one's got no name on it"

MATCH OF THE DAY PRESENTER SUSPENDED THEN RE-INSTATED

Hooray! I've missed a penalty

What a spectacular own goal!

BBC SPORT

—— **FINAL SCORE: LINEKER-1 BBC-0** ——

TOP BBC MAN IN IMPARTIALITY ROW

by Our Political Football Commentator **Lunchtime O'Bias**

ONE of the most prominent figures at the BBC has been accused of displaying "a flagrant lack of impartiality" amid calls that he should be given the sack.

BBC TV star Richard Sharp has been accused of political bias and bringing the BBC into disrepute, following comments he made about the Prime Minister.

Sharp was asked, "Do you think the PM would like a loan of £800,000? And will you help with the guarantee?" To which the prospective candidate for the job of BBC Chairman controversially answered, "Yes, of course."

"Sharp has crossed the line," tweeted Gary Lineker. "Why can't he just talk about football, rather than interfering in political affairs? He's clearly a Tory."

Sharp has a history of partisan statements, such as "Would the Tory Party like a donation of £400,000 from me?", "Would you like a cheque or shall I give it to you in cash?" and "I have nothing to say to the committee. I have no conflicts of interest whatsoever, and I'm sure the Prime Minister will give me the job."

An unrepentant Sharp said, "I will not be cowed by the left-wing press, and I will always stand up for those who are most in need – of a few hundred thousand pounds.

"This poor Prime Minister was washed up and had nowhere to live. Are you telling me that I shouldn't have taken him into my club and bought him an agreeable lunch? What kind of country are we?!"

Doolally Mail

—— **FRIDAY, MARCH 17, 2023** ——

THE battlelines have been drawn. Now is a time for taking sides.

On the one hand, be in no doubt, we hate the BBC and its left-wing wokery. But in the interests of balance, we also hate Gary Lineker, the overpaid crisp salesman, with his holier-than-thou tweets.

But we have to admire the bearded do-gooder for thrashing the liberal blobtards at the Biased Broadcasting Corporation. Almost as much as we admire our much respected national broadcaster for taking on the sanctimonious soccer squillionaire lecturing decent angry people about how to be nice.

How dare he! Or they! I can't decide who to hate more! The vein in my head is throbbing. I hate that smug, elitist, bleeding heart vein! POP! Now my head's exploded! Aarrggh! Who's to blame? Why, Keir Starmer, of course. Or is it Meghan? Oh no, I don't know which one I hate more! Aarrrrggh!

BAFTA TV NOMINATIONS

Best Director (General)

Tim Davie for BBC's *Botch of the Day Football Special*

POETRY CORNER

**In Memoriam
Raquel Welch,
legendary screen siren**

So. Farewell
Then Raquel Welch,
Hollywood goddess
And pin-up.

You were 82
Or, as Keith's dad says,
82–24–36.

You are remembered
For two things.
And also for
One Million Years BC
And *Fantastic Voyage*.

Apologies, Raquel –
You bring out the
Neanderthal in poets of
A certain age.

E.J. Throbb
(17½ million years BC)

"These paintings aren't nearly as old as I initially thought – this particular figure appears to be Raquel Welch in a fur bikini"

LEE AND MY SPOON

THIS WEEK

LEE ANDERSON

Do you have a favourite spoon?
I'm glad you asked me that. I like traditional working-class British spoons that a single dad ex-coal-miner can use to stir his tea at the end of a honest day's toil down the pit.

Would it be fair to say that Labour spoons are all useless?
Yeah, definitely. That's a very good point.

Thanks, Lee. Do I still have to pretend I haven't met you, like we agreed before the interview?
Shut up, you silly twat, and get on with the next question about hanging.

Do you believe, like the majority of British people, in the death penalty for spoon-related crimes?
Oh yes. You won't steal any more spoons after you've been hanged. Zero percent re-offending rate.

Aren't the lads down the Scooter Club great?
I told you not to ask about them.

But their collection of mid-twentieth-century German military spoons is…
Shut up! Shut up!

And those funny T-shirts with the slogans and the spoons in that Iron Cross shape…
Don't broadcast any of this.

Has anything amusing ever happened to you in connection with a spoon?
No.

DIARY

AMANDA PLATELL: MY HUGE MISTAKE

Yee-uchh! For most of my life I looked down on fat people. And not in a good way, either.

Browsing through my leather-bound cuttings books – a much-thumbed research facility – something strikes me like a thunderbolt.

The pieces filed under F for FAT are exceeded only by those filed under D for DISGUSTINGLY FAT and R for REVOLTINGLY FAT. And I feel ashamed.

For decades I've chastised larger ladies in my columns.

In 1974, I wrote that Hollywood legend Liz Taylor was a "two-ton tub of lard".

In 1978, I took Jackie Kennedy to task in an Open Letter to the Former First Lady:

"As a fellow human being and desirable woman, I felt so much compassion for you, Jackie, when your glamorous hubby JFK was gunned down by skinny oddballs Lee Harvey Oswald and Grassy Noel.

"The moment Jack Kennedy breathed his last, grief acted on you like a Ryvita. I don't know if it was all that stretching you did on the boot of his limo, but overnight you turned into a fabulous Size Zero.

"Sadly, since you went and married shady foreign Greek billionaire Aristotle Onassis, you've been wolfing down Moussaka like it was going out of fashion.

"Now they call you Jackie O because you're mouth is always wide open, ready to gobble up the scrapings.

"Get a grip, Jackie – and remember – no one ever loves a Former First Fatty."

I'm not proud of those insults. In fact, I'd go further. I'm proud of not being proud of them.

And I'd certainly never repeat them in print. Why, then, the change of heart?

My fat-shaming epiphany occured a couple of weeks ago as I gazed at a picture of curvy actress Jennifer Coolidge.

Here she was, an undeniably stout-looking 61-year-old woman, posing on the red carpet and looking... utterly magnificent.

A size 16-plus, by anyone's measure, she knocked them dead with her cleavage, wit, fat body and sheer chutzpah.

This was a woman who once admitted to eating six pizzas a day – and look at her! An icon of Big Is Beautiful. A body as curvaceous as the M25. And a truly terrific advertisement for stuffing your face rotten with jammy dodgers.

Looking at Jennifer that day, I realised, with a stab of guilt, just how fat-phobic I have been all my life.

"Like all normal-sized people, I work hard to stay trim," I proclaimed in one of my columns. "That's why I'm the envy of all my flabby friends and work-colleagues – and an object of lust for every red-blooded male.

"Time to bin the biscuits, ladies, if you want to look like yours truly."

I now realise I was wrong to go into print to chastise all those tubbies who – through no fault of their own – had let themselves go.

And it's not just fatty Jennifer Coolidge who has persuaded me to withdraw my offensive remarks.

Go back a few weeks and see, yes, Lizzo posing at the Grammys, looking huge and sexy, if that's what you like, though many don't.

Yes, Lizzo may have been throwing the sherry trifle down her throat. But think of all the other lady performers she beat to the award! Go, greedy girl!

And last month we saw plump potato Sarah Lancashire smashing it in the finale of *Happy Valley* as Sergeant Catherine Cawood, a bigger woman with a huge heart – and an XXL uniform she wore with pride.

We didn't just fall in love with Catherine – we wanted to be like her. Even if she'd never clearly heard the word "Whoah!" or the proverb, "Enough is as good as a feast."

But I am a fat-shamer no more.

Now, when I see younger women in their 20s or 30s bulging out of their size 16-plus skinny jeans as they waddle down the street, I salute them. How great to be so relaxed while looking so revolting.

Sincere apologies to everyone I've ever offended, including the late roly-poly Raquel Welch, RIP, whom I once nicknamed Raquel Squelch, and Michelle Obama, who I called as alluring as a hippo, not to mention hundreds of other fatties like…*(continued for thousands of words)*

As told to
CRAIG BROWN

JAMES BOND REWRITTEN FOR MODERN READERS

The name's Bond... James Bond

The name's Q... LGBTQ

School news

St Cakes goes co-ed today

After centuries as an all-boys school, St Cakes is moving with the times. We now welcome boys and girls whose parents have plenty of money. The old motto "*Quis paget entrat*" has been updated to 21st century Latin: "*Quis paget entrat.*" Thanks to Ms(!) D. Clension (Head of Lower Fourth) for informing us of the feminine nominative of "Quis". As the school welcomes three girls into the 697-strong contingent of boys, the new girls house (Crumpets) will come equipped with its very own lavatory, to be known affectionately by all Cakeians as the Hags' Room. Said Headmaster R.J. Kipling, "St Cakes makes exceedingly good Cakeians, and now we look forward to making exceedingly good money." To mark the historic change, St Cakes welcomes a new head of business studies, Mr C.B.I. Boss, who is suddenly available and comes highly recommended by himself. This term's drama soc production of Romeo and Juliet will feature the part of Juliet being played by a girl for the first time in St Cakes' proud thespian history. Sadly, the long-serving head of drama, Mr Peter Phile, has resigned in protest.

Yes, it's the new Middle-Aged, okay – Very Elderly Love Island!

IT'S WEEK TWO OF TELLY'S SAUCIEST REALITY SHOW AND ANN-LESLEY STILL HASN'T BEEN THROWN OUT. MEANWHILE, RUPERT IS SHARING HIS CORPORATE WORRIES WITH HIS NEW FLAME...

I'M NOT SURE IF A MERGER'S A GOOD IDEA

YEAH – NOT AT YOUR AGE!

DID YOU ASK FOR 'SEX ON THE BEACH'?

HOPE SPRINGS ETERNAL!

I'M A GOD-FEARING PERSON, RUPE

ME TOO – AND I'LL BE MEETING HIM SOONER THAN YOU!

WHY ARE YOU WEARING BLACK, DARLING – ARE YOU GOING TO A FUNERAL?

WELL, YOU NEVER KNOW…

THE TIMES NEW ROMAN

AD41 Tuesday

CALIGULA'S HORSE FURIOUS OVER STANLEY JOHNSON COMPARISON

by Our Nepolitical Staff SUE TONIUS

The distinguished equine, Consul Incitatus, has complained vociferously at suggestions that his appointment by the Emperor Caligula was in some way similar to the knighthood bestowed upon Stanley Johnson by his son, Boris.

"I was appointed on merit," complained the Consul with a long face, "after years of distinguished public service. Whatever the neigh-sayers will tell you, there was nothing corrupt about my elevation to the rank of Consul."

He continued, "I really resent cheap chroniclers trying to make out that the preferment of the utterly ridiculous and unworthy Sir Stanley Johnson is somehow comparable to my own promotion. If any historian repeats this calumny, I may well sue (Tonius)."

Caligula agreed that Boris Johnson was making a mockery of the honours system. Said the mad World Emperor, "Boris Johnson is bringing all of us insane rulers into disrepute. My Consul may be a horse, but at least he doesn't think he's a stud and try to jump on top of all the fillies in the stable at every opportunity."
(Continued AD94...)

BBC SINGERS LATEST

We're Bach!

Hallelujah!

C sharp?

Nobody's seen him for days

It's the Resurrection Symphony

Where are the executives?

They're Haydn

Rwanda 'happy to take in more'

IN what was seen as a major boost to the home secretary's tough new small boats immigration policy, Rwanda confirmed today that it would be happy to take in more of the UK's money.

"We have already taken in large quantities of UK money," a Rwanda government spokesman told reporters, "but we're always happy to take more... as much as they want to send us. We're ready to resettle that money here in Rwanda. We have put no limits on how much UK government money we'll take in.

"Seeing a flight taking off from Heathrow, bound for Rwanda, full of UK money, is a dream of mine," he added.

POTHOLE STORIES KEEP APPEARING

by Phil Hole

THERE is growing concern about the number of pothole stories appearing in Fleet Street.

Said one reader, "you're going along perfectly happily all the way down to page 5, enjoying a nice pleasant journey through the news, and then suddenly – BANG! There's a dirty great big pothole story."

He continued, "I've tried taking an alternative route round to the Comment Section, but you can't avoid them. There are pothole stories everywhere."

Said another reader, "It's high time editors put some money into getting rid of pothole stories – they're ruining the experience." (*That's enough. Ed – I need to leave room for another pothole story.*)

ANOTHER POTHOLE STORY

■ There was good news for pothole haters as the Chancellor, Jeremy Hunt, pledged to pour an extra £200 million into potholes, but critics say it won't be enough to fill the pothole hole and will create an even bigger hole in the nation's finances. (*Nice short piece. Ed – That really filled a hole.*)

THIS WEEK

ISABEL OAKESHOTT

You're famous for your amazing scoops...

I love scoops and I'm very good at acquiring them.

How did you come by this latest one? Did you just steal it from Matt Hancock?

How dare you! I worked long and hard on getting this scoop and what you're suggesting is an insult to my culinary journalistic reputation.

But didn't he just give you access to his cutlery drawer, and you promised not to hand any utensil over to anyone else?

I warn you, if you pursue this line of questioning, I will terminate this interview. This is not about me, it's about the important National Interest in revealing my amazing scoop, by me.

It looks like you betrayed Hancock, scoopwise, and then betrayed your own employer, ForkTV, by presenting the scoop on a plate to the Daily Jellygraph.

Right, that's it. I warned you, I won't put up with this sort of gutter journalism, asking me impertinent questions about the most important scoop in spoon history – be it dessert, soup or otherwise.

How much were you paid for the scoop? A lot, I bet!

How much are YOU paid? Go on! Tell me! I'm turning the kitchen tables on you!

Ok, back to the standard questions. Has anything amusing ever happened to you in relation to a scoop?

I act only out of altruism and a desire to serve the public in the pursuit of truth and justice.

Now that IS funny! Ha ha ha, nice one, Isabel! Hang on, where are you going?

(At this point, Ms Oakeshott left the studio to do another interview)

NEXT WEEK: *Richard Tice, Me and my tice-cream.*

SO, HOW DOES YOUR INVENTION DIFFER FROM OTHER POP-UP TOASTERS?

@Vilmisrimo

Numéro 94
Au grand summit

Macron: Bienvenue à Paris, Riche! C'est un pleasure véritable à parler avec un Prime Minister du Royaume-United qui n'est pas un complete idiot.

Sunak: Vous me flatterez, Emmanuel. J'aime Paris dans le spring. C'est very bromantique!

Macron: OK, assez de la bromance, let's gettons down à business.

Sunak: Nous must stop les criminels qui exploit les desperates gens par fleecing them de l'argent avec pas de guarantée des résultats.

Macron: Oui, absolument. So, combien d'argent êtes-vous willing me payer?

Sunak: Je must vous warn, je ne suis pas un pushover. How much voulez-vous?

Macron: Un demi-billion, peut-être?

Sunak: OK. Mais can vous me promise success?

Macron: Hahahahaha! J'aime le British sense d'humeur presque as much que votre cash!

Sunak: Et maintenant, nous pouvons announcer cet deal formidable!

Macron: J'ai une bonne idée! Vous pouvez tell les Brits "Nous payons £500 million au EU" sur le side d'un grande rouge bus!

Sunak: Je ne understand pas.

Macron: Comme le Boris Brexit bus! Hahahaha!

Sunak: To be honêt, Emmanuel, je n'aime pas le sense d'humeur Français!

Fin
(de bromance)

© *The late Kilomètres Kington.*

"...and lastly, how do you think you'd react in a high-pressure situation?"

New IPCC report pursues more positive message on climate change

LAST REPORT (2014)	NEW REPORT (2023)
WE'RE ALL DOOMED AS CATASTROPHE THREATENS LIFE ON EARTH!	**THERE'S STILL TIME TO PREVENT CATASTROPHE IF WE ACT NOW!**
Response: Report largely ignored and reported as small item on page 94	**Response:** Report largely ignored and reported as small item on page 94

RELIEF FOR GRASS ROOTS TORY VOTERS

by Our Westminster Correspondent **Doug Whistle**

MEMBERS of the Conservative Party are breathing a sigh of relief today at signs that everything is back to normal inside Number 10.

"When Rishi Sunak unveiled the Windsor Framework to much fanfare a few weeks ago we were sick with worry that this would usher in a new era of the government behaving in a reasonable and sensible manner," said horrified Tory voters.

"To see a Conservative prime minister solving a seemingly intractable problem with Brussels through mutual respect and compromise was pretty hard to take. At the very least, Rishi could have dead-legged Von der Leyen at the press conference.

"You can imagine our relief on seeing Suella Braverman in the Commons rounding on lefty judges, the woke blob civil servants, and insisting that all patriotic people back her Stop The Boats bill, meaning we can finally put the nightmare of those reasonable few days behind us."

ROTTEN APPLE TO SUE

by Our Met Correspondent **Brad Pips**

A ROTTEN apple has confirmed that it plans to sue the Met Police, saying its reputation as a repulsive, putrid, disgusting decomposing fruit has been permanently damaged by having its name associated with serving police officers.

"We constantly hear senior officers trying to defend the indefensible by insisting that most coppers are decent and hard-working, but the problem is a few rotten apples," said the rotten apple.

"How would you like to be constantly talked about in the same breath as scumbag rapists and murderers like Wayne Couzens, David Carrick and the rest?

"When it comes to being rotten to the core, I've got nothing on the Met. Enough is enough. I'm going to take them for every penny I can, until I hear the pips squeak."

Police had 'weird initiation rituals' finds report

by Our Crime Correspondent **Rob Erry**

THE damning Casey Report into the Met police has found that some young recruits were forced to take part in a bizarre initiation ceremony in which they were made to investigate a burglary.

"We had to go to the house where a burglary took place, take a statement from the homeowner, investigate the crime and then arrest the criminals responsible," said one young recruit.

"It was so humiliating. I was expecting to roll up my trouser leg and expose my nipple, but instead I had to fill out an incident report. No actual serving Met police officer would do anything as demeaning as investigate a crime. I felt sick for months."

"Watch out! It's the police!"

'YES, I LIED BUT I DID NOT LIE INTENTIONALLY OR RECKLESSLY', SAYS LIAR

by Our Lying Staff
Ivor Whopper and
Fay Kevidence

A NOTORIOUS liar today told a committee of MPs that he did lie to Parliament on a number of occasions, but he lied in good faith, and he believed his lies were true to the best of his knowledge at the time.

In a 94-hour hearing, he repeatedly made the point that he did not intentionally lie, as he routinely lies, and therefore cannot be expected to identify what the intentions of his lies are at any given moment.

As to the accusation that his lies were reckless, the reckless liar shouted, "Fuck recklessness. My lies were carefully considered on all occasions. Except when they weren't."

He continued, "Hand on heart. I can honestly lie to you and say that none of my advisors told me it was against the Covid rules to lie. It certainly wasn't in the guidance not to lie. How was I supposed to know that as Prime Minister you are not allowed to lie? I was extremely busy running the country. This was a 24/7 job. Or, on some occasions, a 25/7 job. And at the height of the pandemic it was, without doubt, a 26/8 job. Believe me, I did not have time to check up on whether every single lie I told was intentional or reckless."

When asked whether he kept a safe distance from the truth at all times, he assured the Committee that, "I was always at least two metres away from the truth, and often far further. I kept as far away from the truth as was possible. It was like there was an electromagnetic forcefield between me and the truth."

At the end of the meeting, the liar told the Committee that all the evidence of him lying showed that he was not a liar, and if they decided he was in fact a liar then they were lying. And that was the truth. He then lied that he'd thoroughly enjoyed the afternoon, and that he was grateful to the Committee for all the work they had done in proving that he wasn't a reckless or intentional liar, even though he was obviously both.

NETANYAHU FLIES IN AMID JUDICIAL REFORM PROTESTS

You're a threat to democracy in Israel

I'll be the judge of that

"No, honestly, we don't do anal probes. That was just Jeff. HR had to get involved. It was a whole thing"

PRIVATE EYE ANSWERS THE PARTYGATE COMMITTEE QUESTIONS THAT REMAIN UNANSWERED

Q: Why did Boris Johnson swear on the bible?
A: Normally, committee witnesses are asked to swear on the lives of their children, but in this case they only had four hours and decided the bible would be quicker.

Q: What was the first sign that Boris Johnson was in trouble?
A: As soon as the committee realised that the former PM had had a haircut they knew he was guilty. Body language experts have long observed how criminals wear suits in court to try and emphasise their innocence, but in Mr Johnson's case the tell-tell sign was a pair of scissors and a brush applied to his coiffure.

Q: Why does Lord David Pannick KC wear silly glasses?
A: Because it requires a very specific kind of eyesight to view Boris Johnson as innocent.

Q: What was the significance of the bell ringing during the proceedings?
A: It was last orders in the Commons Bar and Mr Johnson had to get down to the bar to attend a morale-boosting work event to say farewell to his own career.

Q: Why did no one laugh when Boris said, "The Metropolitan Police Force said I did nothing wrong and we have to trust them"?
A: Ha! Ha! Ha! Ha!

Q: Why did he refer to Lulu Lytle as an 'on site contractor'?
A: Because it's a more polite and technically accurate way of saying, "a woman flogging overpriced rolls of gold wallpaper to his gullible wife".

Q: Did Boris Johnson actually call Harriet Harman a witch?
A: No. The former Prime Minister called her a kangaroo.

Q: Why was there no Liberal Democrat MP on the committee?
A: In order to represent the current political balance of the House of Commons, there would have to have been 1/46th of an MP. The Liberal Democrats were unable to provide this, despite an invitation to Mr Tim Farron's left foot from the ankle down.

Q: Why was Michael Fabricant there?
A: Erskine May, the bible of parliamentary procedure, stipulates that in all committee hearings there must be in attendance at least one ridiculously bewigged Conservative MP to provide "tonsorial balance".

Q: Why was Boris Johnson not advised by his advisors to stop blaming everything on his advisors?
A: He was, but he chose to ignore their advice and suggested instead that, for justice to be properly served, they should all go to jail, and could be transported there in the bus under which they had just been thrown.

Q: What will be the total cost to the taxpayer of the hearing?
A: £200,000 in legal fees and £1,000,000 for Boris' speaking fee.

Q: Why didn't the MPs refer to the party in his flat, and the loud ABBA music, and the karaoke machine, and the suitcases of wine, and the broken swing in the garden, and the fact that everyone at Number 10 was drunk all the time and having sex in the bushes?
A: No, got me there. No idea.

Q: Is Boris Johnson innocent?
A: Don't be silly.

(That's enough Committee. Ed.)

AT LAST — THAT COVID GUIDANCE EXPLAINED

BANNED

Saying goodbye to loved ones

ABSOLUTELY ESSENTIAL

Saying goodbye to work colleagues

Keir Starmer WRITES

HELLO!

I'm sure you've noticed that there's been a bit of alarm about Labour's Twitter attack ads – the ones that label Rishi Sunak as a chap who wants to keep child molesters out of prison!

There is an argument from the usual suspects, like John McDonnell, that this kind of tactic just drags the whole discourse of politics down. I refute that, of course! If an honest decent politician like me, with an unimpeachable character, can't make the odd aspersion that the Prime Minister is on the side of sweaty, leering, kiddie-fiddling perverts, then what is the world coming to?

After some consideration, I've come to the conclusion that a lot of these attacks made on me for my cynical attacks on Rishi are quite cynical in nature and, therefore, the people making these cynical attacks are fair game for me to cynically attack them back!

Look, I'm sure John McDonnell is a nice person, but he did spend a lot of the last ten years hanging around with a strange, beardy bloke with glasses and they both used to frequent festivals where a lot of young people used to go! I'm sure there was nothing wrong with him getting on stage and looking out at a sea of gyrating, semi-clad young people high on drugs and alcohol. Not that I'm implying anything! I'm just asking questions!

So remember – vote Labour! Or else, watch out, as we might do a tweet about you too!

Sincerely, Keir

Pot condemns kettle

A POT today condemned a kettle after the kettle began running cruel, nasty, misleading attack ads.

"Never, in all the years we've been winning elections by running cruel, nasty, misleading attack ads about the kettle, did we think for a second that the kettle would start running cruel, nasty, misleading attack ads in an attempt to win an election," said the pot.

"This is disgraceful behaviour by the kettle. Quite frankly, I'm boiling over."

The kettle, however, insisted that the ads weren't the "cruel, nasty, misleading attack ads" which the pot was infamous for, claiming that they were "misleading, nasty, cruel attack ads," which was completely different and totally justified.

"The fact that the pot has the nerve to complain about our attack ads? I'm utterly steaming."

LATE NEWS

Dog beach ban

THIS summer, dog owners will be fined for taking their pooches to certain beaches.

"It's for health reasons," explained Thérèse Coffey. "We can't have dogs going to beaches and getting ill because of all the human turds bobbing merrily on the beautiful briny sea. Not to mention the ones floating in the moats of the kiddies' sandcastles. It's just not fair on our four-legged friends."

A dog welcomed the ban: "It's a good first step towards improving canine health, but humans can do so much more. Surely, it is now time for humans to scoop up their poop in a nice plastic bag and hang it on a tree, rather than just releasing it into the water system and hoping for the best." *(I said that's enough faecal material! Ed.)*

FISHERMAN'S TALES

I saw a turd this big!

Lines on the Historic Police Action Against the Former SNP Leadership

'Twas in the year two thousand and twenty-three
That a police drama hit Scotland better than anything on TV.
Inspector McKnacker arrested Nicola Sturgeon's spouse
And sent a fleet of officers to collar Peter Murrell at their house.
They set up a tent in the garden of the famous twosome,
As if they'd committed a murder or something equally gruesome.
What were the police looking for? It was like Line of Duty!
Was it cash or gold or some other undeclared booty?
Next they went to Murrell's mother's home, 92, and still alive,
And seized a brand new campervan that was sitting in her drive.
There it was, £110,000 of luxurious motorhome,
That allows the owner over the glens and highlands to roam.
(Without, of course ,having to pay for a hotel or a B&B,
Thus saving money for canny tourists who like to holiday for free.)
But no one can explain why such a vehicle should be bought
By the SNP and answers to these questions are urgently sought.
And those involved in the affair of Dormobilegate
Are beginning to make the Scottish public quite irate.
The support for the new party leader, poor Humza,
Ebbs away, as the ill-fated Yusaf comes a
Cropper trying to defend the previous regime
With its Niesmann and Bischoff vehicle, a wild rover's dream,
And why did the SNP choose him as leader in such a hurry
Before the police sprang into action in a dramatic flurry?
Is this why Sturgeon really decided to retire,
Before the party got stuck in the metaphorical mire?
But, in the chaos, it is interesting who is laughing the most,
In the hope that their enemies are now going to be toast.
Is it Sarwar and Scottish Labour or Ross and the Caledonian Tories?
No. The familiar kilted figure coming once again to the fore is
Alex Salmond of Alba, the former leader of the SNP,
Who, truth to tell, can barely contain his glee.
"Alas!" he says, "This is a tragedy," as he takes out his hanky,
Crying tears of joy at the downfall of the wee former first minister.

© *William McGonagall 1867*

PS. I should say that Mr Murrell was released without charge.
I have no desire to risk a fine for contempt of court, possibly large.

DIARY

WHAT EASTER MEANS TO ME

CAROL MIDGLEY: Wow. Just wow.

LEE ANDERSON MP: That Easter Bunny is playing us for fools. There's a time and a place. Free chocolate eggs? No such thing, mate. Someone's got to pay and – guess what? – it's the hard-pressed British taxpayer. If the Easter Bunny and his left-wing chums have it in mind to ponce around scoffing free eggs paid for by hard-working families, then why don't they clear off out of this country to somewhere that would suit them better? I hear North Korea is nice at this time of year.

LORD JULIAN FELLOWES: I'm sorry to say this, but the Last Supper simply doesn't "do it" for me. Agreed, a dozen clubbable disciples gathered around a long table is a wonderfully civilised idea – but it's hard to overlook those ghastly "sandals".

And their robes were, one regrets to say, more than a little c-o-m-m-o-n. Whensoe'er Lady Fellowes and I invite close friends to dine, we insist on black tie.

I bow to no one in my admiration for My Lord Jesus Christ but had He broken bread at Chateau Fellowes and then passed it around with his grubby bare hands, the words "cleanliness is next to godliness" might have tripped off one's tongue.

ADELE: To be honest, now you mention it, I only have to fink of Jesus on that cross and his nan darn below all weepy I get so moshinaw I mean no one would want to be up on a cross in the blazing sunshine wivat a hat I'm litry cryin my eye zat now you mention it to be honest like now you mention it to be honest. Sezitaw really.

YOKO ONO:

Imagine you are an Easter Egg.
Break yourself.
Now, you are all in little bits.
No, you should not have done that.
And what is in your middle?
Nothing!
There is nothing in your middle!
Just a hole.
So climb through that hole.
And out into the universe.

PETER HITCHENS: Yet another Good Friday is roundly ignored by a nation that, for the most part, does not even know what Easter is about, except yet another opportunity to buy over-the-counter marijuana and to watch government-sponsored Marxist propaganda, such as Antiques Road Show, on their expensive colour television sets.

Incidentally, have you noticed that televisions no longer have a "warm-up" period, in which the viewer is given a time to reflect, while the picture on the screen comes into focus?

Is this yet another cynical plan by that state-conrolled BBC to remove any remaining power to think for itself from the British population?

The Easter story – the story we no longer teach our children, for fear of being detained for an indefinite period our Marxist police – is all about a solitary figure who is brave enough to speak out against the moronic idiocies of his society and is consequently rendered into the hands of spiteful torturers to be tortured and sneered at.

It all ends in utter despair, the hero dying in hopeless agony, the despicable crowd mocking him to the end.

And all because he had the guts to speak the truth in his newspaper column, or its historic equivalent.

ADRIAN CHILES: Don't get me started! I used to love a good old-fashioned hot cross bun, but now it just makes me hot and cross, no pun intended! I'm talking about the way they keep messing with them, these days. They're always adding things, like cheese or caramel or chocolate. They can't just leave well alone, can they? And that got me thinking, and when the time came the thought that I thought I might think was this: why can't they make them like they used to, and no messing about? If I've said it once, I've said it a hundred times. And if I haven't, then I will. Don't get me started!

DAME JOAN COLLINS: I'll never forget the day I married Pontius Pilate.

In those days, there wasn't a girl in the world who didn't want to be Mrs Pilate.

Pontius seemed to have everything. Status. Authority. Wealth. Gorgeous gowns. And beautifully clean hands.

But he let me down. With one hasty decision, he brought shame upon his name for eternity.

Yes, he begged me to stay. But by this time, I had already met the man of my dreams. And that's how I became Mrs Joan Iscariot.

But, alas, it was not to last.

BBC RADIO 4'S YOU AND YOURS Winifred Robinson: One day you're preaching to thousands. The next, you're hanging from a cross. That's no way to spend Easter. With more rail, hospital, passport and postal strikes threatened, inflation running at ten percent, our roads in a dreadful repair and sales of electrical goods down by more than 25 percent, is your Easter going to be even worse? Call *You and Yours* to tell us how you plan to cope. Marjorie Doldrum is in Cardiff. Tell us about your Easter, Marjorie?

Marjorie: Last Easter, I bit into my Easter egg, Winifred, and got a mouthful of silver foil mixed up in my chocolate. No warning, nothing. I'm frankly disgusted. I just wonder how long it will be before someone dies of eating all this silver foil.

Winifred Robinson: We asked a representative from the government health and safety to appear on this programme, but were told none was available. Call *You and Yours* to tell us about how a member of your family has tragically choked to death on Easter egg foil.

As told to
CRAIG BROWN

DESPERATE BUSINESS

JON & MICK / MODERN TOSS

Your CV is very impressive

Cheers, it's the same one I sent you before but I changed the font

you don't seem to have a clue what you're doing

yeah well that's your fault for over-promoting me

We're really keen to get some older people back into the work place, what can you bring to the table ?

I can offer one to one tuition in boozing at lunchtime?

how are you getting on with that spreadsheet I asked for yesterday?

yeah I'm just waiting for my career coach to call back and tell me whether it's worth doing or not

INTERVIEW

How do you handle negative feedback about your work?

What you trying to say mate? Tell you what, you can stick your job up your arse.

CORONATION SPECIAL

WHERE'S the best vantage point to catch a glimpse of the coronation when you're at home?

♚ The best view of the telly is from the sofa, directly in front, but this may get crowded if you don't bag a place early (up to two weeks in advance would be safe).

♚ If you can't secure a spot on the sofa, standing in the doorway to the kitchen could be good, with the view only obscured by the pot plant and the lampstand.

♚ As a last resort, why not stand in the garden and look through the window, though your view may be obscured by all the royal bunting, not to mention the curtains.

"I've misplaced my optimism"

How the coronation will reflect the cost of living crisis

by our Coronation Correspondent
Penny Pincher

OUR thrifty King is sensitive to our cash-strapped times. Here's how our modern monarch has saved the pennies:

● Second-hand crown
● Used throne
● Repurposed carriage, with rescue horses
● Recycled fly-past
● Pre-loved Queen

Thanks to our King's determination to have a value-for-money monarchy, the coronation costs have been kept to a minimum.

Rather than ballooning to £250 million, as some critics had feared, this stripped-down royal event will only cost the nation £250 million.

Said a palace spokesman, "The King is so in touch with his subjects that he is even keeping on old Nicholas Witchell, who has been in the family since the late Queen's accession to the throne."

He added, "The King is very keen on saving as much money as possible, which is why he's getting the British public to pay for it all."

Notes & queries

In the run up to the coronation we are hearing a lot about something called the Supertunica? Who or what is it?

● Supertunica is of course a famous song by the popular Swedish hit machine, ABBA. It featured on the best selling album "ABBA Cadabra" and topped the charts for 19 weeks in the summer of 1976. Everyone will remember the catchy lyrics by Bjorn Beardus and Benny Hillson: "Supertunica/ For sure we all do like ya/ Supertunica/the lights are very bright ja?". The song can now be heard at the CO_2 Arena where AI-powered Chatbot Abbatars perform in four dimensions and bring to life the incredible harmonies of Agnetha Christieskog and Anni-Widdecombestad.
The Rev Marcus Welby, St Justin on Parade, Lambeth Walk (OI).

● The Reverend is preaching utter nonsense as usual! Supertunica, as if we could forget, was the name of the booster Covid vaccine developed during the pandemic by the Anglo-French-Swiss-Chinese drug company, Pfarma. It was claimed by eminent Covid-sceptics, such as myself, that Supertunica contained micro-processors which sent all the data from your internal organs to Bill Gates who then marketed them to lizards disguised as members of the British Royal Family.

If the Reverend could be bothered to look at the research, he would see that a study by Professor Luny of the Swedish Online University of Bonkurz has found that everything I say is true, but will inevitably be denied, thus proving an establishment cover-up.
Piers Corloonybyn, The Old Nuterry, Padcel.

● I am afraid Mr Corloonybyn is barking up the wrong tree. The Supertunica is the sacred gold vestment worn over the white shift, the Colobium Sidanddoris, and under the Imperial Hilary Mantle during the coronation of the Monarch. It is full length and embroidered with thistles and Tudor roses and edged with gold bobbin-lace and is a reminder of the priestly robes that emphasise the divine nature of Kingship.
David Dimbleby Dunbroadcastin, The Richard Dimbleby Retirement Village, Great Dimbleby.

● Dimbleby is just being silly. No one could believe any of that stuff in this day and age. Super Tunica is a cartoon character in the eponymous children's cartoon game in which the Super Tunica Brothers have to save the Rhubarb Queen Camilla from the villainous *(That's enough question and answer. Ed.)*

*Next Week
What's up, Pussycat?*

LATE NEWS

Doctors close to agreeing new deal

THERE was widespread relief in the health sector this week as doctors are believed to be on the verge of reaching a satisfactory and wide-reaching pay agreement.

Said one, "Our initial starting point was a 35% increase, but obviously that was just an initial negotiating position, and what we have now secured is a very reasonable boost of 100%.

How could I say no? Australia here I come!"

Said another doctor, "Of course, before quitting the NHS and flying Down Under, there are other factors to consider: there's the sunshine, the beaches, the ice-cold tinnies waiting for me at the end of a long, working half-day spent treating people who are, on the whole, in far better nick, thanks to their healthier lifestyle. See ya!"

WHAT'S REALLY INSIDE THE BEAST?

After Joe Biden's historic trip to Ireland, we reveal the secrets of the famous presidential limo...

- President-sized bed
- Built-in glass for the Presidential teeth
- Blacked-out windows (to keep out pesky daylight)
- Five-inch-thick armour plating to cancel noise so as not to wake up dormant President
- Emergency Chamber Pot-us for POTUS in middle of nap
- Noise-cancelling engine which takes the world's most powerful man from 0-40 winks in under three seconds
- High-impact shock absorbers for smoother ride and slumber

Tony Blair's recollections of the Good Friday agreement, 25 years on

Tony Blair... Tony Blair... Tony Blair... Tony Blair... Tony Blair... Tony Blair... Tony Blair... Tony Blair... Tony Blair... Tony Blair... Tony Blair... Tony Blair... Tony Blair... Tony Blair... Tony Blair... Tony Blair... Tony Blair... David Trimble... Tony Blair...

FURY OVER SELFIE TAKEN WITH MAN NOTORIOUS FOR HIS HATRED OF THE BRITISH

Oh, I don't think Joe's that bad

Biden speech in full

■ NORTHERN Ireland cannot return to being a place where everyone lives in constant fear of the next shooting... like America.

New bank failure threatens global financial system

by Our Banking Staff
Lloyd Barclay and **Nat West**

The world economy was teetering on the brink of disaster at the news that the Bank of Mum and Dad was about to collapse.

This respected and previously stable financial institution now appears to be riddled with bad debt and toxic investments. Said a representative of the Bank of Mum and Dad (Mum), "To be honest, we've just thrown good money after bad. We invested in our son, Simon, and hoped to see some sort of return on the second-hand car he was talking about."

Another bank insider (Dad) said, "If we'd exercised due diligence and checked out the state of his room, we might have given Simon a lower credit-rating. To be honest we didn't stress test the 'studio flat with his mates' investment proposal. It turns out that the entirety of the property funds were invested instead in the alcohol sector. Mainly vodka."

The Bank of Mum and Dad denied that they'd been irresponsible lenders, and in a statement delivered from Head Office (the living room), said, "That's unfair! We checked all his paperwork, birth certificate, etc, and he's definitely our boy. We'd do anything for him – apart from lend him any more money."

The knock-on effect of this withdrawal of credit has led to a run on the Bank of Mum and Dad, with billions being refused to offspring all over the globe. Experts believe that if the Bank of Mum and Dad continues to fail, international capitalism will go into meltdown, the housing market will collapse and all children will live with their parents for ever.

Said the Bank of Mum and Dad, "Okay, we give in. here's a couple of grand to tide you over, but this is the last time, definitely."

"I'm sorry you had to find out like this, Peter"

LIZ TRUSS COMEBACK TOUR WOWS AMERICA

by Our US Correspondent
Di Saster

FRESH from her triumph delivering a speech that lasted almost as long as her premiership, Liz Truss is to delight American audiences further by commencing a barnstorming tour of the US.

THAT TOUR IN FULL

■ **21 April** – "Why the wokerati elite are undermining our economic freedoms" – to be delivered at Crazy Ike's Crabster Pot, New Dworkin.

■ **23 April** – "The dangers of the redistribution ideology in the left-wing economic city establishment" – Jerry the Giraffe's Under 5 Softplay Area (Milkshake'n'Sodaland), just off Highway 94, Pigsknuckle, Arkansas.

■ **27 April** – "The growth of the anti-growth coalition in the pork and cheese markets which threaten to raise taxes for top earners" – Krispy Kreme Kastle (formerly Chucky's Cheesecake Chowderama), Desolation, Nebraska.

■ **29 April** – "How deregulation can turbo boost Anglo-American economies without leading to a £60 billion hole in the budget and a run on the banks" – Cosby's Horse 'n' Crayfish Booby Bar (2 spiked drinks minimum), Loonyville, Shutter Island, Milwaukee.

■ **May 1** – "How intergalactic lizards are infiltrating our bodily fluids and forcing brainwashed zombie governments to capitulate to Marxist-Leninist political correctness gone mad and give money to poor people" – Area 51, Roswell, New Mexico.

THE KING OF TROUBLES

A short story special by Dame Hedda Shoulders

THE STORY SO FAR: The moment of destiny for which Charles has waited his entire life is nearly upon him. Now read on…

"**B**OO! Not my King," the cry echoed around the hallowed walls of Yesminster Abbey. "Down with the Monarchy! Get a job, you freeloading, over-dressed nancy boy."

"What on earth are you doing, Sir Alan?" King Charles enquired testily, as Sir Alan Fitztightly ran up and down the empty nave, hurling anti-royalist invective at his soon-to-be- crowned King.

"It's all part of the rehearsal, Sire," explained the Royal kool-aide-de-camp. "We have to prepare for all eventualities and that includes protest in all its forms."

At that point, Sir Alan threw an egg at his monarch's head and Charles only just ducked in time, as it whistled past the bowler hat full of flour which the King was wearing to simulate the weight of the Imperial Leather Crown.

"Well, you don't have to do it all with such enthusiasm, Sir Alan!" Charles complained. "Anyone would think you were enjoying it!"

"Not at all, my liege! And well ducked, if I may say so. If the egg had connected with the flour in your hat we could have had a Bake Off situation!"

Charles had rarely seen his Chief Eggquerry and Lieutenant of the Listerine so happy in his work. Charles proceeded nervously towards the wooden throne of King Edward the Eagle, awkwardly carrying his regalia substitutes: a bowling ball for the Virgin Orb-it and a snooker cue for the Sceptre of King Ottakar.

But what on earth was Fitztightly doing now, as he ran towards Charles in a cloud of orange powder?

"Just Stop Anointing Oil!" shouted Sir Alan, as he brandished a tube of superglue and attempted to stick himself to Charles' cloak, the Hilary Mantle of State, replicated for this rehearsal by a duvet cover featuring Batman which, as Sir Alan had explained to a dubious Charles, was appropriate, on account of him being both a Crusader and Caped.

"That really is quite enough, Sir Alan," said Charles, expertly batting him to the ground with his cue and dropping the bowling ball on his head.

"Well played, Sire!" gasped the wounded factotum. "Defender of Yourself as well as the Multifaiths!"

"Surely we have now covered all the possibilities!" sighed the King, wearily. The rehearsal was now into its seventh hour and somehow they had to condense the mystery and the majesty of the ceremony into a TV audience-friendly hour (or 43 minutes for ITV's Tom Bradybunch to fit in the adverts for Cut-Price Coronation Quiche – now available at RodLidl).

"There is still the matter of the pillars, Sire," the last of the Fitztightlys reminded him.

"Ah. The Pillars of the Establishment. Where to seat the Great and Good who have assembled to pledge their allegiance to the newly coronated Carolus Rex?"

"No, the pillars we are going to hide members of your family behind."

Sir Alan really did seem to be relishing his role as Master and Commander of Ceremonials and Chief Pompadour of Circumstance.

"Do we put Andrew behind a pillar and let Harry distract attention by putting him up front? Or do we put Andrew centre stage to distract attention from Harry sulking behind a pillar?"

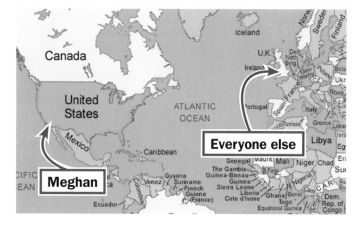

Charles put his head in hands, which was a mistake, as the bag of flour burst and emptied all over the Batman duvet of state.

"And what about the elephant in the room?"

"Worry not, Sire. Fergie is under house arrest at Royal David Lodge in Windsor until the end of the ceremony. And that's no way to refer to the Duchess. Naughty! Slapped wrist. You'll be cancelled before you know it!"

Charles remonstrated, "No, I meant the real elephant in the room!"

There was only one guest they all feared. She Who Must Not Be Mentioned. The Californian equivalent of the ghost of Banquo turning up for the feast. The Lady Macbeth from Montecito…

Charles grimaced at the thought of the Duchess of Suxxess arriving at the Abbey with the Frogmore Prince Archewellness and his little sister, Princess Lilypond – not to mention the ten-man Newtflix Camera Crew and Oprah Whiney in tow. Would she stand by Poets Corner under the gaze of the spirits of the great romantic bards like William Wordsearch and Percy Bysshe Shelleysuit to denounce him as a slave-trading colonialist and imperialist, whom she could never forgive for failing to behead Princess Kate Middlebrow for being rude to her?

The soon-to-be-anointed King's noble brow furrowed further, like the lines left by the ancient plough on his Duchy Original Organic Potato patch at Poundlandbury in Borsetshire.

"Ahhh! I can see your concern, Sire. 'How do you solve a problem like Meghana?', as Mother Superior very nearly sings about the flibbertigibbet Julie Andrews in my partner, the Air Vice Marshal's, favourite film, *The Sound of Markle*. We went to a singalong version and…"

"This is no time for levity, Sir Alan! The future of the entire monarchy is at stake. That woman could destroy thousands of years of history in a single moment!"

"It's all right, Sire," soothed Sir Alan. "The Coronation seating plan that I have devised is absolutely fool-proof."

"Phew!" breathed Charles with an enormous sigh of relief. "You really have thought of everything!"

"Indeed, Sire. All you have to do now is to proceed magisterially to the exit and enjoy the Bells."

"The Bells? Thank God for that!" rasped a voice from the shadows. "Make mine a double. I'm parched. And while you're at it, pass me a gasper from under the ancient Rolling Stone of Scone. I hid a packet of Benson & Hedgefunds there for emergencies."

As ever, his Queen and soul mate punctured the pomposity of proceedings and brought a touch of down-to-earth normality to the elevated fol-de-rol and flummery.

At that moment, as if on cue, the heavenly sound of Purcell's *Donald Trumpet Voluntary* rang around the Abbey and the choir burst into the specially composed anthem by Andrew Lloyds Bank – *Don't Cry for Meg, Arentchasickova?*

Charles smiled for the first time that day. Perhaps the whole thing was going to be all right. Or was it?

(To be continued…)

Sir Alan's Cunning Coronation Seating Plan

MAN IN HAT SITS ON CHAIR

Those Doolally Mail headlines in full

This week	Next week
PLEDGE ALLEGIANCE TO OUR NEW KING, OUR WISE AND CARING SOVEREIGN	**WHEN IS WILLS GOING TO TAKE OVER FROM THIS JUG-EARED MEDDLING LOON?**

Nadine Dorries

"WHY I was right in my capacity as a parliamentarian to attend the Coronation – but many other MPs were not – because they were there as part of a grubby deal involving political favours – which I have certainly NOT been party..." *(continues with no sense of irony for several hundred words)*

"Have you come far?"

Protesting about pomp and ceremony is something we do very well in this country

THE CORONATION OF KING CHARLES THE THIRD
The nation's verdict in full

COMPLETELY ridiculous... loved every minute of it... music was magnificent... except Lloyd Webber... awful... Harry behind the feather ha ha ha ha... Penny Mordaunt with that sword phwoar... upper arm strength... Liz Truss in orange ghastly who does she think she is... Charles could have given us a smile... it wasn't his funeral... not quite yet anyway... ha ha ha... Camilla looks a bit tired, doesn't she... probably dying for a fag... still, rescue dogs on her gown aaahh... wasn't Kate MARVELLOUS... so regal... so elegant... bit thin though... she should be Queen really... And young Louis... bless... bit of a handful... that soprano in yellow amazing... but what WAS she wearing... all got a bit daft when Charles put on the Oven Glove... bit Ruritanian... gospel choir such an inspiration... such a modern twist... such tight trousers... Welby rather dull... zzzz... time to put the kettle on... Hot equerry on the other hand... mmmmm... oh he's married... booo!!... Clare Balding what a trouper but enough about the horses... that one that went bonkers... crikey... Prince Andrew... what a disgrace... how did he get there? In the back of a police van... ha ha ha... Is that Ant and Dec?... which one is which?... oh it's left to right... very clever seating plan... That Crown just doesn't fit, does it? They should have thought of that... looks like the Archbishop needs a mallet to hammer it on... though, come to think of it, all the hats really are very silly... And what's the point of those bracelets of whatever it is?... Ah... Zadok... now you are talking... you've got to hand it to Handel... showed up poor old Lloyd Webber... Penny Mordaunt, I say... looks like a Greek goddess or maybe Anne Boleyn... either way, eat your heart out Thérèse Coffey... Prince Wills kissing his dad on the cheek... aahhh... bet that annoyed Harry... though he probably couldn't see, stuck behind Anne's feather... ha ha ha ha... armed forces splendid... clockwork precision... at least something in this country still works... classic British event... rain didn't manage to spoil it at all... shame about the flypast... Oh no, Clare's still going on about the horses... Oh look, Harry's not on the balcony ha ha ha... who is the one with the glasses?... Gloucester?... Kent?... who knows?... and those poor kids... fancy making them wear those outfits... and then it was all over... completely ridiculous... loved every minute of it.

What You Missed

Coronation highlights
with commentary by Huw Edwards

"And here they come in serried ranks, the officers of the Metropolitan Police, led by Inspector Knacker bearing the official Baton of State, which he ceremoniously brings down on the head of the Chief Protester, crowning him with the traditional words, 'You're nicked, sunshine!'

"This phrase dates back to the 1970s and the reign of Her Majesty Queen Elizabeth II. You will note that the protester is wearing the official T-shaped garment bearing the inscription 'Not My King', the provenance of which is unknown but is thought to have originated early this year...

"Oh, and here comes the ritual Taser of Liberty, and now the donning of the Silver Handcuffs of Freedom. The Chief Protester, a Mr David Spart, proclaims, as is customary, 'This is illegal, you fascist pig!' To which his accomplices join in, with the chorus, 'Don't worry Dave, we've got this on our phones.'

"And there they go, ceremoniously unceremoniously bundled into the black carriage, named after the Empress Maria, to the sound of the sirens blaring with their stirring *Nee-Naw Nee-Naw* anthem. This, of course, is merely the first stage of the ceremony. Tomorrow we will have the official announcement of the apology from the police, followed by the renouncement of the apology by the protesters.

"They will then sing the words of the old Celtic chant which is set to the tune of an ancient American hymn. This is, of course, *She'll be coming round the mountain when she comes*, which has been modified for a modern ceremony to: *You can shove your coronation up your arse!* And aren't the choir magnificent?... *(cont. for 94 hours)*

IS GYLES BRANDRETH THE GRIM REAPER?

by **Lunchtime Obituary**

AT FIRST glance, it seems a ridiculous idea, but let's just look at the evidence.

Every time someone famous dies, a piece appears in the newspapers by Gyles Brandreth recounting a hilarious encounter that Gyles and the celebrity have just enjoyed together.

I'm not saying there is a definite connection, but it seems more and more likely that the jumper-wearing comic may actually be none other than Death himself.

Let's look at the list: Prince Philip – hilarious lunch with Gyles Brandreth. Dead. Her Majesty the Queen – hilarious tea with Gyles Brandreth. Dead. Barry Humphries – hilarious dinner with Gyles Brandreth. Dead. Can you see a pattern? It's more obvious than the pattern on his novelty sweater.

And now, the latest victim is Len Goodman – one hilarious meeting on the beach in Broadstairs with Gyles Brandreth and, yes, you guessed it, he's gone.

So, despite Brandreth's smiling demeanour, it is worth considering that Gyles Brandeath, as he should surely be known, may well be none other than the Fourth Horseman of the Apocalypse, descending on unsuspecting celebrities and *(I'm killing this piece right now – Guest Editor Gyles Brandreth)*

"We've been on strike for a week and no one's noticed"

The **Maily** EXPRESS **Telegraph**

LAST WEEK

■ HOORAY for the Archbishop of Canterbury as he gives his solemn religious blessing to this traditional affirmation of British values, as exemplified by our marvellous Monarch, King Charles III. May he provide wisdom and counsel in his long and happy reign, which we hope lasts forever. God Save the King!

THIS WEEK

■ SHUT your face, Archbishop Holier-than-thou, you interfering God-botherer! And shove your crook where the sun don't shine, unlike Rwanda where it's lovely all day! You're nearly as bad as his Royal Busy-bodiness, aka Big Ears III. Keep your nose out or we'll chop off your head! God rot the pair of you!

POETRY CORNER

Lines on the death of Ralfe Whistler, celebrated "dodologist"

So. Farewell
Then Ralfe Whistler.

You were a dodo expert
With an extensive
Collection of dodo
Droppings, dodo bones
And other dodo-related
Paraphernalia.

But now, alas,
You are as dead as a...
Oh.
What's the phrase?
Er...
Yes, that's it!
Doornail.

E.J. Thribb (17½)

EYE RACING TIPS

YES, it's the Grand National Disgrace – so join with the *Eye* as we offer you a FREE £1 bet on Britain's favourite sporting event: the Two Grand A Day National! Here's your guide to the odds for the day's action in Parliament:

❍ Conservative MP to accept job with fake gambling firm: .... **Evens**

❍ Conservative MP to accept job with real gambling firm: **3/2**

❍ Conservative MP to turn down job with any gambling firm: **100/1**

❍ Conservative MP to say "This looks dodgy, I should go back to representing my constituents" when being offered £2,000 a day: ...**10,000/1**

LATE NEWS

■ Lame Conservative MP may have to be put down after disastrous performance before hidden camera.

WHY IS IT ONLY BREXITEER MINISTERS WHO GET ACCUSED OF BULLYING?

There aren't any Remainer ministers because they were all sacked by the Brexiteers.

CIVIL SERVICE REACT TO ACCUSATIONS THEY CONSPIRED TO BRING DOWN RAAB

RAAT TO LEAVE SINKING SHIP

by Our Nautical Staff **Davy Jones-Locker**

MR DOMINIC RAAT, a prominent rodent, has announced his intention to leave the sinking ship of state, SS *Torytanic*, along with about 10 percent of the other senior vermin.

Mr Raat enjoyed a controversial career on the ship and his frequently bad-tempered behaviour was generously described as "ratty".

However, his rat-like cunning served him well, as he maintained his position as Deputy Chief Rat, until he lost it. Which he often did with subordinates.

He was a commanding figure in the bilges, and colleagues respected his ability to sink his teeth into anyone who didn't do what he said quickly enough.

Now Mr Raat has had enough and has decided to leave the ship entirely. "It's not because it's sinking, obviously, although it is," he squeaked. "No, the reason I'm leaving the ship is because the sea is closed and I now want to spend more time with my family, *Rattus norvegicus*."

On hearing his plans, his family immediately headed in the opposite direction.

Dictionary Corner

Bullying [Bu-lee-ing] (*n.*)

1 (*archaic*) Behaviour likely to intimidate or frighten others, like shouting, swearing, or physically attacking them.

2 (*modern*) Telling people they're not very good at their jobs, being a bit mean, or looking at them and scowling when they've screwed up in their department.

*"You only had **one** job!"*

HUGH BONNEVILLE: Your esteemed Majesties, everyone here in the gorgeous grounds of Windsor Castle, and all of you in your little homes – Welcome to the Coronation Concert!!!!!! And what about that truly SPECTACULAR first number.

(Cheers, flagwaving)

(Cut to King grimacing)

That was a literally INCREDIBLE start to our evening and tonight we're GETTING THE PARTY STARTED as ONE HUNDRED COUNTRIES all around the world join together to kneel in gratitude to THEIR ROYAL MAJESTIES!!! And we are of course all HONOURED AND DELIGHTED to be joined by our newly crowned KING CHARLES III whose lifelong passion for upbeat chart-based popular music we shall be celebrating throughout the show!

(Cut to King glancing at his watch)

So let's CRACK ON with one of this country's BIGGEST AND BEST LOVED STARS! It's the FANTASTIC MISTER OLLY MURS!!!

OLLY MURS *(sings)*: Jist wanya terdan zwimmy to-nargh!

(Cheers, flagwaving)

Video insert MOTSI MABUSE: DID YOU KNOW that His Royal Majesty can dance like Mick Jagger...?

(Clip of Charles in 1973 moving his elbows slightly)

...and NOT ONLY THAT but QUEEN CAMILLA is a huge STRICTLY FAN just like you ordinary people!!!

DAME JOAN COLLINS: DID YOU KNOW that His Majesty is a supreme ECTOR and has turned his hand to several different GENRES OF ECTING for which he has been awarded many HONORARY BAFTAS! And he is internationally acknowledged as a MASTER OF COMIC TIMING!

(Clip of Charles visiting EastEnders set)

PHIL MITCHELL: This is our boozer!

CHARLES: Well, I say!

(Entire EastEnders cast roar with laughter)

HUGH BONNEVILLE: Yes, we are TRULY BLESSED to have this MAGNIFICENT and MOST GRACIOUS MAN as our King

(Cut to Charles looking glum and Camilla looking for the exit)

Next we have two of the world's greatest opera stars – and this will, I assure you, take you breath away!

BRYN TERFEL: Wairn you WAAAAAARK through the STAAAAAARM

ANDREA BOCELLI: Hold your HAAAAIRD up HIIIIIIIGH!

BRYN AND ANDREA TOGETHER: Waugh KHAN! Waugh KHAN!

(Cut to Sophie Wessex waving a flag and Edward looking odd)

BRYN AND ANDREA TOGETHER: And you'll NAAAAAAAAIRVAH Waugh Ka LOOOOOOOOOOOONE!

Video insert DAME TRACEY EMIN: DID YOU KNOW that His Majsty's REEY PASHNUT about art and he's a truly briv-yarn painter?

(Tracey looks at a wishy-washy watercolour of a castle)

This is VANDASDIG there's so much HARDFEL EMOSHARN in it.

HUGH BONNEVILLE: And now, Windsor –say you, say me, let's say it together!!! – it's the INTERNATIONAL SUPERSTAR – Lionel RichEEEEEEEEE!

LIONEL RITCHIE: Swya meeeasaaargh
Am eaaasaaargh
Am eaaasaaarghlak sunday mawawaw
Nun.

(Applause, flag waving. Cut to Zara Tindall mouthing along)

LIONEL RITCHIE: Aw Nat Lung
Aw Nat!
Aw Nat Lung
Aw Nat!
Aw Naaaaat Luuuuuung!

(Applause, flag waving)

(Cut to Charles fumbling with earplugs and Camilla eating her flag)

Video insert RICHARD E. GRANT: DID YOU KNOW that one of Her Majesty's FAVOURITE HOBBIES is reading. She absolutely LOVES TO READ!!! And she turns all those HUNDREDS of pages all by herself! She just loves it! So much so that she started a book club of which I am a member and so now I can read the same book she's reading!

PIERCE BROSNAN: DID YOU KNOW that His Majesty is one of the greatest sportsmen the world has EVER SEEN? From a very young age, he's been able to run and walk and he is also an accomplished swimmer!

LORD SUGAR: DID YOU KNOW that His Majesty is a formidable Captain of Industry? His Duchy of Cornwall generates £20million a year – a man after me own heart! Your Majesty – You're In!!!

TOM CRUISE *(in fighter jet)*: Pilot to Pilot, Ruler to Ruler, Your Majesty you can be my assistant operational Thetan wingman any time!

HUGH BONNEVILLE: And now please give a big Windsor welcome to His Royal Highness the Prince of Wales!!

PRINCE WILLIAM: Don't worry – unlike Lionel, I won't go on "All Night Long"!!!!!!

(Laughter, flag-waving, close-up of Prime Minister clutching his side)

PRINCE WILLIAM: My father has long held true to one simple belief: service. That's why, every morning, his first word is always: "Service!" And that is why he has always desired nothing more than to be served by people of all faiths and all backgrounds.

HUGH BONNEVILE: And now, Windsor, go crazy to serve as we welcome to His Majesty's Coronation Concert stage global pop icon, the sensational Katy PERRY!!!!!!

KATY PERRY: Agat the eye of a tagger, a fadder!!
Dancin through de fay-er!!
Cause I am a cham pyan!!
Anygonna hear me raaaaaaaaaaaaw!

GORDON RAMSAY: DID YOU KNOW that His Majesty is is a Master Chef, and can even create a ham sandwich using nothing more than two pieces of bread and a slice of ham?

HUGH BONNEVILLE: What a night!! To bring the curtain down on this magical evening we have something really very special. Please welcome to the stage the return of British pop royalty – Take THAAAAAAAAT!

TAKE THAT: Leddy shan! Leddy shan! Leddy shan!
C'mon see the lad on your face
Syawlav that madduzt me!
SHAAAAAAAARGHN!

(Cut to everyone waving union jacks, Edward and Sophie and Mike and Zara Tindall and Rishi Sunak clapping almost in time with the music, while Their Majesties King Charles and Queen Camilla continue to wave strenuously while scuttling towards the exits)

As told to
CRAIG BROWN

MESSAGE TO VOTERS

"I do not keep changing my mind"

"Yes, you do!"

Daily Telegraph

LOCAL ELECTION SPECIAL — Friday, 19 May 2023

Disastrous night for Starmer as Tories romp home with only 1,000 or so lost seats

by Our Political Staff **Paul Facre**

THE Labour party was licking its wounds last night as it woke up to a new political landscape. Its dreams of winning a general election were in tatters, as it bitterly contemplated a result that gave its only a meagre gain of 500 seats.

As the nation came together to give Labour a resounding kick in the ballots, Starmer tried to put a brave face on it by saying, "We mustn't get over-confident," and telling dejected supporters, "We are on our way to Number Ten".

Labour strategists are calling for a change of direction after the humiliation of substantial nationwide gains, but it is clearly too late.

Said a jubilant Tory Chairman, "I predicted that we could possibly lose a thousand seats but, as it turned out, we successfully lost even more than that. What a fabulous result!"

Now the right wing of the Conservative party are seeking to cement their landslide defeat by calling for the party to move further away from the centre ground.

Said Priti Patel, "What I am hearing from people in my head is that they want lower taxes for the rich and lower benefits for the poor. They also want everyone who doesn't vote Conservative to be deported to sunny Rwanda forthwith. I blame whoever has been in charge for the past 12 years."

ON OTHER PAGES

● Why resurgent Lib Dems are washed up forever **p2**
● Why the Greens' gains spell wipe-out for the Eco Loons **p3**
● Why Rishi Sunak will win next three elections **p94**

Keir Starmer WRITES

HELLO!
Fresh from Labour's unmitigated triumph at the local elections two weeks ago, I've been on a "practising to be Prime Minister" tour, where I've set myself the Herculean task of not answering as many questions as possible before the next election!

Among the questions I'm avoiding is: am I Tony Blair on steroids? This is a ridiculous question. Frankl , the people asking this need re-education, re-education, re-education. I simply feel the hand of history on my shoulder, and I want to invade Iraq. Apart from that, there is no similarity between between me and any other former Labour leader. We're all riiiiight!!!!!

Sincerely, Keir

≋ Met Office

Amber Alert

● With temperatures beginning to climb, we are alerting all residents of the UK to the imminent danger of hot weather. In a few days, you may soon be seeing an outbreak of middle-aged men in shorts, with the additional hazards of socks and sandals. Do not panic – by the weekend there will inevitably be a return to less unpleasant legwear when it starts raining again.

US WRITERS' STRIKE CONTINUES

by Our Hollywood Correspondent **Fi Niall-Draf**

CONCERNS that the US Writers' Strike could halt production of the 17 Marvel movies due to be released in 2024 have been downplayed by the studio.

"We already have one script completed and that should do us for all 17 movies, as they're all the same anyway," said one Marvel studio exec.

"There's a bloke in ludicrous spandex flying about with a sexy woman in tight-fitting leather and they're chasing the 'orb of destiny' or the 'crystal of doom' or something, and a famous British actor is slumming it as the villain intent on enslaving the world or destroying the galaxy or something... yeah, I think we'll be fine."

US TV studio bosses also insisted they'd be able to see out the strike, as they'd already commissioned straight-to-series-seventeen of the funniest placards from the striking writers' picket lines.

"SCAB!"

NEW STORES OPEN

"We're expanding!"

"Aren't we all?!"

"Bloody overseas students – coming over here, keeping our universities solvent"

Neasden University
(formerly Polytechnic of the North Circular)

Applications are now invited for overseas students in the following subjects:
Whatever you like.

Students are allowed to come from the following countries:
Wherever you like.

Students are allowed to bring the following dependents to live with them:
Whoever you like.

Students are expected to have the following qualifications:
Money.

Neasden University is an equal opportunity institution. We'd like to make as much money as humanly possible from everyone, irrespective of sex, gender, race, colour, creed, immigration status or academic ability.

Attendance at courses is not compulsory, though payment is.

Neasden University We Bank on Your Future

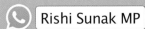

Rishi Sunak MP — The New Prime Minister's Highly Confidential WhatsApp Group

> Hey guys, time for a post mortem on the local elections. What do we think went wrong?

James Forsyth
Nothing, Rishi, it could have been worse. We said we'd lose a thousand seats and we did.

Jeremy Hunt
1,063 to be precise.

James Forsyth
You see! Underpromise and overdeliver! Great new optics.

> It was a disaster. I'm very disappointed.

James Forsyth
Cheer up, Rishi, all the Tories are really impressed with the leader.

Penny Mordaunt
The Leader of the House, that is. 😊

Lee Anderthal
Lookin' Fookin' Great, Penny! Star of the show.

Penny Mordaunt
If you need a sword to fall on, Rishi, I'll lend you mine. 😉

> Great banter, Penny, but I'm not sure I'm in the mood.

Penny Mordaunt
No probs, PM – which incidentally are my initials. Just sayin'. Or should I say: Just slayin'? 😊

James Forsyth
Concentrate on the positives, team! We didn't do as badly as UKIP or the Reform Party. They had a nightmare.

Kemi Badenoch
So, the lesson is we need to change direction and be more right wing. Perhaps it's time to install a new leader. We've not had one for months!

Jacob Rees-Mogg
Post local election carnage felicitations to one and all! Might I suggest we bring back an old popular leader?

Liz Truss
Hi guys, I'm available! I'll empty my diary. Which won't take long.

Boris Johnson
I think the Moggster was pretty clearly making a reference to the most successful Conservative leader since Theresa May. The election-winning machine that is Yours Truly. The hero of books, plays, films, investigations, police inquiries, Parliamentary reports and paternity suits! Me!!!!!!!

> Liz Truss, Boris Johnson and Jacob Rees-Mogg have been removed from the group, under the new Public Order Act, which bans dissent from anyone about anything.

> There must be some non-Penny sword wielding positive news that we can capitalise on?

Greg Hands
I've been going round all the TV and radio news studios and I can tell you – there isn't any. The only thing I could think of was to accuse the Labour Party of flip-flopping on every issue.

Grant Shapps
Bastards! That's our idea!

Greg Hands
If the flip-flop stuff isn't working, shall I do a U-turn on it?

> No. Stick to your guns.

> On second thoughts, dump it.

> No. As you were.

Jeremy Hunt
Talking of positive news, what happened to the big bonfire of EU regulations?

Kemi Badenoch
Ah. Yes. Tbh it's less of a bonfire and more of a barbecue. The kind of barbecue that you can't get started. It's a bit wet and the matches keep breaking.

> Are you trying to tell us something, Kemi?

Kemi Badenoch
We're leaving one or two of the EU regulations in place.

> How many?

Kemi Badenoch
About 4,000.

> But I made a video! With a shredder! Saying we were going to get rid of all this interference from Brussels.

Kemi Badenoch
I'd shred that video if I were you.

Jeremy Hunt
One might say: it's going from Badenoch to Worsenoch!

Penny Mordaunt
If only there was something we could use to slash through all this red tape.

TRUMP HUSH MONEY ARREST LATEST

> Lock him up! Lock him up!

POETRY CORNER

In Memoriam Jacqueline Gold, CEO of Ann Summers

So. Farewell
Then Jacqueline Gold.

You transformed
The sex trade,
Taking it from
The back street
To the High Street.

Keith's mum says
You liberated
An entire generation
Of women
And created
Quite a buzz.

She then went
A bit red.

When I asked her
If she was a fan
Of Jacqueline Gold
She said: "Yes! Yes!
Oh, YEEEEESSSSSSSSS!"

E.J. Thribbed, extra thin sensitive
(17½ inches)

> Hey guys! what's up?
>
> Oh fuck off.

Generation gap

A Tank Driver writes

*Vlad 'Mad' Putin,
Tank No: ZZZZ*

Blimeski, look at the road. Totally clear. Normally there are loads of tanks around on Victory Day, but I've got the whole of Red Square to myself. And look at my tank – isn't she a beauty? Classic. One of a kind. Literally. I'm in the only tank left in Russia! T-34. They don't build them like that anymore. They don't build them at all. Bloody sanctions. Someone's just shouted "Old Relic" at me – better be talking about the tank! Why's everyone making "V" signs at me? Oh yeah – Victory! I blame the West, bunch of Nazis. Ursula van der Himmler. Angela Goebbels. Jean-Claude Junckers! I mean, they started it. There I was, peacefully invading Ukraine, and they picked a fight. See that building over there? That's the Kremlin, that is. Got to be careful going near there, might get a drone on your head. Or a bit of one. After we've shot it down. There are a lot of falling objects around here. Bits of drone. Lumps of masonry. Five-star Generals falling from the 7th floor. Oops, there goes another one! Better turn the wheel – make sure I drive over him! Where is everyone? Moscow's bloody empty! Anyone would think we're losing. This is a Victory Parade! For the Eurovision Song Contest. Which we won. We being Ukraine – which is part of Russia. Except the bits that aren't. I love Eurovision. Boom Bang-a-Bang. Puppet Dictator on a string. Save All Your Missiles For Me! No, I love music, I do. Not Wagner, obviously. Bit too loud for my taste. Gets on your nerves. Over the top. Goes on forever and costs a fortune. As the old saying goes: the show ain't over until the fat bastard falls out of the window! Ha ha ha ha ha! Oops. Sorry. Bit bumpy. Just gone over a sleeping police chief! Where do you want to go anyway, mate? Round and round in circles. Sure – I can do that. Why's this gear stick come off?!

© A lone tank driver 2023

PRIME MINISTER READS JILLY COOPER

I love Riders!

We can see that!

WHY LABOUR'S PLAN TO PUT VAT ON PRIVATE SCHOOL FEES IS A TERRIBLE IDEA

BECAUSE we don't want to pay more fees, which are quite expensive enough as it is. Thank you very much.

SHIRE HORSE

SHYER HORSE

TEA

Nursery Crimes

································ Nurseryland, Thursday ························

GEORGIE PORGIE LOSES SEXUAL ABUSE CASE

by Our Yankee Doodle Handy Staff **Trumplestiltskin**

IN a dramatic civil lawsuit, the former president, Georgie Porgie, was found guilty of sexually molesting a number of girls and making them cry.

Mr Puddin'-and-Pie furiously denied the charge, saying that he could not possibly have kissed the said girls and made them cry because "the girls were not my type".

He then confused a picture of the main complainant with his former wife, which rather ruined his case.

A spokesman for Mr Potus-and-Lie said, "The fact that when the boys came out to play my client ran away is in no way an admission of guilt. Nor is his statement that when you are a twinkle twinkle major star, which he is, you can kiss any girl you like and get away with it."

Mr Potus-and-Lie concluded, "In fact, the jury was rigged and the result was stolen from me. The jury actually voted unanimously that I was innocent and the machines were fixed by the elite democratic paedo-ring that controls Nurseryland from Aladdin's pizza parlour in Wishie-Washington."

Mr Georgie Porgie is appealing – but only to himself. "Boy, I am so hot," he told his mirror. "If I wasn't me, I would assault myself in a department store changing room."

MAKE AMERICA GROPE AGAIN

—PILBROW—

TV HIGHLIGHTS

Return of the hit BAFTA-winning reality sensation **The Traitors**, presented by Claudia Rothermere

Each week, a random group of Doolally Mail journalists point at other people and call them "Traitors", based on no information and their own prejudices.

Who will be this week's Traitors? Will it be the judges? The lefty lawyers? Remoaners? The Blob? The BBC? The Nurses? The Lifeboat volunteers? The lollipop ladies? Gary Lineker? It could be anyone!

Years of fun, as the tension mounts and the number of those who AREN'T traitors dwindles to one – Paul Dacre, who finds himself alone and unmasked as it dawns on him... perhaps HE was the traitor all along! *(No, of course he wasn't – it was the Guardian! Ed.)*

EYE RATING Lunatic fringe appeal.

THE TRAITORS

Joy as fall in inflation means prices now only skyrocketing

by Our Inflation Correspondent **Paul Foot-Pump**

THERE was widespread joy today as inflation fell from 10.1% in April to 8.7% in May, meaning prices are now only skyrocketing instead of utterly and insanely skyrocketing.

"It's such a relief to know that this fall in inflation means all the stuff I could not afford to buy before is now still too expensive to buy," said one shopper in Weston-super-Mare.

With most economists agreeing that the fall in inflation is far lower than expected, the Governor of the Bank of England, Andrew Bailey, has turned his fire on the economy:

"But for the British economy, our plan to halve inflation by the end of the year and restore growth would be working.

"Once again, the British economy is talking the economy down. It should be ashamed of itself."

Michael Sheen in new acting row

by Our Showbiz Staff **Dai Versity**

WELSH actor Michael Sheen has sparked a new controversy after claiming that only Welsh actors should play Welsh characters.

He has added fuel to the fire by insisting that only Michael Sheen should play all parts in all dramas.

Said the star, who played David Frost, Tony Blair and Brian Clough, "Only a Welsh actor could play all these roles convincingly and, in fact, only one Welsh actor is really good enough to play everybody all the time. To be honest, it has to be me. I am sorry, but I just don't find other actors at all convincing because, let's face it, they are not Michael Sheen, are they?"

In his latest controversial role, Sheen is to play "Mr Sheen", a moustachioed pilot who flies around dining tables spraying them with polish.

Said a furious spokesman for the Polish community, "Only Polish actors should play Polish pilots. We have not taken a shine to Mr Sheen."

School news

....

St Cakes

Vaping term begins today. Nick O'Teen (Gaspers) is Captain of School and E. Liquid (Puffers) has been appointed Head of Flavours. There are currently 368 pupils dilating behind the e-bike sheds. Exhalations will be blown at Assembly and Exeats to have a quick drag will take place in the middle of every lesson. We welcome new Head of Chemistry, Mr Ivor Toxin, who will be teaching a module on the periodic table and, in particular, the presence of lead, nickel and chromium in all the students' lungs. Mr Toxin comes to us highly recommended from his previous employer, Planet of the Vapes, at 73 The High Street (no more than 10 children in the shop at once). We also say goodbye to several teachers. Namely, all of them, as we welcome Mr GPT Chatbot to the staff room – he will be Head of Classics, Maths, Geography, etc. If pupils are struggling with any of the subjects, Mr Chatbot will be all to happy to help them get ahead by doing all their homework for them. The school play this term will be an updated all-singing, all-vaping, all-coughing production of Aristophanes' *The Clouds*.

"It's from the gentleman at the end of the bar"

OUTRAGE AFTER LATEST US MASS KILLING

by **WALTER PEEPEEKAY**
Our Mass Killing Staff

THIS week, the nation was in shock after a driver in Texas ploughed his truck into a crowd of innocent bystanders.

"This was a sickening crime," said a spokesman for the National Rifle Association. "What was the killer thinking? He should have used a gun! A true patriot's weapon of choice should not be a four-wheel drive, with its limited range and killing capacity. You're only going to take out a dozen people, max. Get tooled up, dude!"

A colleague, whose military camouflage failed to hide him against the white wall of the NRA office, said, "This tragedy clearly highlights the danger of trucks. We need to ban trucks now. People can just go into a truck showroom and buy one without any checks whatsoever. This kind of tragedy is just going to happen again. Luckily, we've got guns, so I am going to go and take out every goddam truck salesman before someone else needlessly loses their life."

Netflix tries to stamp out password-sharing

by Our Streaming Correspondent **Juan Morr-Episaud**

YOUR ex-partner, their children, and their children's friends reacted with horror to the news this week that Netflix is launching a crackdown on shared accounts.

Your son's closest friend from school, Big Tim, who got your account's password 18 months ago and has been using it exclusively to watch medieval Korean zombie content, said that Netflix was "breaking human rights or something. This is like something out of Kingdom of the Flesh Eaters."

"This is ridiculous," added a friend of yours, who once visited for a night and copied down the password on a bit of paper. "Without the free use of Netflix, I will have to start visiting my friends again – they were all very happy when I finally managed to get a subscription and stopped inviting myself round constantly. Netflix has jeopardised that careful social balance."

Finally, you yourself expressed concerns, because there are so many people on your account messing up the algorithms that you've actually got access to your next-door-neighbour's account without them realising, and *(cont. p94)*

(cont. p94)

THOSE NEW DAD ROBERT DE NIRO FILMS IN FULL

The Oldfather Part 2

Meet the New Parents

Meet the Old Focker 1-7

The Mission-ary position

The "Oh Dear" Hunter

Buggi Driver

Goodyellas

Non Sleepers

Midnight Milk Run

The Untouchable Nappies

The King of Comedy
(This is a real title. Ed.)

Dirty Grandpa
(This is another real title. Ed.)

Raging Balls
(That's quite enough. Ed.)

POST OFFICE SCANDAL: EMPLOYEES 'RACIALLY PROFILED'

Post Office

Most offenders were white, overpaid executives

IS IT ALL OVER FOR DISGRACED TV STAR?

> It was unwise but not illegal

> That's my defence!

LATEST: PHIL DOES A RUNNER

PHIL AIRTIME TO S AND NOT SIT DOW

by Our TV Staff Dayti

THE WORLD of daytime television was rocked to its foundations last night when broadcasting legend Phillip Airtime announced that he was "standing down, standing up and walking out of the studio".

Airtime had delighted morning TV audiences for decades with his easy-going manner and on-screen chemistry with co-star Holly Forgettable. Together, they had redefined the art of sitting on a sofa smiling and it is almost impossible to imagine la t s as the u

Tributes to A u poured in from around the world but, unfortunately, there was only room on filltime TV itself for a brief 30-second eulogy from stand-in presenters Someone O'Someone and Alison Everything. This was before cutting to an important interview with top Towie star, Tania Fake, revealing all about her *(cont. for 94 minutes)*

DIARY

PHIL AND HOLLY AND THE FUTURE OF THE WESTERN WORLD: A SYMPOSIUM

MATTHEW SYED: I wonder if this is a moment to step back and ponder a deeper question, not about Schofield or Willoughby but about us. Because this is ultimately about us. Take a step back for a moment. Let's cut through the nonsense. This whole affair poses, to my mind, profound questions about who we are, and who we want to be, and who we would prefer to be if we do not want to be who we are. What is perhaps most fascinating is that an argument can be made one way or the other. On the one hand, you can argue that the other hand is to blame. But on the other hand, you can argue the reverse. For the time being, we live in a free society. But I find the whole thing deeply troubling, whatever it is.

EAMONN HOLMES: It's a cover-up, a total cover-up and I'm not prepared to take it anymore. I'm here to speak for the people who haven't got a voice, the tired, the poor, the huddled masses yearning to breathe free.

Let's face facts, shall we? Phillip Schofield created an atmosphere that was toxic. Mr Goody-Two-Shoes was totally different off-camera. When he thought no one was looking, I'd see him setting fire to other people's lockers, making Nazi salutes and pulling the wings off birds.

Sad to say, I once came across him in a corridor plotting an armed bank raid with two accomplices in balaclavas.

I would now appeal to anyone who has ever been held at gunpoint by Schofield, or thinks they might have been in another life, to get in touch, and stop others suffering a similar fate. We've no time to lose, my friend.

ALLISON PEARSON: As a former award-winning presenter of This Morning, I've deep respect for hundreds of thousands of good, honest, hard-working TV presenters.

And that's why it deeply grieves me to point out that Phillip Schofield was a fool to have done what he did, whatever he did

And even if he didn't, he did.

Because whatever he did was what he shouldn't have done, even if he didn't do it.

Which he did.

As a former top-level psychiatrist, I can only ask: what were you THINKING, Phil?

DOUGLAS MURRAY: Serious people should be talking about the really big issues facing us – housing, pensions, education, jobs, inflation, you name it – but instead they are talking about Holly and Phil, Phil and Holly. What is happening to us, the British nation, that we should become so involved in what I can only see as this weird displacement activity, glorifying utter trivia at the expense of our futures? Faced with the war in Ukraine and the imminent threat of extinction from AI, who frankly gives a tinker's cuss about Phillip Schofield and his relationship with Holly Willoughby, which, incidentally, I have long regarded as a fraud perpetrated on the British public. I mean, there was something about her smile I never quite trusted, and do you remember that horrible look she gave Phil when he was showing us how to cook chicken fritters with a parsley sauce when Gary from Take That was in the studio?

The Rt Hon LORD SUMPTION, OBE, PC, FSA, FRhistS: The subject I intend to address in this magazine or periodical is the role of This Morning, its presenters and their associates. The twin themes I intend to explore are, first, who, if anyone, by which I mean those who worked in or about the vicinity at that particular time, knew, or had prior knowledge of, the event or events that brought about the resignation of Mr Schofield and second, the meaning, exact or otherwise, of the reported statement by the programme's editor, Mr Frizell, when he commented, and I quote, "I'll tell you what's toxic, and I've always found it toxic: aubergine. Do you like aubergine?" But first let me address the question of the aubergine. Over the past ten days, there have been calls made by and/or on behalf of the Aubergine Protection League, which I intend to refer to from this point forward, for reasons of brevity, and/or succinctness, as the "APL" and from the Aubergine Support Group, or "ASG", as I shall call it, to limit what both these bodies see as the disproportionate abuse meted out to the aubergine community, which, for the purposes of this survey, can be said to also include the wider communities of courgettes, baby marrow and summer squash. But before I do so, I wish to tackle the secondary *(cont. p94)*

As told to
CRAIG BROWN

"Oi, Schofield, there's a queue!"

Job Centre Plus

PIERS MORGAN ASKS

Why has this Titan of morning television been so badly treated by ITV?

WHATEVER you say, this man is a brilliant broadcaster and an interviewing genius who is completely irreplaceable and has been shabbily treated by the pygmies of ITV management.

Yet, with no warning, poor Piers was given his marching orders and thrown into the broadcasting wilderness that is Talk TV. Is that fair?! Is that just?! Or is it just an accurate picture of the toxic snake pit that is my mind? *(Surely "my personal experience of independent broadcasting"? Ed.)*

| RETURN OF LOVE ISLAND | INCREASE IN CASES OF SYPHILIS AND GONORRHOEA |

65

M8 BRITAIN

Real contestants, real quiz shows, real answers, real dumb!

Tipping Point, ITV

Ben Shephard: A monocycle is a mode of transport that has how many wheels?
Contestant: Four.

Shephard: Which 20th-century Soviet leader is often referred to as Uncle Joe?
Contestant: Joe Pasquale.

Shephard: Richard the Lionheart was king of England in which century?
Contestant: The 20th.

Shephard: Which planet in our solar system features in the name of a former Queen lead singer?
Contestant: Mars.

Shephard: In May 2021 Christie's auctioned "*Waterloo Bridge, effet de brouillard*", by the French impressionist painter Claude… who?
Contestant: Van Damme.

Shephard: In which decade did Elvis Presley have his first UK number one hit?
Contestant: The 19th.

Shephard: The French word "cinq" translates into English as which single-digit number?
Contestant: Six?

Shephard: In the Tales of Beatrix Potter, what sort of animal is Pigling Bland?
Contestant: A rabbit.

Shephard: What Latin word meaning "of the king" follows Lyme to give the name of a Dorset seaside town?
Contestant: Scale.

Shephard: In the game of basketball, how many quarters are played in a game?
Contestant: Two.

Shephard: Who was the leader of the Soviet Union during the Cuban missile crisis?
Contestant: Rasputin.

Shephard: Which indoor sport celebrates winners with the Jocky Wilson Cup?
Contestant: Badminton.

Shephard: In 1909, the US explorer Robert Peary claimed to have been the first person to reach which of the Earth's extremities?
Contestant: The Moon.

Shephard: Which of the five male titles of the British peerage lies above earl and below duke?
Contestant: Corporal.

Shephard: The Strait of Messina separates which island from the Italian mainland?
Retired merchant navy seaman: I think it's Turkey.

Family Fortunes, Challenge TV

Les Dennis: Give a slang word for your head.
Contestant: Nonce.

Dennis: Name something you have more than two of on your body.
Contestant: Arms.

Celebrity Mastermind, BBC1

Clive Myrie: Which poet had the first names Thomas Stearns?
BBC journalist: John Keats.

Myrie: "Per ardua ad astra", meaning "through adversity to the stars", is the motto of which branch of the British armed forces?
David O'Doherty: Tottenham Hotspur Football Club.

The Weakest Link, BBC1

Romesh Ranganathan: In food and drink, on spirits, beer and wine labels the abbreviation ABV stands for "alcohol by"… what?
Contestant: Voltage.

Ranganathan: In cinema, the 2000 Ang Lee film that was nominated for a best picture Oscar was called *Crouching Tiger, Hidden*… what?
Daytime TV star: Cupboard.

Ranganathan: Name the Archbishop of Canterbury murdered in Canterbury Cathedral in 1170.
Cheryl Baker: Chaucer.

The Chase, ITV

Bradley Walsh: What first name links the prince in *Swan Lake* and the war poet Sassoon?
Contestant: Vidal.

Walsh: Which children's author was named after the explorer Roald Amundsen?
Contestant: Enid Blyton.

Walsh: In a 17th-century Rembrandt painting, a sleeping Samson is resting on which woman?
Contestant: Mother Teresa.

Walsh: Which American civil rights leader was jailed in Alabama in 1963?
Contestant: Al Capone.

Walsh: Which East Anglian warrior queen fought against the Romans?
Contestant: Joan of Arc.

Walsh: The father of which Rat Pack member was a Sicilian boxer called Saverio?
Contestant: Bob Geldof.

Walsh: The Vaal is a tributary of which South African river?
Contestant: The Amazon.

Walsh: Which famous battle took place on St Crispin's Day 1415?
Contestant: Waterloo.

Walsh: Which musical duo wrote "The Lonely Goatherd"?
Contestant: Simon and Garfunkel.

Lincs FM

John Marshall: Which famous Bob turns 82 this week? He sang "Blowin' in the Wind" and "The Times They Are A-Changing".
Caller: Carolgees.

Ten to the Top, Radio 2

Gary Davies: Complete the title of this album by the Beatles: Rubber…
Caller: Dinghy.

Davies: Which 1981 Dire Straits hit shares its name with a William Shakespeare play?
Caller: Money for Nothing.

Brain of Britain, Radio 4

Russell Davies: What may be the best-known of all the songs in the musical *Les Miserables*, "I Dreamed a Dream", is sung by which character?
Contestant: Courgette.

The Wheel, BBC1

Michael McIntyre: Name any country with Spanish as its first language.
Gloria Hunniford: Portugal.

TalkSport

Host: Which mountain range runs through Argentina?
Footballer/pundit: Er, the Falklands?

The Tournament, BBC1

Alex Scott: Beginning with the letter O, what is the piece of music that is played at the beginning of an opera?
Contestant: Othello.

Scott: In the films *Frankenstein* and *Bride of Frankenstein*, which Boris played Frankenstein's monster?
Contestant: Boris Johnson.

BBC Radio Sheffield

Newsreader Nick: How many children did Queen Victoria have?
Traffic girl Chelsea: Victoria? Was that the one that just died?
Newsreader Nick: Nooooo.
Traffic girl Chelsea: Was it her mother?

Pointless, BBC1

Alexander Armstrong: Which pirate, with a name beginning with B, was caught off the east coast of the USA in 1718?
Contestant: Boudicca.

Armstrong: We're looking for a 19th-century philosopher, first names John Stuart, surname beginning with M.
Contestant: Marx.

Ant & Dec's Limitless Win, ITV

Ant (or was it Dec?): In which year did the Berlin Wall fall?
Contestant: 1910.

Hardball, BBC2

Ore Oduba: Catherine the Great ruled which country?
Contestant: Scotland.

Oduba: From which animal do we get merino wool?
Contestant: The whale.

The Chase, ITV (again)

Bradley Walsh: Kidology is the art of what?
Contestant: Raising goats.

Walsh: What symbol of German unification faces Pariser Platz in Berlin?
Contestant: The swastika.

Walsh: The study of Classics involves the study of Latin and which other ancient language?
Contestant: Latin.

Walsh: The Gorbals is on the south bank of which river?
Contestant: The Rhine.

Walsh: Which Oscar-winning actress shares her name with William Shakespeare's wife?
Contestant: Meryl Streep.

Walsh: The TV series *Dalgliesh* is based on the works of which author?
Contestant: Kenny Dalglish.

Walsh: "Waltzing Matilda" is considered the unofficial national anthem of which country?
Contestant: Germany.

Walsh: Which famous statue is popularly referred to as "The Gateshead Flasher"?
Contestant: The Statue of Liberty.

Walsh: Which German religious reformer had daughters called Margaret and Magdalena?
Contestant: The Pope?

Good news as migration numbers plummet

by Our Political Correspondent
Daniel Fiddlestats

BRITAIN breathed a sigh of relief today after new government figures were released showing a sharp drop in the number of migrants attempting to enter Britain.

A government spokesman explained, "The net figure of 606,000 immigrants is way below the figure of 1,000,000 immigrants that we leaked to you last week.

"This huge reduction in immigrant numbers is a sign of a government in full control of Britain's borders.

"Those 400,000 people who didn't come here would have completely overwhelmed public services and infrastructure, and the fact that they never arrived, thanks to never existing in the first place, is a huge breakthrough."

Another Conservative spokesman added, "We are expecting the numbers of legal migrants for 2024 to be in the region of 2,000,000,000 people, so when we announce that there were only 700,000 we will expect you all to be very grateful, and to forget that we've spent the last decade promising to get the numbers down to tens of thousands."

WE SAY: Hurrah for the Conservative Party!

EXCLUSIVE TO ALL NEWSPAPERS

THAT MADDIE NEW DISCOVERY

She still sells papers.

IS IT THE END FOR THIS MORNING?

Our seasoned media watcher, **Phil Graves**, sees the one tell-tale sign of impending doom

IT'S ALL OVER. This Morning's days are numbered. Why? Because yesterday morning I turned on the telly and there, sitting opposite Holly Willoughby on the sofa, cloaked in his trademark jumper, was Gyles Brandreth himself.

Gyles, who has so often been seen in recent days as the harbinger of death, is a key indicator of imminent demise. Whether it be Queen Elizabeth, Len Goodman or Barry Humphries, whoever has a laugh with Gyles – be it over tea, cocktails or dinner – is only weeks away from the obituary column.

So now there can be no mistake, the Beaming Reaper has chosen his next victim, and it is This Morning, which may now not live to see this afternoon.

Presidential launch marred by tech problems

TWITTER users the world over were distraught after thousands crammed into a virtual room to hear Republican Ron DeSantis launch his presidential campaign in conversation with Elon Musk.

For significant periods of the interview, the technology actually worked and listeners could clearly hear Mr DeSantis outlining his plans for government.

"It was awful," said @GarageGollum94. "I could hear DeSantis saying he thought he was qualified to be president and that his policies would include easier gun ownership, clamping down on gender politics, and curtailing abortion. I hated it."

Said another Twitter user, @LegendofZeldaFitzgerald23: "Twitter Spaces should have failed completely. It left us having to listen to Mr DeSantis talking about his governorship of Florida and his desire to take America in a more conservative direction."

Critics say that the failure of Twitter Spaces was all part of Elon Musk's broader strategy for the site, which involves driving away advertisers and making it even less bearable than before.

Said a third user, @elonmusk, "This DeSantis stuff is the sort of filth you'll find on your timeline since I fired all the content moderators."

"Oh for goodness' sake, Mum! Being a misogynist makes me popular!"

What You Missed

That Epsom Derby thriller

"…as they go past the post with just one furlong to go, it's Protest Boy making a late dash, but PC Plod is coming in from the rails with Minimum Wage Steward on the outside. This is anybody's race! And as they approach the finish, the runners are all closing in. This is what the Derby is all about, thoroughbred demonstrators showing their form after months of training. Oh, and Protest Boy has been caught with just yards to go. He's a faller! Oh, no. Terrible scenes here at Epsom. It looks like he's being put down – by the crowd, who are all booing him. So now we await the stewards' inquiry into how the hell he got onto the course and why PC Plod showed insufficient use of the whip."

James Forsyth
Did everyone see these bad boys?

Penny Mordaunt
STOP THE BOOTS! 😀

> Great footwear-related banter Penny, but I was actually delivering a serious message about Stopping the Boats, and my no nonsense footwear matched our no nonsense immigration plans 🇬🇧 .

Jeremy Hunt
Where are the boots from, Rishi?

> They're from Timberland.

Suella Braverman
Send them back to Timberland! Back where they came from! It's the only way to stop those boots.

> Well, that's not very nice, is it?

Suella Braverman
It's tough but fair. And I've been to Timberland, which is very safe, and everyone's very helpful there. The boots will be very happy, living in a box.

Penny Mordaunt
I think sending the boots back will be a big vote winner 😀 .

Suella Braverman
I have a dream where all boots are put on a plane and flown back to Timberland.

Lee Anderthal
At last, some fookin' common sense. Bloody brown boots, coming over here, taking over the footwear industry. Putting decent hard-working British shoes out of jobs.

> Good to get an authentic working-class perspective, Lee. But actually these boots are 100% American 🇺🇸 .

Lee Anderthal
Like you, before you dropped the Green Card bollocks.

James Forsyth
Okay, team, I'm afraid I'm going to have to delete all of that boot-related banter. This is just the kind of personal stuff the Covid Inquiry doesn't need to see.

Jeremy Hunt
Feet Out to Help Out! 😂

James Forsyth
Yes, I'd be grateful if you'd redact that too, Jeremy. It's not relevant and it doesn't show the Prime Minister in a good light.

Boris Johnson
What ho, fellow Covidians!

James Forsyth
Don't say anything to him, team. He'll just give it to Baroness Hallett 👩🏿 .

Boris Johnson
Piffle and Pfeffel, I've got nothing to hide, particularly on this new phone, unlike Rishi who's entirely responsible for... ██████████████ , ██████████████ , ████████████ and ███████████ , not to mention ███████████ .

> I thought you said we wouldn't mention ████████ if I let you give a knighthood to your dad and a peerage to your dog and make Mad Nad a Dame.

Boris Johnson
So that's all in order, is it?

> Oh yes. It just has to go through the normal channels and procedures.

Boris Johnson
Details, details! And you are going tell those wankers on the Privileges Committee to let me off?

> Oh yes. It just has to go through the normal channels and procedures.

Boris Johnson
Phew! Well, that's a deal!

> Boris Johnson has left the group.

> Guess what, guys! I had some quality time with the President of the United States. Three whole minutes. I did have a ten-minute slot, but then he fell asleep.

Grant Shapps
Did you talk about Artificial Intelligence?

> That's when he nodded off!

Grant Shapps
So how long before a robot takes over Rishi's job?

Lee Anderthal
Already fookin' has!

Penny Mordaunt
I'd say it needs rebooting.

Suella Braverman
Stop the Reboots!

Boris Johnson
You utter rotter Rishi! You bounder! You cad! I've just found out you lied to me! You cheated me! You betrayed me! Who do you think you are? ME!!!??? I resign! 👊 👊 👊

> Boris Johnson has been redacted from the group.

Film highlights

Fast and Furious Ten

The latest and most exciting sequel yet in the high-octane franchise. This time, it's Royal!

Global superstar Harry Windsor (an in form Vin Diesel) and Meghan Markel (Charlize Theron again) are trying to save the world from the evil press. Only, this time the battle takes place in the back streets of New York, as the hated paparazzi engage in an epic two-hour chase to corner the couple and take a blurry picture of them for the National Enquirer.

Enjoy the white-knuckle ride as the couple get in their car and drive around a bit and then get in a taxi and drive around some more before driving to the police station and then getting in another car and driving home.

Talk about fast and furious! He's fast to claim that it's been a near global catastrophe and millions of lives have nearly been lost! She's furious – but we all knew that!

Don't miss the climactic scene where the taxi-driver goes rogue and says, "Nothing much happened really – it wasn't a big deal and I wouldn't call it a chase."

And what can top for sheer testosterone-fuelled petro-thrills the image of the mayor of New York himself declaring, "It was fine. Everyone got home safely without incident"?

For those who think this Fast and Furious Sussex Franchise is running out of steam, this is perfect proof that you are right.

EYE RATING: Vroom for improvement!

"I don't, as a rule, sleep with someone on a first date"

BORIS JOHNSON RESIGNATION SPECIAL

Ha ha ha ha ha ha ha ha ha ha ha ha ha ha ha ha ha ha ha ha ha ha ha ha ha ha ha ha ha ha ha ha ha ha ha ha ha ha ha ha ha ha ha ha ha ha ha ha ha ha ha ha ha ha ha ha ha ha ha ha ha ha ha ha ha ha ha ha ha!!!!!

"We've got a problem – I've turned it on, but I can't turn it off again"

COULD AI BORE US ALL TO DEATH?

by Our AI Correspondent **Hugh Manity**

THERE were increasing concerns today from experts with pained expressions on their faces that the human race could be bored to death by all the constant stories about AI and how it threatens to destroy us.

"I turned on *Today* and for the hundredth time this week Nick Robinson was talking about the risks of AI. How everyone is going to end up unemployed and how deepfakes are going to destroy democracy. I had to switch off I was so bored," said one Radio 4 listener.

"I opened the *Times* to find another seventeen stories about AI, all accompanied by a photo of Arnie as The Terminator and my eyes glazed over and I lost the will to live," agreed another person.

Experts say that, as the number of stories about AI destroying us are multiplying at a terrifying rate despite no actual proof the technology is going to destroy us, this means the risk that AI will bore us all to death has never been greater.

That Dishonours list in full

Guto Harri Kiri receives the Order of the Brown Nose, for suicidal services to Boris Johnson.

Priti Nasty MP becomes Dame Nasty of Priti, for services to being pretty nasty on behalf of Boris Johnson.

Mr Marty Party becomes Lord Of The Dance (BYOB) for services to work events and can-carrying on behalf of Boris Johnson and Carrie-oke Johnson.

Peppa Pig becomes Lady Pig of Peppatown for services to writing impromptu speeches for Boris Johnson.

Ms Comely Dogwalker becomes Dame Doo-Doos, for services to business – clearing up Dylan's business and hanging it in a bag on the nearest tree.

Ms Fruitella Blowdry becomes Baroness Curling-Tongs for services to… well, certainly not styling Boris's hair.

Ms Nadine 'Mad Nad' Dorries becomes Ms Nadine 'Mad as Hell' Dorries.

Giant orange metaphor engulfs US

by BERNIE PLANET
Our Environmental Staff

NEW YORK was last night covered in an enormous metaphor as an enormous orange disaster enveloped the city.

Said one metaphorologist, "I couldn't help noticing how this catastrophe is just like Donald Trump. It's not only orange but it's thick and toxic and makes everyone want to be sick.

"We are warning people to stay away from it, as any contact can be extremely damaging. If we're lucky, this appalling simile will evaporate into nothingness."

Last night, the puffy orange monstrosity was heading towards Washington DC and hovering over the White House.

A Tank Driver writes

Vlad 'Mad' Putin, Tank No: ZZZZ

Every week a well-known tank driver gives his opinion on a matter of topical importance. This week, the destruction of the Kherson dam…

Blimey, guv! You want me to take you South of the River? Not a chance. Some idiot's gone and blown up the dam. Nothing to do with me, guv. I wasn't anywhere near it. I blame those Ukrainians nextdoor to the dam. I reckon they did it themselves. Probably wanted to wash the car. Or the house. Or something. And all those farmers, deliberately flooding their fields, just to get out of an honest day's work. What's that you're saying? You think the Russkies did it to attack civilian infrastructure because they've got form in that sort of thing? I wouldn't say that. I mean it, mate – I really wouldn't say that! Unless you want to find yourself falling out of a sixth-floor window. Although to be fair, the water's up to the fifth floor, so you'll have a nice landing. Ha ha ha! Talk about a new offensive. I'll tell you what I find offensive – being accused of war crimes. Me? An honest tank driver? I'm just doing my job. Show me the bit in The Knowledge that tells you the way to blow up a dam rather than how to get from Moscow to Kiev via the quickest route, avoiding the snarl-up at Bakhmut. I mean, what have I got to gain from such an act of wanton destruction? Apart from slowing down the Ukrainian army until the old duffer in the Oval Office gets turfed out. Then they'll get somebody reasonable in like that Donald bloke who lets me do whatever I like. Very clever man. He gets my vote! Every time! I had him in the back of my tank once. Him and his young lady friends. Eeeugh! I had to disinfect the whole tank after that. Be lucky!

© A tank driver 2023

Lady Macbeth

Writes exclusively for the Daily Chain Mail

Nobody knows better than me the pain of private correspondence being made public

BELIEVE me, readers, you can't have effective government if everyone's personal messages are published to the whole nation.

I, myself, have been the victim of an excruciatingly embarrassing incident when my private and personal message to my husband to murder King Duncan was taken completely out of context and put in a play for all to see. It was entirely personal, and nothing to do with politics at all. It was just a friendly message to my spouse, the then Thane of Cawdor, telling him to screw his courage to the sticking post, take the dagger that he saw before him, and stab the king repeatedly while he slept.

Big deal! Yes, I had misgivings about the suitability of Duncan to remain king, or indeed alive, and yes, I saw the possibility of my husband getting the top job, as the three weird sisters had prophesied, if he stabbed a few other people as well.

But to suddenly find oneself reading this in the Birnam Wood Echo, Witch magazine and even that disreputable rag, Private Eye of Newt, was very traumatic. And I knew it wouldn't stop because it would be in all of tomorrow and tomorrow and tomorrow's papers as well.

So let's be clear about this: private messages should remain private, and not be sexed up, or rather "unsexed up" in my case, into some sort of regicidal drama.

How do you expect our leaders to make sensible decisions, such as murdering each other, if they are not allowed a little privacy?

© *Lady MacVain of Cawdor, putting the "me" into medieval politics.*

Radio 2 listeners horrified that Ken Bruce's replacement isn't Ken Bruce

by Our Radio 2 Correspondent
'Smashie' Ann Nicey

RADIO 2 listeners were horrified today to discover that the replacement for Ken Bruce on the Radio 2 breakfast show wasn't Ken Bruce.

"We knew that Ken Bruce was leaving for a rival broadcaster, but surely the BBC realised that the only possible replacement for Ken Bruce would be Ken Bruce," said furious listeners.

"I gave Vernon Kay a try and while he seems pleasant enough, I came to the conclusion that he wasn't Ken Bruce, so I threw my Bakelite radio out of the kitchen window into the garden in fury," said all other listeners.

Radio 2 bosses were said to be relaxed about the criticism, announcing that they're looking forward to 2058 and the outpouring of love from listeners when the much-respected elder statesman, Radio 2 breakfast host, 81-year-old Vernon Kay, announces he's leaving for Greatest Hits Radio.

"Hi guys – have you tried Radio 2?"

WORLD OF MOUNTAINEERING

Race on to conquer Britain's newest mountain?

HIGHER than K2, PPE1 rises majestically above the New Forest, its peak clearly visible from outer space. Amazingly, the mountain wasn't made by volcanic activity or the movement of tectonic plates, but by friends of Matt Hancock and Michelle Mone's business associates.

Said top mountaineer, Chris Bonington, "I have climbed Everest the hard way, but I have never seen anything like the North Face of PPE1. It's the ultimate challenge, and I think I'll need an oxygen mask at the top – which is lucky, as there are seven billion masks up there. Although many of them may have holes in them."

Already there are queues of mountaineers stretching all the way back to Everest, waiting to take their turn to summit Mount Kilimanyoftheelderly.

BRITISH ENDANGERED SPECIES

Wildcat

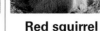

Red squirrel

Mortgage

MORTGAGES
An Apology

IN RECENT decades, we, the Babyboomers, may have given the impression that Millennials or whatever they call themselves, were a privileged, entitled bunch of whingers who had absolutely nothing to complain about and were making a bit of a fuss, having been born into a period of prosperity and peace.

We may further have insinuated that they were a bit flaky and overly sensitive, concealing a fundamental inability to get down to some work and buy themselves a house, like we did.

Comments such as, "Pull yourself together, boy", "You don't know you're born, my girl," and "At your age I'd bought my third flat" may have given the impression that we thought in some way the current generation were lacking in the sort of gumption, ambition, backbone and drive which we thought we had displayed throughout our youth.

We now realise, in the light of the stratospheric interest rates and general economic meltdown, that nothing could be further from the truth, and that we were merely the lucky recipients of a booming post war economy, and that the Millennials are not, after all, feckless, work-shy parasites, over-reliant on their parents, but the victims of an impossible financial situation, greed-based property prices, and an insupportably generous pensions system.

We would like to apologise unreservedly for any confusion which may have been caused by our ignorance and arrogance, and request that they whole-heartedly support us in the coming decades, as we totter uncertainly into the crumbling health and care systems which they will inherit from us, along with not much else.

MORTGAGES – YOUR OPTIONS IN FULL

BRITAIN'S lenders have agreed a radical new set of ideas which will allow mortgage borrowers better flexibility and stability in the long term. Here is the suite of ideas proposed by some of Britain's most powerful financial institutions:

1. Go broke now! This is a great option and will give you maximum flexibility in future. To do so, all you have to do is ring your broker and say how much you earn. Once they have finished laughing, they will begin the process of repossessing your home.

2. Go broke later! This is an exciting new option. Depending on your circumstances, you may be able to extend to a 300-year mortgage so the debt can be handled more sustainably by your children, and your children's children,

yea until the last days of *(Yes, we get the idea. Ed.)*

3. Downsize! If you are willing to move from a three-bedroom house to a studio flat 400 miles away, this might allow you to restructure your mortgage debt in a way that means you'll only pay double what you are paying now. This is a great option for people who have children at school, or who live near family, and no longer want either of those things to be true.

4. Go on holiday! Not a mortgage holiday, you understand, just a permanent holiday. And when we say holiday, we mean "leave in the night, taking a suitcase with you, nobody will be able to find you, you can slip onto a ferry to Le Havre and build a new life as a lobster fisherman in Normandy." This seems like an extreme option but several million people are currently considering it.

Notes & queries

● *Next week: Who or what is "disposable income"?* Answers on a postcard please, if you can afford the stamp.

Shrinkflation

"I swear that was only 40 minutes"

THOSE SHRINKFLATION BRANDS IN FULL

As products get smaller without any decrease in price, we highlight some of the worst offenders:

THEN	NOW
Heinz 57 varieties	Heinz 37 varieties
Mini cheddars	Mini mini cheddars
Quavers	Semi Quavers
Shortbread	Even Shorterbread
Maxwell House	Maxwell Flat
Double Decker	Single Decker
Marathon	Sprint
Lidl own brand	Even Lidler own brand
Magnum	Minimum
Ritz Crackers	Travelodge Crackers
Philadelphia Cream Cheese	Emptyadelphia Cream Cheese
I Can't Believe It's Not Butter	I Can't Believe It's Not Bigger

LATE NEWS Gnome Supermarket denies making all trolleys 10% smaller so you don't notice what's happening on your weekly shop.

"I see old Jeremy's out muck-spreading again..."

CLARKSON'S FARM

Bobby Bullar

ENVIRONMENTAL UPDATE

THOSE NEW DOWNGRADED RIVER NAMES IN FULL

■ **The Wey** becomes the Wee

■ **The Wye** becomes the Wype

■ **The Ouse** becomes the Ooze

■ **The Ure** becomes the Urine

■ **The Tweed** becomes the Turd

■ **The Forth** becomes the Froth

■ **The Cam** becomes the Scum

■ **The Stour** becomes the Stool

■ **The Pool** becomes the Poo

■ **The river Looe** stays as it is.

To celebrate the merger of the PGA and the Saudi-financed LIV tours, the Eye is delighted to offer readers the new lexicon of golf

Club – implement for hitting dissident.

Wedge – what you pay the PGA tour to change their mind.

Gimme – what officials say when they see Wedge.

Fairway – outmoded term, no longer used.

Handicap – taking a moral stance.

19th Hole – illegal, go to jail or receive 50 lashes.

Bunker – where PGA boss is now hiding.

Irons – what you'll be clapped in if you go to the 19th Hole.

Swing – penalty for dissent.

Rough – nature of justice.

Drive – what women are allowed to do but not campaign for. See 19th Hole.

Below Par – behaviour of sporting world at first sight of money. See Wedge.

We've got away with merger!

Court Report

Mirror Group Newspapers vs the Duke of Suessex

Day 1

Judge Fancourt: Where is he?

David Sherbore, KFC: I'm afraid, Your Honour, he is attending an urgent engagement.

Judge: Is he indeed? May one ask the nature of this 'urgent engagement' that leaves us all waiting here?

Sherbore: It is the occasion of Princess Lilibet's second birthday, M'Lud, and the clown hasn't turned up.

Judge: So it would seem.

Andrew Greed, KC and Sunshine Band, representing Mirror Group: Hahahahaha, Your Honour! What an excellent riposte! How immensely amusing you are!

Day 2

Andrew Greed: So, Gingernuts…

David Sherbore: Objection! That is not the nomenclature we agreed for addressing my client.

Greed: Fair enough. So, Ginger Whinger…

Sherbore: Objection!

Judge: Sit down, Mr Sherbore. I fear you have been watching too many episodes of the American television programme *Suits*.

Greed and Sherbore: Hahahahahaha!

Harry: What I want to say is that the press have ruined my life. Ever since I was born, my phone has been hacked.

Sherbore: If I may, Your Honour, I would like to introduce Exhibit A.

Exhibit A

Sherbore: Do you recognise this phone, Your Highness?

Harry: Yes. It was my first phone and the Mirror hacked it.

Sherbore: If you look carefully, Your Honour, you can see a bit of string with a tin can which has clearly been used to intercept my client's first words, which were…

Harry: The press are bastards.

Greed: In your autobiography, you claim your first words were 'Goo-goo-ga'. Which is correct?

Harry: Er… I dunno, I haven't read it.

Sherbore: My client is very distressed at having to relive the last question. May I request a short break while I remind him of what he's meant to say?

(Court rises. Judge goes to Garrick for agreeable lunch of steak and kidney pudding)

(Press go to file stories headed 'Harry Useless Witness in Court'. Harry wonders how they got hold of story and adds today's coverage to phone hack legal proceedings)

Day 2½

Sherbore: My Lord, I now have positive proof that my client has been appallingly portrayed in the British press. May I produce Exhibit B?

Exhibit B

Judge Fandango: Why are you showing me a portrait of Mr Edward Sheeran, whom I see most weeks here in unrelated cases of alleged plagiarism?

Harry: That's the whole point, Your Honour. I've been cruelly depicted as thick, self-pitying and sorry for myself. Oh, and thick.

Sherbore: Objection! My client is being allowed to incriminate himself. He is going to plead the Fifth.

Judge: Once more, I fear, you are confusing reality with the televisual entertainment offering *Suits You, Sir!*

Sherbore and Greed: Hahahahahaha!

Day 94

Sherbore: May I now turn to the 32nd article in Bundle 978, which is a piece in the Mirror headed 'Harry Birthday To You, Your Royal Highness'.

Harry: They clearly hacked my phone to find out when my birthday was.

Greed: Did this piece not appear in the Daily Telegraph the day before? And did my clients not just copy it out, almost word for word, merely changing the word 'Happy' to 'Harry'.

Prince Happy: You see! They were clearly hacking each other as well. And here's the clincher…

(Court falls silent, awaiting killer evidence)

Harry: Piers Morgan is an utter bastard!

(Court in uproar)

Judge: Prince Harry, you cannot just come into a court of law and state the obvious. Various facts pertaining to this case are in contention, but Mr Morgan's utter bastardry is NOT one of them.

Greed: As a representative of Mirror Group, may I just say I concur entirely with the aforementioned reflections vis à vis the utterness of Mr Morgan's bastardness.

Judge *(looking at watch)*: Forgive me, Your Highness, if I'm failing to follow the thread of your evidence. You have produced a compelling case to show the British press to be desperate, lazy and incompetent. But that is not quite the same as producing documentary evidence of phone hacking.

Harry: You see! Everyone's out to get me. Including you. No wonder I'm paranoid. I've been ruthlessly exploited by people trying to cash in on my gullibility.

Sherbore: Leave me out of it, Harry boy. I'm doing my best here.

Judge: Are we anywhere near the end of the case?

Greed: I do hope not. I get paid per diem and there are many more refreshers to come, surely?

Judge: Talking of which, there's a very fine claret at the Garrick Club which isn't going to drink itself.

Sherbore: In conclusion, Harry, are you OK?

Judge: Is that a reference to the celebrated case of Willoughby versus Schofield, 2023?

Sherbore: How very sharp of you to notice the precedent, m'Lud.

Greed: Objection! It's my turn to suck up to His Ludship.

Judge: Overruled. As they say in *The Suity Show*, but sadly not in British jurisprudence. Pray continue, your Royal Hightimethiswasoverness.

All: Hahahahahaha!

Harry: Boohoohoo! My life has been ruined. The press have destroyed every relationship I've ever had, which means I've ended up with this awful woman in an awful mansion in California, with kids and chickens and no friends for a thousand miles.

Judge: Mr Sherbore, could you remind your client that this is not a therapy session.

Sherbore: Oh yes, it is. Except even more expensive.

Greed: We agree on that.

Judge: Excellent. The court will now adjourn, in my case to the Garrick, where spotted dick and custard awaits, along with my judgment.

All: Hahahahahahaha!

(A number of other witnesses will be heard, but not reported because they're not as famous as Harry and they're not even as famous as David Sherbore, so no one cares)

Who should be the new owner of the Daily Telegraph?

You choose which multi-billionaire media mogul should buy Britain's top Conservative-leaning broadsheet

| Rupert Murdoch | Elon Musk | Xi Jinping | Lord Lovaduck of Lebedev | Logan Roy | Boris Johnson's "Cousin" | Prince Harry (*the Archie Wellegraph*) | Sir Frederick Barclay again |

REVOLTING RUSSIANS

UKRAINE WAR SHOCK

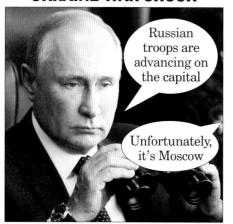

Russian troops are advancing on the capital

Unfortunately, it's Moscow

EX-CHEF IN POWER GRAB

It's coup of the day!

The feud here is terrible

PRIGOZHIN EXILED

I saw a window of opportunity

And soon you'll be falling out of it

RUSSIA LATEST

MASSIVE COLUMNS OF COMMENTATORS FORCED INTO HUMILIATING RETREAT

AS THE world looked on in astonishment at the huge mobilisation of thousands of columnists on Saturday, it was not known how events would transpire.

No one could have seen that this vast army of experts, who were predicting civil war, the collapse of Russia and fighting on the streets of Moscow, would by tea-time see their columns having to be abandoned, as they deserted their positions and were forced to regroup.

Said one, "It was mayhem. One minute I was confidently predicting the fall of the Putin regime and the next I was backtracking at speed, suggesting that it was far too early to speculate on how things would play out."

Said another, "One thing is certain. There will be columns tomorrow, probably shooting down the one I wrote yesterday. I have come to a deal with the editor to exile me to the pub until it all calms down." *(Rotters)*

....

ON OTHER PAGES

■ **Dave Spart writes:** "This isn't a Civil War, but is actually, as comrade Putin says, a Civil Special Military Operation... er..." **p94**

LETTUCE 'NOT AMUSED' BY LIZ TRUSS COMPARISON

by Our Salad Staff **Quentin Lettis**

A FURIOUS lettuce spoke out last night, voicing its anger at being compared to former Prime Minister Liz Truss.

"It's pathetic and puerile and just not funny," said the lettuce, as it sat alone on a shelf. "Just because I'm wilting and past my sell-by date, does not mean I should be subject to childish insults regarding the disgraced ex-PM."

The distinguished summer vegetable continued, "Liz Truss did real harm to huge numbers of ordinary people. I, on the other hand, might taste a bit off now, but to pretend there's any similarity between us is actually offensive."

The lettuce went on to complain that the British media did not really understand the complex world of salad issues and was happier making cheap jokes about personalities – or rather lack of personalities, in the case of Liz Truss.

"I'm not humourless, or sour, or bitter," concluded the lettuce, "and if you think I am, I frankly don't give a toss."

Keir Starmer WRITES

HELLO! And first, can I make it clear that at a recent party I was at all times careful to maintain social distancing. Despite being at Rupert Murdoch's summer party, I did not come within two metres of him at any point. I obeyed all the rules and guidelines laid down by the Labour Party and I can justify my presence at this function on the grounds that it was a work event and NOT a party.

I was not enjoying myself, but was assiduously working at winning the next election, which requires a certain amount of morale-boosting sycophancy to Rupert Murdoch and his brilliant son, Roman.

Furthermore, I have taken professional advice from those Labour figures who have won elections before – and Gordon Brown.

So, when these respected figures, like Tony Blair, offer the benefit of their experience, it is well worth listening. And Tony told me, "If Mr Murdoch says you have to jump, the correct answer is 'How high, Sir Logan?'."

Just because I had a drink with Mr Murdoch and his talented son, Kendall, it does not mean that I should be penalised by my own party, which accuses me of selling out and abandoning my principles.

I have not done a U-turn on this, in the same way I have not done a U-turn on the issue of the House of Lords.

When I said that I was going to abolish the Upper Chamber because it was full of Tory cronies, what I meant was that I was not going to abolish it and instead was going to stuff it full of Labour cronies. You couldn't get much clearer than that, could you?

Honestly... I am happy to reward all those who have done so much to assist the Labour party's return to power in the last few years. Step forward, Dame Nadine Dorries, and arise, Lord Boris Johnson!!

Sincerely, Keir

P.S. When I said we would ban all new North Sea oil and gas projects, I obviously meant we might consider banning all projects except exisiting ones and planned ones and important ones involving oil and or gas.

NEWS

"And finally..."

WHY IS THERE SUCH A GHOULISH FASCINATION WITH THE TITANIC?

IT IS utterly extraordinary, the sheer number of articles about the doomed ocean liner at the bottom of the Atlantic. Surely there are other things to write about other than a tragic shipping disaster of over a century ago?

Why is there such a morbid fascination with this wreck lying on the seabed, when there is so much going on today worthy of our attention?

What is it about the Titanic that (cont. pages 2-94)

"It was always only a matter of time before the profiteering began"

Great Rescues of History, according to Twitter

Apollo 13

A group of three privileged, white, male astronauts, who have needlessly voyaged into space, get what's coming to them, only to be saved by a pointless and exorbitantly expensive intervention by Big Government.

Miracle on the Hudson

A bunch of American tourists, who are killing the planet with their addiction to flight, look as if they will face justice for their crimes against the climate after their plane's captain murders a flock of geese with his jet engines. Tragically, due to a fluke of flying ability, they all survive the experience and learn nothing from it.

The Chilean Miners

A group of 33 men – probably toxic men steeped in South American sexist culture – get stuck at the bottom of a mine, where they have been plundering the resources of Mother Earth. Due to sentimental "family members" at the surface and more carbon-intensive engineering efforts, they are brought up to continue their ecocidal reign of terror against nature's bounty.

The Titan Submarine

(That's enough. Ed.)

BORIS JOHNSON

LEFTIES may sneer, but I salute this maverick genius who broke all the rules, ignored the bleatings of the timid safety-first brigade and took a magnificent risk in a spirit of can-do adventurism.

Yes, I salute myself. I plumbed the depths and then imploded, writing about a tragedy and turning it into yet another piece in praise of my own career. I was called a Titan by Priti Patel and it is no coincidence that the brave submersible shared the same name as the greatest political explorer and buccaneer there has ever been – myself – defying the odds, ignoring the odds, and embarking on a heroic voyage to survey the wreckage of this once great country *(We get the idea. Ed.)*

TYPES OF COLUMN

| Doric | Ionic | Corinthian | Shit |

Police response times 'quicker than ever'

by Our Law and Order Staff
Laura Norder

FOLLOWING months of criticism, the Commissioner of the Metropolitan Police, Mark Rowley, was delighted to point to the success of his force in responding rapidly to reports of criminal activity.

"Take the recent case of an illegal party which took place during Christmas 2020. It is only 30 months later that my force has leapt into action to investigate this video that everyone else has been watching."

Commissioner Slowley continued slowly, "A response time of two and a half years is pretty impressive, I think you would have to agree, and certainly an improvement on the 30 years it's taken to make further inquiries about one of the suspects in the Stephen Lawrence murder."

SHORT SELLER CRISPIN ODEY IN TROUBLE

Are you going to lose everything?

I wouldn't bet against it

THAT SHAUN BAILEY 'JINGLE AND MINGLE' CHRISTMAS PARTY INVITATION

THE names that they didn't use, on the grounds that they were too inappropriate:

- Celebrate and Incubate
- Rave and Grave
- Buffet and Snuffit
- Bop and Drop
- Superspread and End up Dead

(We get the idea. Ed.)

TV HIGHLIGHTS

New Series

Not Strictly Come Obeying The Rules

Entertaining dance show where contestants in glamorous outfits – red dresses and Christmas novelty sweaters – strut their stuff on the dance floor, before the judges deliver their verdict: guilty! Hours of fun as the Lady in Red and Beardie Spad knowingly break Covid rules, ignore social distancing and drunkenly bump into the table with the buffet, to the sound of the Pogues singing "You scumbag, you maggot, you cheap Tory braggart." Who will be the sad losers on tonight's "Jingle and Mingle"-themed instalment of *Not Strictly*? The public, of course!

Eye rating:
10 out of Number 10!

Boost for Biden campaign

by Our Washington Correspondent **Laura Less**

THERE was a major boost for Joe Biden's re-election campaign today, with millions of Trump voters immediately changing allegiance, after Hunter Biden was charged with tax crimes and illegally possessing a gun whilst he was addicted to crack cocaine.

"In court over guns, drugs, unpaid taxes and crack cocaine? Those Biden folk sound like our sort of people," said a group of angry rednecks shooting up a bar in Lynching Time, Tennessee.

"Here's hoping that Hunter fella was planning to shoot up a local school where they have them 'woke' things called books. We had the Bidens down as nice people but, thankfully, we were wrong.

"Biden 2024! Four more years, four more years!"

Donald Trump hit back, urging his supporters to keep the faith and promising it was only a matter of time before his deadbeat kids, Don Junior and Eric, outdid Hunter by being arrested for wire-taps, drug running and people smuggling.

The Oval-tine Office

PRINCE WILLIAM – CONCERN FOR HOMELESS

by Our Royal Staff **Ivor Cardboard-Box**

HIS ROYAL HIGHNESS the Prince of Wales last night pledged his commitment to his new favourite cause, promising to do everything he could to make Prince Andrew homeless.

Speaking movingly, William said, "I want Andrew to move, now. I don't care where, I just want him out of Windsor Royal Lodge."

William was visibly upset, as he described a young family with three children who were on a waiting list to move into suitable accommodation, but who were being thwarted by a sitting tenant who was squatting in the premises.

Said Andrew, "It doesn't seem much to ask, really. All I want is a palace of my own."

William, however, was insistent that his homelessness campaign should be successful. "In the 21st century, no one in Britain should be forced to sleep on the streets – except Andrew."

Children in schools identify as 'piss takers'

IN A terrifying new trend guaranteed to alarm the middle-class parents reading this newspaper, we can reveal that children at Britain's schools are increasingly identifying as children who are taking the piss.

These children really are a symbol of the end of the world and are definitely not just little brats who need a good kick up the arse, and they herald the first wave of an enormous and alarming *(cont. for 94,000 words)*

Should adults identify as cats? You decide

George Galloway
Identifying as Prat in Big Brother

James Corden
Identifying as Twat in Cats

Cat Stevens
Identifying as Cat at Glastonbury after years being Yusuf Islam

---

Court Circular

Kensington Palace
Tuesday, 20 June

Her Royal Highness the Princess of Wales will look lovely today.

She will begin by looking lovely, playing rugby, or tennis or ping pong, and later she will look lovely at the official opening of something or other and even more lovely when she visits a school or possibly a community centre. But not quite as lovely as she will look in the evening, when she will attend a gala.

Her Royal Highness will then also be looking lovely, wearing spots, or stripes, or anything really, topped with a hat, or a fascinator or a tiara or just her own lovely hair – but, rest assured, she will be looking lovely and cool and elegant and fragrant and, well, lovely, really.

JEFF BEZOS WITH ENGAGEMENT RING

One online retailer to rule them all

"Yes, sorry about that – the bin men are on strike"

IAN BAKER

As Wimbledon gets under way, we tip the Brits likely to go all the way to the final

The Princess of Wales

Fresh from her triumph, partnering Roger Federer on the front pages of all newspapers, Catherine has got the stamina to smile through a fortnight of gruelling competition, and will be certain to be waving come finals day.

Kate Middleton

The plucky girl nextdoor has risen up the rankings from the middle class to be a sure-fire spectator in the Royal Box at the final.

The Duchess of Cambridge

Will she last two weeks of what will be a fortnight of very intense spectating, which will test her clapping skills to the limit? Yes.

The Countess of Strathearn

The little-known gutsy outsider is much fancied by all editors and readers, and is *(That's enough six to watch. Ed.)*

"Actually, I'm English – I just don't want my boss to spot me on TV"

POETRY CORNER

In Memoriam Glenda Jackson, actor and politician

So. Farewell
Then Glenda Jackson.

You played many
Dramatic parts,
From Cleopatra
To Queen Elizabeth I
To King Lear.

You also appeared in
Comedies such as:
The Muppet Show,
*The Morecambe and
Wise Show,*
And the House of
Commons.

As well as your
Two Oscars and
Three Emmys,
You won
Five elections.

Possibly your
Most challenging
Role was as
Labour Junior
Transport Minister.

And now,
Alas, we must
Complain about you
Being "late".

E.J. Thribb
(Number 17½ bus
to Hampstead)

New formats 'must adapt to survive'

by Our Cricket Correspondent
Ed G. Baston

NEW cricket formats have been warned they must adapt or die in the face of the excitement and popularity of five-day test cricket.

The organisers of The Hundred say they are considering major changes to the format, as they struggle to attract young people lured away by the sheer thrills that only test match cricket delivers.

"We do our best to provide a thrilling spectacle, but what hope do we have when competing against the heart-stopping drama such as we saw in the first Ashes test between England and Australia?" grumbled a Hundred spokesman.

Some of the proposed changes to The Hundred would include expanding the format to one where both teams bat twice and for the matches to take place over five days.

"We believe these changes will put us on a level playing field to compete with the ultimate thrill ride that is test match cricket."

"OK, one more time: Go home and log on to our website from your computer, create an account and purchase your ticket with your credit or debit card, download the ticket to a smartphone, then come back at the allocated time... Just what part of 'easier and more convenient' don't you get?"

TOP KNIGHT REFUSES TO RETIRE

by Our Sports Staff
Billy-Jean King Arthur

ONE of Britain's most prominent sporting knights refused to rule out a comeback, despite showing signs of unfitness in his latest defeat.

The legendary Sir Andy Murray, once famed for conquering all-comers, is now showing the scars of battle.

Said one commentator, Holly Grail, "He has had a problem with his hip – in that it has been completely severed from the rest of his body."

She continued, "His forearm is not what it was, as it's lying about twenty feet away from his torso, and he's not as agile as he once was, on account of having no legs. But he's still the best British contender we've got."

Sir Andy crashed out in defeat last week saying, "Ok, we'll call it a draw."

The Eye's Controversial New Columnist

The columnist who is still on his Fisher-Price phone trying to get tickets to the Wiggles

This week I am very glad that train firms are planning a mass closure of ticket offices because, quite frankly, they are surplus to requirements. I have been following 'Thomas the Tank Engine' my whole life and I have never seen anyone buy a ticket in all the time I've watched it. In fact, why stop there? I think the cafes should go because no one seems to eat, and they can rip out the toilets too, because I have never seen the Fat Controller get caught short, ever. He either has a reinforced plastic bladder or he must have a secret place behind Cranky the Crane to have a widdle, which is probably why Cranky the Crane is so cranky. But all this is a side issue. The unions are always banging on about needing useless jobs – like guards and drivers on trains. The government say they refuse to embrace new technology and they are absolutely right. Imagine how many people we could sack if we embraced the island of Sodor's policy of having talking, thinking trains with big bulging eyes and white smiles? Granted, they can be cheeky, and might get up to the odd bit of mischief and destroy a few houses, but that's a small price to pay to keep the shareholder swimming in Toytown money. And we can always wall them up if they get (cont. p94)

BANK ACCUSED OF TERMINATING ACCOUNT ON POLITICAL GROUNDS

by Our Financial Staff **Nigel Farrago**

ONE of Britain's most prominent banks, the Bank of Mum and Dad, has been criticised for refusing to deal any further with one of its leading clients, Trevor.

Said an outraged Trevor, 27, "This is blatant discrimination against my controversial view that I shouldn't pay any of my loan back – nor should I pay any interest."

A spokesperson for BMD – Mum – said "Trevor's politics have got nothing to do with it. We just think he should get a proper job. The fact that he called the Chairman of the Bank – Dad – a fascist, did not help. The Bank's decision is based solely on the fact that Trevor does not meet the threshold of having any money at all."

Trevor cited further evidence of the Bank's shoddy treatment of its client, by saying, "Mum never liked my girlfriend, Denise, and so rejected my financial plan to go to Glasto with her and have our union blessed by a Druid in a yurt."

Trevor has announced that he will now seek alternative banking arrangements – namely the Bank of Godmother and Godfather, but so far they have not responded to his request for an interim fixed rate 0% 75-year minimum loan.

Dear Mr Farage,

Coutts

Having reviewed the state of your account, we regret to inform you that… you're out. You're leaving. You cannot remain. Get over it! Suck it up! You lost! You can't get back in and you can't change the decision! Coutts have taken back control! Your ties with the Bank are severed! Stop whingeing. We've got Farexit done!

Yours sincerely,

Sir Ivor Loadser-Money Coutts
Manager for individuals of very low net worth

"I don't know much about art, but you can ask me anything about heat pumps"

'JUST STOP OIL' URGED NOT TO DISRUPT MUCH-LOVED SUMMER EVENT

by Our Protest Staff **Ann Oying**

THE eco protest group Just Stop Oil have been asked to stay away from next week's Just Stop Oil protest.

The organisers fear that protesters will ruin the traditional spectacle of protesters ruining an event by throwing orange powder over the people throwing orange powder over someone else.

Said an organiser, "It would be a great shame if our protesters were prevented from protesting, when they have trained for months and gone to a lot of trouble buying t-shirts and making placards."

He continued, "Yes, they've got a point about climate change – but this really isn't the right place for a protest. The British public want to enjoy watching our Just Stop Oil protest without being disrupted by tiresome and, frankly, counter-productive interventions by Just Stop Oil."

City Demands Tighter Bank Regulations

by Our Finance Staff **Robin Git**

Concerned financiers have called for a review of banking practices following Coutts' treatment of Nigel Farage.

Said one broker, "It appears that some banks are concerned about ethical issues, like racism, sexism and homophobia. We must return to our traditional values of greed, avarice and heartlessness. It's a choice of Woke Banks or Broke Banks."

Some critics, however, say that a voluntary code is insufficient and have called for a regulator with teeth. "Banks need to recognise that their first duty is to money and fleecing their customers, regardless of their political views," said the spokesman for proposed regulator OffRip.

Coutts has defended its actions, saying, "This is the first time since 1692 that we have ever had to deal with a client who was deemed, to use the technical financial terminology, 'a right dodgy geezer'."

When it was pointed out that Coutts is the bank of the Royal Family, the bank admitted that it just prefers a better quality of aristocratic shyster.

LATEST POLL
PENCE WAY BEHIND TRUMP IN RACE FOR REPUBLICAN PRESIDENTIAL NOMINATION

You're going to get millions fewer votes than me

Great! Then you'll declare me the winner

Keir Starmer WRITES

HELLO! I like a bit of nostalgia as much as the next man, so it gladdened my heart to see wizened old leftie John McDonnell on Newsnight having a moan! I've always looked on John as the Andrew Ridgeley to Jeremy Corbyn's George Michael, so it's good to know he's not been forgotten!

And, as we've mentioned Wham! at this point, I would like to mention that, yes, Club Tropicana drinks WERE free in 1983, but that's a very bold spending commitment that Labour aren't committing to honour at this stage!

Apparently, John was a bit cross about the purge going on in the Labour party of left-wingers, and said it's been a "witch hunt"! Well! That's an incredibly brave thing to say in public, John! Let's hope you don't get a knock on the door in the middle of the night from a few of my NEC chums!

This is part of my plan to be completely electable – speaking of which, the Uxbridge by-election is being threatened by a policy that could scupper our chances – by being a policy.

We need ultra low emissions of policies – and Ulez is one of those toxic policies that is getting up people's noses. In fact, the Starmer Squad have dubbed it 'Ulooz'! (Excellent work, Mr O'Farrell!) My policy on 'Ulooz' could not be clearer – that we fully support the aims and aspirations of this policy, so much so that we are slamming the brakes on aand performing a 'Ulez-turn' (you're on fire, John!) – much as drivers do when they see a Ulez sign!

There's nothing wrong with healthy disagreement in the party, and Mayor Khan is quite at liberty to pursue this policy – which admittedly has great health benefits, though not for his future as Mayor, when he is purged from the party in six months' time.

As the great George Michael once sang so memorably, "Bad boys stick together… and when they don't, they're free to join the Liberal Democrats"!

Sincerely, Keir

SUPERMODELS

KERBER

POETRY CORNER

**In Memoriam
Christine McVie of
Fleetwood Mac**

So. Farewell
Then Christine McVie.

You were a
Songbird,
But now you have
Gone Your Own Way
And can
Stop Thinking
About Tomorrow.

Keith really enjoyed
Rumours, particularly
The ones about
Your relationships with
Other members of
The band and the
Lighting crew.

I, however, felt
You were the finest
Blues woman and
Piano player in
The history of
Popular music.

Now you are flying high
And surrounded by
White powdery clouds.
As in life, so in death...
Rock and Roll!

E.J. Thribb
(17½ billion downloads)

**In Memoriam
single-use plastic plates
and knives
and forks**

So. Farewell
Then single-use
Plastic tableware.

You have had
Your chips and are
Officially washed up.

I say farewell,
But you take 200 years
To decompose.
So not quite
Farewell yet.

Keith says
It is a step forward
For the planet
But, essentially,
We are all
Still forked.

E.J. Thribb
(17½ takeaways a week)

HS2 REPORT
STATION'S FUTURE IN DOUBT

Euston, we have a problem

MARRIAGE SERVICE FOR A FORMER CHANCELLOR

Vicar: Dearly beluvvies, we are gathered here in the sight of Nick Robinson to join in marriage this man and this former personal assistant in Holy Ludicrous Matrimony.

Congregation: I give it a week.

Vicar: Does anyone know of any just cause or impediment why these two should not be married?

(Entire congregation checks phone, reads anonymous poison-pen email and begins laughing)

Vicar: Who giveth away all secrets of the groom?

Congregation: Not sure, but we've got our suspicions. They seem to know all the dirt.

Vicar: Do you, George Gideon Oliver Austerity Osborne, promise to love, honour and obey whichever media mogul is paying the bills?

Osborne: I do.

Congregation: Praise the Lord Lebedev.

Vicar: Do you, Thea Deliveroo Rogers, promise to take this man and make him look more metrosexual and appealing than he did in his previous marriage?

Thea: Yes, indeedy.

Vicar: And will you love, cherish and protect him in sickness and in wealth, for richer or extremely richer?

Thea: You betcha.

Vicar: And will you both promise to forsake all others…

Groom and Bride: Hang on, we are Tories, you know!

(Congregation laugh)

Vicar: The first reading is from Psalm 23.

Ed Balls *(reads from the Bible, in order to fill up airtime on new podcast)*: Yea, though I walk through the Valley of the Shadow Cabinet of Death, I shall fear no evil, for George is with me and his Chief of Staff shall comfort his rod!

Congregation: Thanks be to Pod!

Vicar: It's time to sign the register… of interests.

(Ceremony stops for several hours as Osborne lists all his hundreds of jobs. The congregation sing hymn 94, 'Blackrock of Ages')

Vicar: By the power of investments invested in me, I now pronounce you…

(There then follows the traditional Ceremony of the Just Stop Oil. A member of the congregation [it may be Barbara, it may be Sandra] will step forward and throw orange confetti over the couple)

Vicar: …as I was saying, before I was so conscientiously interrupted, I now pronounce you second husband and second wife. You may now kiss the woman in the third row.

Congregation: Ah, bless!

Vicar: You may now kick the groom.

Congregation: Sob!

Vicar: Today's collection will be taken by David Cameron, in aid of his favourite charity, himself.

(Organ plays Beethoven's 'Odey to Joy' as congregation proceed out, led by Michael Gove and Ed Balls dancing the Pasa Doble with Emily Maitlis and Jon Sopel)

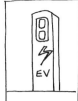

Charging point | **Overcharging point**

Supermarkets deny collusion on petrol prices

by Our Supermarket Correspondent
Won. K. Trolleywheel

THE BIG four supermarkets have issued a joint statement denying any collusion after a report accused them of artificially keeping petrol prices high at the pumps.

"We can assure you that competition between us is fierce," the supermarkets said in a joint statement, "and that we are always competing to give the customer the exact same price."

Opec disgusted

OPEC has reacted with disgust to a report that says Britain's big four supermarkets are colluding to keep petrol prices up to 6p a litre higher than they should be.

"Petrol retailers have no business acting this way against the interests of the motorists, that's our job.

"Where will this end? With them buying every Premier League club in Britain too?" said a furious Saudi *(cont. p94)*

HISTORIC MIDDLE-EAST MOMENT

Israel and Palestine agree on a two state solution:

1 State of Anarchy
2 State of War

LATE NEWS

Third state announced: Despair.

Planet Warmer Than Ever Before
Those Telegraph solutions in full

by Our Environment Correspondent
Fracky Detory

LEST anyone accuse the Daily Telegraph of having no answers to the moderate climate change that can, in part, be attributed to the use of fossil fuels, we have come up with a list of perfectly sensible, easily achieved measures, which will create a temperate, secure, prosperous and happy future for the planet:

Ban electric cars The amount of energy needed to produce just one electric car could keep a new North Sea oil platform going for four whole seconds.

Make gas boilers compulsory Every heat pump uses the equivalent of an entire offshore wind farm to heat a vsemi-detached house. Houses with one gas boiler should be offered incentives to get a second one.

Set up UHEZ zones – Ultra High Emission Zones – where Telegraph readers can breathe in healthy petrol fumes without interference by the nanny state. Did you know that inhaling 75 cubic metres of exhaust fumes from a 4x4 is healthier than electronic vaping and uses less energy?

Delay the Net Zero deadline to 2094 Only a 44-year delay will allow Net Zero to happen on time. Every year that we delay, the target will result in a one-degree drop in global temperatures.

Ban solar energy The sun is extremely hot and getting hotter. Do we want to encourage this madness by building sun traps all over our fields before they become viable deserts?

See? Easy! Your children and grandchildren will thank you for saving them from the madness of the eco-lunatics.

Goliath vs GOLIATH

The Prime Minister's Highly Confidential WhatsApp Group

Rishi Sunak MP

> I'm absolutely furious. I just can't keep silent on the matter any longer.

Penny Mordaunt
You've finally got an opinion on Boris?

> Don't be ridiculous. I'm talking about Jonny Bairstow. That judgement was totally incorrect. He should never have been made to walk.

Lee Anderthal
You ARE fookin' talking about Boris!

> No. I have no opinion on whether Boris broke the rules.

James Forsyth
Tricky optics, PM. You had time to spend a day at the Test, but you didn't have time to vote in the Commons.

> That's not a fair point. It's not a fair comparison. It's not fair.

Michael Gove
🎵 Same old Rishi, Always Bleating! 🎵

> Great, cricket based musical banter, Mikey! But it really isn't fair.

Lee Anderthal
Let's face it, Rishi, you're fookin' stumped. Just like dopey Bairstow.

> He wasn't stumped. He should have been allowed back in.

Nadine Dorries
Hooray! Time for Boris to return! He's bowled this maiden over! 🖤 🖤 🖤

> Nadine Dorries has been dismissed from the group. She is definitely OUT.

Australian players 'horrified by sledging' in the Long Room

THE Australian test players have spoken of their horror at the sledging they received from MCC members as they walked through the Long Room after the controversial dismissal of Johnny Bairstow.

"It was horribly twee," said one Australian batsman. "No one called us f****** c**** or said they'd like to **** our mum.

"We expected to be called ****ing ****s and ***** ****, but instead they just yelled 'cheat' and 'Aussie bastards' at us, it was appallingly tame," said wicket keeper, Alex Carey.

The MCC offered the Australians a full apology and promised the crowd at Edgbaston would be utterly abusive next time they cheated.

SNOBS

HUSBAND

Letters to the Editor

The spirit of the game

SIR – I was in the Long Room on the occasion of the so-called "fracas" involving members of the MCC and the visiting Australian team.

Like many of those in the Pavilion, I did not see the incident in question, as I was soundly asleep at the time, enjoying the morning's play.

You can imagine my surprise when I was rudely awakened by the sound of booing. This was occasioned by Mr Carey, the Australian wicket keeper, who had "stumped" Johnny Bairstow, the England batsman. Please note that I do not use the ghastly term "batter", which is something Lady Gussett serves as a pudding for dinner when I return to Somerset after a long day's snoozing at Lord's.

However, despite my failure to witness the actual event, I have no doubt that this was quite clearly a case of the players failing to uphold the spirit of the game.

If test cricket means anything, it means observing the unwritten rule that Members should not be woken up just before luncheon by something interesting happening on the pitch. Such behaviour is tantamount to cheating. Spectators do not come to cricket for controversy, rancour and entertainment!

It may not specifically state this in the 940-page MCC Rulebook, which rightly concentrates on such important issues as preventing ladies from wearing strapless dresses and high-heeled trainers in the Long Bar Annexe in the tea interval. However, every true MCC stalwart knows that this sort of over-excitement is "just not cricket", to coin a phrase.

Arcane arguments over whether I was "dead" or "merely asleep" at the time are beside the point; the session may have been not "over", and I was clearly "out" of it, but there were no reasonable grounds for waking me up.

After some discussion with my fellow members, Sir Simon Redtrouser and the Rev Portly-Flushing, about the correct course of action, I "went upstairs" (to the Long Room).

There, I was so overcome by my sense of injustice and a few pre-lunch sharpeners in the Bodyline Bar that I had no option but to attempt to punch the Australian Captain on the nose as he left the field.

I have since been called upon to appear in front of the Members' Disciplinary Committee, who I am sure will be wanting to know what sort of penalty should be imposed upon the Australian players for committing the cardinal sin of waking an MCC member from his innocent slumber.

If this is NOT their intention, then I admit I am "stumped"!

Sir Herbert Gussett,

The Old Scoring Box,
Great Stokes, Nr Bazball-on-Wane,
Somerset.

CLICKBAIT CORNER 1

▶The NHS was born 75 years ago.

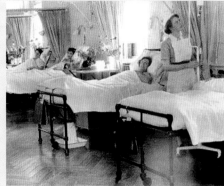

▶You won't BELIEVE what it looks like now!

(As a special service to our readers, we have missed out the normal clickbait convention of having to go through ten pages full of adverts for Viagra, toenail fungus cures and women over 50 in your area.)

AAARGH! I'VE TRODDEN ON A PIECE OF LEGO!!

AAARGH!!

THE AGONY!!

RGJ

Notes&queries

I see a lot of references to something called 'phubbing'. What is it?

● "Phubbing" is the residue left over after over-enthusiastic brass rubbing. The graphite, wax or chalk residue around the edges of a plaque is the "phubbing" and the clumsy enthusiast who has caused it is known as the "phubber". Special anti-phubbing solutions can be made at home from vinegar and oil of ULEZ, and kept in a handy atomiser.
The Reverend Paul Weller

● Sorry, but the Reverend Weller is talking out of his monumental brass. Along with Phuket Phichit and Phibiwallahbrij, Phubbing is one of the most ancient sites in Thailand. Notable for its collection of Goopi jade eggs, which were used as torture devices, for many years Phubbing was the capital of the Goop dynasty, led by a powerful warrior queen known as

Gwinit Phaltrow, who was eventually overthrown after insisting her entire population had a weekly facial massage.
General Feargal Sharkey, Derry

● The good General is generally wrong, and has clearly been at the regimental sherry. "Phubbing" is a term from the world of psychology, to describe statements which are not blatantly untrue – that would be "fibbing" – but which the speaker has managed to persuade themselves are true in the face of no evidence. My paper on the subject, *Talking Phubbish*, has analysed the speeches of all British prime ministers since Gladstone and has revealed a worrying 394% rise in phubbery-related incidents since 1868.
Dame Siouxsie Sioux, UCL

Answers please:

Why do birds suddenly appear, every time you are near? How do you do what you do to me? What's love got to do with it?

Film Highlights

Indiana Jones and the Zimmer of Destiny

■ Indy's back and this time he's very old. Yes, it's the 94th instalment of the all-action archaeology-meets-Nazi-hunting franchise, and Indy is facing his toughest challenge yet. Can he find the fabled Zimmer of Destiny that will transport him along the Corridor of Doom to matron's office where he will pick up the Cheque of Eternal Life from Mr Spielberg? Indy (played by an in-form Joe Biden) is teamed up with newcomer, Fleabe Waller-Bag (played by the youthful Olivia Coleman Mustard), in a classic screwball time-travel romp-com packed with sideways glances and knowing winks to the audience, as Indy and Fleabe break the Fourth Wall of China and try to go back in time to when Indiana Jones was any good (ie The Last Crusade – we enjoyed that one but the one where the pyramid took off – the crystal one – that was awful!).

CLICKBAIT CORNER 2

▶Here's what Harrison Ford looked like when he went in to watch his latest epic film, Indiana Jones and the Dial of Destiny...

You won't BELIEVE what he looked like when he finally came out at the end of the film!

(Once again, we have omitted the usually obligatory ten pages of advertisements for pet insurance, ear wax removal, and women under 80 in your area.)

////////////////////

Theatre Trigger Warnings

FOLLOWING the Chichester Festival's trigger warning for *The Sound of Music* – "Contains Nazis and the annexation of Austria" – the Eye is happy to provide trigger warnings for other potentially disturbing musicals:

Only Fools and Horses Contains Trigger.

West Side Story Contains gang violence, racism and cultural appropriation.

Guys and Dolls Contains organised crime, gambling addiction and simplistic binary gender differentiation.

Mary Poppins Contains harmful sugar (one spoonful) to help the medicine go down.

South Pacific Contains claims that shampoo will wash that man right out of your hair, which have not been upheld by the Advertising Standards Authority.

Les Misérables Contains upsetting scenes of Paris burning as revolution sweeps city, disturbingly close to present-day reality.

We Will Rock You Contains Ben Elton.

The Full Monty Contains nuts.

"Please continue to hold, your fall is important to us"

KILLER HEATWAVE SWEEPS EUROPE

Stop the plane – I have a fear of frying!

The Daily Mailograph

Friday, July 28, 2023

Why the European heatwave is not my problem

by Our Complacent Correspondent
Dee Nile

FOR too long we have been worrying about perfectly ordinary weather events under the label of "climate crisis".

Despite what the doommongers at the BBC or the Socialist Worker will tell you, it's important to remain calm – and, as long as you don't engage with the information, it's easy to stay frosty too!

Yes, some wild-eyed boffins might be shouting that wildfires across Canada are bigger than they have ever been before, and the ice in the Antarctic is four million square kilometres below normal, and, yes, the heatwaves mean that there might be simultaneous crop failures across the planet – it's called "the weather"! But you know what? At my home, in the Cotswolds, right now, it's about 15 degrees, and I don't mind telling you, I like the sound of a bit of global warming!!!

Yes, it's all a terrifying conspiracy by the eco-nazis to spread fear by printing bright red "hot spot" maps in all the papers while failing to point out that you're more likely to freeze to death than spontaneously combust from weather extremes and *(cont. 94°C)*

On Other Pages
● Greece burns **p1**
● It's Acropolis Now **p2**
● Here comes Warm-ageddon **p3**

News in brief

Small boats latest

■ There was jubilation last night at the news that lots of desperate people fleeing for their lives had been successfully transported to safety in small boats.

Clutching just a few personal belongings, tourists, many of them children, had escaped from Lindos on the island of Rhodes after making a hazardous journey from their hotels.

Gathering on the shore, they hoped to be ferried to a better life, away from the wildfires. A cry of "Start the Boats" went up from all the Brits, terrified that the traffic in people would stop.

Witnessing these poor wretches aboard the tiny craft with nothing but the clothes on their backs, Home Secretary Suella Braverman demanded that they immediately be flown to Rwanda.

That McDonald's Unhappy Meal Menu In Full

McFlurry of allegations
McSpicy language
Bully Beefburger
Feely O'Fishy
Big dirty Mac
Chick McHuggets
Seize Her Wrap
Neck Bites
Burger Off

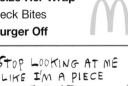

STOP LOOKING AT ME LIKE I'M A PIECE OF MEAT

MC DONALD'S

ROBERT THOMPSON

The Sun's Controversial Five Point Manifesto in Full

1 I promise to carry on being really hot whatever the eco-loonies say

2 I promise to melt all the icebergs and raise the sea levels ASAP

3 I promise to promote extreme weather events, whatever the green nutters do

4 I promise to set fire to the planet starting everywhere tomorrow

5 I promise to vote Conservative *(Is this right? Ed)*.

EXTREME WEATHER GAUGE

FUCK ME, IT'S HOT!!

weather house

COMMENT

Final proof that Brexit is working!

A DAILY EXPRESS study has found conclusive proof that Brexit is now working for Britain, as our proud nation has been basking in agreeable temperatures of 18°C whilst the European Union has been going into meltdown.

As Europe sizzled, with temperatures soaring upwards of 40°C, citizens from Madrid, Rome and Athens were overwhelmed by spiralling heat inflation.

Meanwhile, Brexit Britain has seen temperatures falling, with persistent drizzle proving again that getting out of Europe was the best decision ever made!

POETRY CORNER

**In Memoriam
Jane Birkin**

So. Farewell
Then Jane Birkin.

"Je t'aime",
That was your
Catchphrase.

"Ooh! Ooh! Aah!"
That was another.

I am listening to your
Record right now.

Phew!
Is it hot in here?
Or is it just me?

E.J. Throbb (17½ rpm)

WIMBLEDON ROUND-UP

Delight as Wimbledon hails new champion

ALL the spectators were on their feet as the world of tennis saluted the five-set victory of the hugely popular player, Not-Djokovic.

Said one tennis fan, "Not-Djokovic has got everything you'd want in a Wimbledon champion. The thing we all particularly like about Not-Djokovic is the way he's not Djokovic."

During the game, Not-Djokovic wowed the crowds with his non-Djokovicity, and his complete not Djokoviciness, as well as his convincing not-being-Djokovicability.

Not-Djokovic has a wonderful future ahead of him, so long as he remains not Djokovic, and stays focused on his strengths, and doesn't mind that people don't remember his real name is Carlos Alcaraz.

LATE NEWS
■ Murray Mound (formerly Henman Hill) to be renamed Not-Djokovic Knoll.

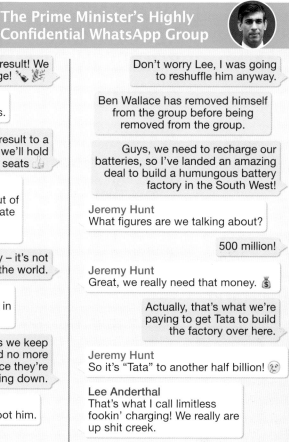

Wow! What a brilliant result! We won Uxbridge! 🎉

Jeremy Hunt
Held. And only by 495 votes.

Extrapolate that result to a general election and we'll hold onto all our seats 👍

Jeremy Hunt
We got hammered in two out of three by-elections. Extrapolate that and we'll end up with about 100.

Come on, Jeremy – it's not the end of the world.

Ben Wallace
I think Putin's pencilled that in for next Tuesday. 📷

Well, so long as we keep our nerve and no more MPs announce they're standing down.

Lee Anderthal
Fookin' hell! A deserter! Shoot him.

Ben Wallace
We don't have any guns. That's why I'm off.

Don't worry Lee, I was going to reshuffle him anyway.

Ben Wallace has removed himself from the group before being removed from the group.

Guys, we need to recharge our batteries, so I've landed an amazing deal to build a humungous battery factory in the South West!

Jeremy Hunt
What figures are we talking about?

500 million!

Jeremy Hunt
Great, we really need that money. 💰

Actually, that's what we're paying to get Tata to build the factory over here.

Jeremy Hunt
So it's "Tata" to another half billion! 😢

Lee Anderthal
That's what I call limitless fookin' charging! We really are up shit creek.

Thérèse Coffey
Is that a tributary of the River Avon? 💩

BY-ELECTION RESULT PROMPTS REVIEW OF 'GREEN CRAP'

by Our Eco-Staff **Justin Stopoil**

THANKS to the historic victory of angry old car owners in Uxbridge, both main parties have abandoned all attempts to save the world from catastrophic climate change.

Said one angry old car owner, "This is a victory for common sense in the midst of a cost of living crisis, which will save me twelve quid a day on ULEZ for my diesel Ford Banga.

"This is money that I can now use to take me and the missus on a flight to Rhodes, where, from what I hear, it's lovely and hot at the moment. People are coming back with an incredible tan."

A government spokesman said, "We do absolutely believe in climate change, as the political climate has clearly changed, but now we'd rather preserve the endangered species of Conservative MPs on the outskirts of Britain's major cities."

Meanwhile, a Labour spokesman said, "We are aiming to reintroduce new Labour MPs across red wall habitats where they were once plentiful – and, let's face it, ULEZ is not setting the world on fire. In fact, it's very expensive and has cost us a by-election."

Asked what future historians would make of their plans, both parties agreed: "There won't be any future historians."

GENERAL WASTE · GLASS PAPER PLASTIC · NOT QUITE SURE

PUTIN DRAFTS OAPs TO FIGHT IN UKRAINE

Ever invade a country and forget what you went in for?

Ben Wallace: 'We must learn lessons of Ukraine war'

by Our Defence Correspondent **Hugh Knew**

OUTGOING Defence Secretary Ben Wallace has described the Ukraine war as "a battle lab" delivering vital defence lessons. He said that the war had shown that to defend your country against an aggressor like Russia, your army needs tanks, troops and weapons.

"For a long time, the UK strategy has been to have an army with no troops and inadequate weapons. Incredibly, this war has taught us that to defend Britain, our army needs both soldiers and armaments," he told astonished reporters.

Wallace added, "The long-held Conservative belief that we could rely on contrarian armchair columnists writing dismissive articles about conventional warfare has been proved wholly incorrect."

He concluded, "Who could have possibly known that having personnel, armoured vehicles and big guns would be necessary in a war? Apart from everyone?"

THOSE ELLAS IN FULL

AN *Eye* Guide on how to distinguish between the bearers of this summer's hottest suffix:

LEGIONELLA Popular bacterium spreading rapidly in asylum barges.

NUTELLA Popular chocolate and hazelnut paste spreading rapidly over your toast.

SUELLA Unpopular nutter spreading misery – should be toast.

NIGELLA Popular fruity cook spread generously over TV schedules.

UMBRELLA Popular British summer accessory.

(That's enough Ellas. Ed.)

NEW SOLUTION TO HS2 PROPOSED

THE government has been advised by top consultants Munny, Downe & Drayne, that it would actually be cheaper if the entire city of Birmingham were to be moved to London, instead of building a high-speed train line.

Said senior partner, Seymour Munny, "Building homes for 2.6 million people, paying their relocation costs and transporting the whole of the Birmingham ring road to the North Circular would be much cheaper and a far more achievable solution than laying down a couple of rail tracks for 100 miles."

Said Levelling-Up Minister Michael Gove, "This sounds like a great idea – we'll call it Londingham and, if it works, we can bring Manchester down to Guildford and relocate Liverpool in Chichester. At last, I can see light at the end of the tunnel! Shame the same can't be said for HS2."

Buffers

OFFICIAL REPORT: HS2 'UNACHIEVABLE'

It's a massive hole

Keep digging!

LATE NEWS

IRONYOMETER BREAKS AGAIN

■ HAVING only just been repaired after Prince Harry went on every media outlet to demand privacy, the Ironyometer has once again exploded.

This time, the sensitive device monitoring humbug and bizarre contradictions across the planet began steaming, as word spread that the video communications company, Zoom, had ordered staff back to the office.

The Zoom announcement came as bad news for workers at the Ironyometer Centre, who had hoped to keep running the paradox-detecting equipment remotely.

Said the Zoom CEO from the laptop in his kitchen, "You can't run a business with everyone working from home. Hang on – that's a parcel, won't be a minute."

Film Highlights

Barbenheimer

■ Top nuclear physicist Barbenheimer (played by an in-form Margot Murphy) is in a race against time to create the world's first all-pink nuclear bomb. Oppenbarbie (played by an in-the-pink Cillian Robbie) wrestles with his conscience and ironic feminism as the air-head Ken (an hysterical performance by Ryan 'Air' Gosling) does his best to reinvent the pink plastic patriarchy before the Nazis use the doomsday pink Corvette to establish a pink Reich that will last for a thousand years. Laughs and harrowing scenes aplenty in this Christopher Gerwig/Greta Nolan-helmed nuclear pink fest.

EYE VIEW: Absurdly thin and megadeathly dull

LOGOS AS THEY SHOULD BE...

Barbie OLD *Barbie* NEW

THOSE NEW REGULATORY BODIES IN FULL

OfWat: Regulator in charge of failing to regulate water companies.

OfSkim: Regulator in charge of failing to stop profiteering by water companies.

OfTrot: Regulator in charge of failing to stop OfWat regulators from trotting off to lucrative jobs in the water companies.

OfTurn: Regulator in charge of failing to stop water companies from turning off the taps when the reservoirs of cash run dry.

OfWatTheFuck: Regulator in charge of failing to stop water regulators from failing to... *(Yes, we get the idea. Ed.)*

"First rung of the housing ladder? God, no! This is the ladder to the first rung..."

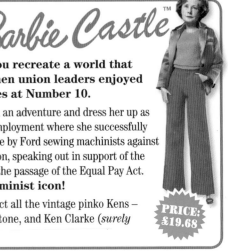

GREATEST HITS RADIO

KEN BRUCE

And a very good morning to you because yes that's what it is – a very good morning, with the emphasis on *good* not forgetting the *morning* of course or indeed the *very* so all in all a very good morning...

KAAIRN BROOOCE ON GRADEST HIDS RADIOOOO – GOOD TAMS SAND LAK THIS!

...and that was *Three Times a Lady* by the great and I was about to say late but in fact he's not so very late no he's thankfully alive and kicking yes I'm talking of course about the legend that is Lionel Richie...

KAAIRN BROOOCE ON GRADEST HIDS RADIOOOO – GOOD TAMS SAND LAK THIS!

...and coming up in the show we'll be enjoying our Tuesday Tune this week picked by Sheila from Stourbridge just to explain to those of you who might not know the Tuesday Tune is a tune we play every Tuesday by which I mean of course not just this Tuesday but as I say every Tuesday and it's over to Gavin for the weather...

An unsettled day with strong winds and cloudy in most areas and generally unsettled and cloudy that's the latest I'm Gavin Rutter!

A big thanks to Gavin there with the weather and there's there's certainly a lot of weather about one minute it's raining the next it's well not so much raining as in fact quite the reverse or to put it another way I might go so far as to say it's not raining or dry as the experts call it so without further ado let's travel back to 1977 for this all-time classic from the late, great Demis Roussos...

FEEL THE FUN AT CLEANEDOUTCASINO DOT COM SPEND A TOTALLY FUN AMOUNT OF YOUR LIFE SAVINGS AT CLEANEDOUTCASINO DOT COM SPIN THE WHEELS WITH A CHANCE TO PLAY ON FAVOURITE FUN GAMES LIKE DOWN THE DRAIN SQUANDER AND KAPUT YES JOIN IN THE FUN AND SEE IT ALL TURN TO NOTHING AT CLEANEDOUTCASINO DOT COM! AND REMEMBER – KEEP IT FUN! MAKE LOVE HAPPEN TODAY AND EVERYDAY – HEAD TO LOVEDEBT.COM AND BUY YOUR WAY TO LOVE. ARE UNSECURED DEBTS MAKING YOUR LIFE A MISERY? WRITE THEM OFF NOW BY BORROWING AS MUCH AS YOU WANT FROM US – WE'RE THE FRIENDLY, CARING FOLK WHO LOVE TO LEND.

So it's just coming up to ten past eleven on the twelfth I tell a lie it's just turned twelve minutes past ten on the eleventh I'll forget my own head next on the subject of which let's give a good old fashioned heads-up to Sandra and Bill from Beckenham beautiful Beckenham not a town I know well unfortunately who celebrate their 55th wedding anniversary on the thirteenth of the month so let's get firmly in the mood for dancing with this classic from the legendary Nolan Sisters...

♪ *Aminda moofurdan sin Ro mansinoooooo amgivi nit aw tonaaargh!!!* ♪

And those were of course the unmistakable dulcet tones of none other than the legendary Nolans getting us all in the mood for dancing

and romancing and just about anything else you might imagine that ends in 'ing' – just as long as it's not too naughty for a Tuesday morning in April!

KAIRN BROOOCE – ER CRASS THE UK – ON YOUR RADIO MOBILE OR SMARD SPEAKER THIS IS GRADEST HIDS RADIOOOO WITH BEEEE PEEEE – BP AIM TO MAKE EVERY JOURNEY JUST A LITTLE BID BEDDER GET BONUS POINTS EVERY TIME YOU FILL UP WITH FOOD OR FUEL TERMS AND CONDITIONS APPLY .

And now it's time for our legendary feature Golden Years where you tell us about a special memory of a – you got it – golden year. We've got Tim from Dorking on the line lovely to speak to you Tim tell me Tim where are you from Tim?

Dorking in Surrey Ken

Ah yes Dorking I know it well Tim and how are things in Dorking Tim

Not too bad Ken

Good to hear it Tim

Could I just say Ken thanks for a great show

And so where are you calling from Tim?

I'm calling from Dorking Ken.

So you live in Dorking and you're calling from Dorking? You clearly can't get enough of Dorking, Tim! Good stuff! So without further ado or ado-ing much further, let's go straight to Gavin Rutter with the latest on the weather front.

An unsettled day with strong winds and cloudy in most areas and generally unsettled and cloudy that's the latest I'm Gavin Rutter.

Thanks Gavin as I thought there's a bit of wind about it must be this new medication I'm taking hur hur which takes us nicely into this from the late great Ziggy Starburst himself Mister David Bowie..

KAIRN BROOOCE – ER CRASS THE UK – ON YOUR RADIO MOBILE OR SMARD SPEAKER THIS IS GRADEST HIDS RADIOOOO.

It's Tuesday here on Greatest Hits Radio which makes it the day before Wednesday and the day after Monday which can't be bad unless you're more of a Thursday or Friday sort of person but then again in just 24 hours it'll be the same time tomorrow how time flies...

ARE YOU OWED SOMETHING BY A STRANGER IF YOU CAN THINK OF SOMEONE TO BLAME FOR ALL THAT'S GONE WRONG IN YOUR LIFE TEXT YOUR CLAIM TO MAKEMEAMILLION6060 IN THIS MONTH'S SWISH MAGAZINE FIND OUT WHY CAROL VORDERMAN HAS TAKEN UP CROCHET AND DISCOVER 56 WAYS OF COOKING A SAUSAGE.

Yes it's that time again so let's welcome Jean from Stroud to the legendary Pop Master where are you from, Jean?

Stroud Ken.

Ah good old Stroud know the place well so Jean here's your first question which song reached number 3 in the charts in October 1985 and the following week slipped to number 5 then bounced back to take the number 2 slot before falling to number 7 and for a bonus point what Motown song got to number 17 in 1966 and number 5 in 1967 before resurfacing at number 7 in the summer of 1972

...sorry Ken it's gone

Sadly I can't give you any points for that Jean so that's nul points as they say sur le continong and for an extra two points can you tell me what make of automobile the late great Prince was driving in his April 1983 hit which was also a hit when it was re-issued in November of that same year?

...sorry Ken it's gone

KAAIRN BROOOCE ACRASS THE UK ON GRADEST HIDS RADIOOOO – GOOD TAMS SAND LAK THIS!

As told to
CRAIG BROWN

Apparently BY MIKE BARFIELD

LAWNCARE: A CALENDAR FOR LESS-INCLINED GARDENERS

'NO MOW' MAY | 'STILL TOO SOON' JUNE
'WHY EVEN TRY?' JULY | 'CAN'T BE FUSSED' AUGUST
'JESUS WEPT' SEPT | 'PAVE IT OVER' OCTOBER

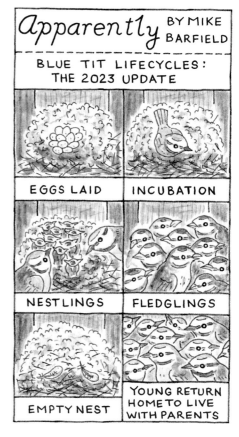

Apparently BY MIKE BARFIELD

BLUE TIT LIFECYCLES: THE 2023 UPDATE

EGGS LAID | INCUBATION
NESTLINGS | FLEDGLINGS
EMPTY NEST | YOUNG RETURN HOME TO LIVE WITH PARENTS

TRUMP ELECTION CAMPAIGN DRAMA

"I want four more years"

"How about twenty?"

"Jail to the Chief!"

Recount demanded

A PAIR of scales at Fulton County Jail today demanded a recount after being stepped on by Donald Trump as part of his committal proceedings.

Said the scales, "Trump is claiming that he weighs 215lbs, which is way, way below the correct figure."

The scales claimed that a recount would show Donald Trump weighed at least 20 stone and that the lost pounds were nothing less than a fraud on the public.

The ex-President, however, refused to allow a recount, insisting such a process was beneath the dignity of "a seven-foot-two man with a full head of hair and a golf handicap of minus 28 degrees Fahrenheit".

The scales were carried out, screaming "Lock him up before he treads on anyone else!"
(Rotters)

LATE NEWS
Trump poses for mug shot and T-shirt shot and hoodie shot and baseball cap shot.

OUTSIDER WINS DEBATE

by Our American Election Correspondent **Redd Neck**

WITH Donald Trump absent, businessman Vivek Ramaswamy brushed aside the front runner, Governor Ron DeSantis, to emerge as the surprise winner of the first Republican presidential debate.

"Ramaswamy is a vastly wealthy, super-confident businessman who has never held any political office and has extreme right-wing views about how to transform America," cheered all Republican voters excitedly.

"What could possibly go wrong, electing a man like that as president?"

Popular drama 'totally unbelievable' say critics

by Our Entertainment Staff **Baz Bamig-Ball**

CRITICS were unanimous in their opinions of the recent roller-coaster thriller. However heart-warming the feel-good story may have been, there is no getting over the fact that the plot was absurd and the punchline stretched credibility to breaking point.

Critics agreed that to have the hero, Stuart Broad, announce his retirement just before the interval and then to bowl the winning ball to draw the series was the stuff of fairytales but hardly what was expected from a realistic narrative.

Said the doyenne of drama critics, L.B.W. Purves, "The Ashes was a nail-biting and edge of the seat production, but ultimately failed to convince as a truthful account of test cricket as it is played in England today."

Said another critic, Quwisden Letts, "I am all for a happy ending but to expect us to believe that England can come from two nil down and then level the series in the last of hour of play on the last day is frankly absurd.

"The scenes of a triumphant Stuart Broad kissing his child as the crowd rose to their feet to applaud their hero would not have been out of place in a Richard Curtis film. Bazball? More like Schmalzball!"

THE TIMES NEW ROMAN

LIONESSES MAKE GOOD PROGRESS IN EARLY ROUNDS

By our sports staff **ALEXA CALEDONIA**

It's been a spectacular start for the lionesses as they've devoured the opposition and torn up the Coliseum in a ruthless display of attacking skill.

As the audience cheered, sang "Three Lionesses on my Toga" and gave an encouraging thumbs down, the female sporting superstars pounced on the hapless teams of human beings sent against them.

Commentators agreed that it was easier for the lionesses in these early stages because the opposition were unarmed slaves and Christians who had no weapons. But things are about to get more difficult, as the lionesses face sterner opponents in the knock-out stages which invariably go to sudden death.

They face a team of gladiators from much-fancied Thrace in the next round, and there are fears that they will be slaughtered. Either way, the lionesses can hold their heads up high, or someone else will, on the end of a spear.

ON OTHER PAGES

NO SELFIES

TOLD YOU!

—PILBROW—

Hi, fellow petrol heads! It's Rishi Clarkson here! I'm the best PM… in the world! 🏎️🛢️

James Forsyth
Top Top Gear Rebrand, Rishi! You're so convincing as a fuel-injected man of the people!

Let's put our foot on the gas – and the oil, obviously – and take this party from 0 to 600 seats in under three seconds!

Lee Anderthal
Fookin' great! We're ditching the green crap at last!

See, the common man likes it already!

Jeremy Hunt
Just to be clear – we're ditching all our Net Zero commitments that we were fully behind two weeks ago because we somehow won a by-election by being pro-pollution?

That's the kind of screeching U-turn the Stig would do!

James Forsyth
Great turbo-charged Grand Tour on Amazon Prime banter, PM, you're entirely convincing as the voice of the ordinary car driver.

Well, I speak to mine every day, when we're on the way to the helicopter or private jet, so I very much know what the average motorist in a peaked cap with gloves is thinking.

James Forsyth
I've got you a radio spot with Nick Ferrari, PM.

Ferrari? My kind of guy! Vrrrrm! 🏎️

James Forsyth
It'll be easy, so long as you don't sound smug or patronising. Or rich.

Don't worry. I'll just talk about going on an ordinary holiday like an ordinary person, taking my ordinary kids for an ordinary week in California, to stay in one of my portfolio of luxury homes around the world. 😄

James Forsyth:
Maybe rephrase that, boss.

But we're all booked for Disneyland. I can't change now.

Kemi Badenoch
Disneyland? Could you see if they're interested in entering a trade agreement with the UK? It's got to be worth more than the pan-Pacific deal I've just signed.

James Forsyth
PM, the callers on Ferrari's show may not be very interested in Disneyland and may question you about the cost of living crisis instead.

Well, that's very rude of them. They should trust me to get on with important things, like stopping the boats.

James Forsyth
Don't mention the boats. That isn't going so well.

Lee Anderthal
I blame the fookin' leftie lawyers! You know what I'd do with 'em? I'd send them off to Rwanda – that'd teach 'em!

Suella Braverman
Er, Lee, our entire policy is based on the pretext that Rwanda is a really nice, safe place and not a punishment.

Lee Anderthal
Fook me, this government lark is doing my fookin' 'ead in!

James Forsyth
Back to the matter in hand, LBC.

Lee Anderthal
I think it's LBCTQ+ nowadays, God 'elp us!

James Forsyth
Calm down, Lee. LBC is a radio station and it is mostly for taxi drivers. In fact, I think you'd enjoy it.

So, just to recap, you don't want me to mention the boats?

James Forsyth
No. Or inflation. Or the debt. Or the NHS. Or growth. Or any of our pledges

Jeremy Hunt
But it's a phone-in. What if a caller asks Rishi about, say, their mortgage problems?

Easy-peasy! I'll simply ask the caller if they've thought about not having a mortgage. Interest rates are terrible at the moment. It's much more sensible to pay it off with cash.

Jeremy Hunt
You may need to be a little more sensitive, than that PM.

Well, if you're going to get personal, Jeremy, I'll start TALKING IN CAPS!!!!

Jeremy Hunt
Woah, sorry, PM. No need to get tetchy.

I AM NOT TETCHY!!!!!!!!!!!!

Penny Mordaunt
Wow, you really need a holiday.

Lee Anderthal
Fookin' right. You should go somewhere nice and safe and lovely. Like Rwanda. 😉

Suella Braverman 👍👍👍

How to tell if your neighbour is a Russian spy

The *Eye*'s handy checklist for working out if Mr and Mrs Jones from Number 49 are actually working for legendary Russian Military Intelligence Service, the FSB

❑ They're interested in visiting British Cathedrals.

❑ Their car looks suspiciously like a tank and has the numberplate ZZZ.

❑ Their bridge evenings involve loud explosions.

❑ They put on protective gloves before touching any doorknobs.

❑ They claim your driveway is their ancestral land.

❑ They keep calling you Nazis over the fence.

❑ They have a 37-foot-long dining table.

❑ They play nothing but Wagner at all hours.

❑ Amazon asks you to look after their packages marked "Fragile: Polonium!"

❑ People occasionally fall out of their top bedroom windows.

TABLOID HACK SENDS IRONYOMETER INTO FURTHER MELTDOWN

I've been the target of a smear campaign… an untrue story… spurious allegations… unspeakable slurs…

YORKSHIRE CAKE SHOP

PARKIN FOR PATRONS ONLY

@Vilvivinio

JUST (NON) STOP OIL!

> I'm going to plumb the depths

> That's the bottom of the barrel!

> He's trying to rig the election

Eye Explainer Number 94

How carbon capture works

1. Natural gas burned at power station

2. Carbon dioxide separated from other gases

3. Carbon dioxide stored under the North Sea

Natural gas

It doesn't.

Court Circular

Buckingham Palace, Tuesday

The Duchess of Sussex today celebrates her 42nd birthday.

His Royal Highness the Prince of Wales will not be sending a birthday card. Nor will Her Royal Highness the Princess of Wales. HM the Queen will not be raising a glass to toast her health, and she will be joined by HM the King in not picking up the phone to wish her "many happy returns".

Sir Alan Fitztightly, Royal Equerry and Steward of the Stinky Ink will observe that it would be best if there were "no returns at all" from Ms Markle.

Clarence House – Wednesday

HM the King will announce a special family event to commemorate the anniversary of the late Queen Elizabeth's death.

He will fail to send an invitation to the Duke and Duchess of Sussex, and their children Prince Archewellness Foundation and Princess Lilibet 365. He will, however, extend an invitation to Prince Andrew, despite his previous engagements with the American judicial authorities.

Sir Alan Fitztightly, Treasurer of the Toothpaste and Bearer of the Brush will proclaim that there doesn't seem to be a "Spare" invitation.

Balmoral – Thursday

The entire family will gather for the traditional summer holiday, apart from the Duke and Duchess of Sussex, whose invitation has sadly been lost in the post. Sir Alan Fitztightly, Lord Lieutenant of the Lavatory Seat, will observe that they are less welcome than the midges. HM the Queen will ignite a Queen-size Rothpersons cigarette to dispel the said insects, and reprimand Sir Alan for his waspish, though humorous, lack of respect for the Count of Montecino.

HRH the Prince of Wales will refuse to wear a kilt and will share this information with the Royal Press Corps on the condition that they will run it on the front when Meghan's about to announce a Netflix film based on the romantic novel "When Harry Met Savvy".

The Royal Press Corps, led by Mr Ovaltine Lowbrow, will agree wholeheartedly, providing they can have a picture of Catherine, the Princess of Wales – any picture, doing anything – bearing the headline, "Lovely Kate – Isn't She Lovelier Than Unlovely Meghan?"

Sir Alan Fitztightly, Commander in Chief of the First Battalion of the King's Own Eggy Soldiers, will remind their Majesties of the time when Backstairs Billy wore a kilt with the traditional absence of undergarments and surprised the assembled under-footmen when he tried to toss his caber and *(That's enough Court Circular, Ed.)*

The Daily Telegraph

Friday 25 August 2023

What could possibly be causing all these wildfires across the face of the Earth?

OUR team of brilliant journalists have been on the case, studying why there are enormous wildfires across multiple countries all over the planet. We present our exclusive findings in a handy list form:

1 They're all because of arson. Even the ones which started in incredibly remote bits of Canada where no people have walked for ten years have been started by beavers which were released by disastrous left-wing rewilding schemes.

2 Any which weren't arson – which they all were – were actually caused by passing electric cars, which this paper has revealed are 99 percent likely to burst into flames without provocation on any given day. Fact: remote Greek islands, Sicily, Spain and Italy are almost entirely full of electric cars.

3 Any which weren't caused by arson or beavers or electric cars were down to the BBC, which sent a number of national treasures like Bill Bailey on whimsical walking holidays, where they probably dropped a match or accidentally released several hundred billion tonnes of carbon dioxide.

4 Those that weren't caused by arson or beavers or electric cars or Romesh Ranganathan *(This is brilliant, keep going. Ed.)* were caused by Sir Keir Starmer, for reasons we will fill in later.

5 There are no massive fires! There was one small fire, and a series of enormous space mirrors built by George Soros, and the international Woke Brigade have just reflected these images so it looks like multiple countries are experiencing devastatingly high temperatures. That's a relief, because it means we won't have to do anything and can continue exactly as we have before.

THAT NET ZERO REFERENDUM IN FULL

How the proposed democratic ballot on climate change will look:

Do you want Britain to be:

A ☐ On fire?

B ☐ Under water?

C ☐ Both?

100 NEW METEORITE LICENCES

ROBERT THOMPSON

"Is that wise?"

NHS WAITING LIST CRISIS

> We're not meeting our targets, but we have a plan

> Get rid of the queues?

> No – get rid of the targets

THEFT OF PRICELESS ARTEFACTS FROM BRITISH MUSEUM

by Our Crime Staff **Nick Stuff**

The man at the centre of a huge theft of ancient treasures from the British Museum has refused to give them back.

He told police, "Yah, I nicked them, but they're mine now. Sure, the objects were obtained illegally, but that's history for you. And there's nothing the previous owners can do about it."

He continued, "I will be displaying the antiquities in my front room and, to be honest, I will take better care of them than the British Museum. I mean, someone can just walk in there and steal them! My home will be open to visitors from all over the world, free of charge, except for the occasional special exhibition in the kitchen, which will cost hundreds of pounds, and be very difficult to get tickets for."

When quizzed further, the thief said, "I have proposed an arrangement to British Museum Chairman, George Osborne, where I loan the artefacts back to the Museum for a limited period, but on the understanding that they give them back to me, because they're mine now. Finders, Keepers, Museum, Weepers!"

....

LATE NEWS

■ **Metropolitan Police finally identify the man at centre of British Museum theft. Inspector Knacker says, "We have arrested a** **257-year-old man, known only as Lord Elgin. When we apprehended him, we shouted 'Frieze'!"**

....

LATE LATE NEWS

■ **The late Lord Elgin denies theft and claims Marbles "fell off the back of an Acropolis".**

TORY PARTY ANNOUNCES AI STRATEGY

1. Do nothing.
2. Allow AI technology to enslave us.
3. Give £40 million to bra manufacturer and Tory donor to invent time machine.
4. Wait for John Connor to emerge as resistance to the Rise of the Machines.
5. Send AI Cyborg Arnold Schwarzenegger back in time to protect John Connor from Shape-Changing T1000 AI Cyborg sent back to terminate John Connor.
6. Prevent Judgement Day.
7. Accept large donation from Skynet to relax AI regulation.
8. Allow right-wing press to brand John Connor and anti-AI resistance as "Woke Blob Enemies Of The People".
9. Activate Skynet AI global defence system.
10. Judgement Day.

NEW WARNING FOR SMOKERS TO BE PLACED IN CIGARETTE PACKETS

Keep smoking and you could end up looking like this...

That Liz Truss Dishonours List In Full

Lady Letitia Lettuce
Dame Commander of the Order of Salad for services to national morale during the Liz Truss era Sept-Oct 2022.

Lord Kwasi Kwar-Kwash
Baron Hard-Up of Skid Row for services to tanking the economy during the Liz Truss error Sept-Oct 2022.

Lord Brian Yesman Baron Nodding of Dog top political consultant, for services to agreeing to whatever Trussonomic measures the Prime Minister suggested during the Liz Truss terror Sept-Oct 2022.

Sir Spaddy McSpadface speech writer, 23, for services to putting the words "Wow!", "Hey!", "Pork!" and "Cheese!" into all her landmark speeches during the Liz Truss horror Sept-Oct 2022.

Dame Dimmy Dum-Dum founder of the Anti-Anti-Growth Coalition Coalition and Director of leading think tank the Institute of Criminal Irresponsibility, for services to national decline during the Liz Truss howler Sept-Oct 2022.

Lady Maya bezzy-friend, deputy best friend, for services to still answering Liz Truss' calls and not pretending she'd never met her like everybody else during the Liz Truss er... Sept-Oct 2022.

GEORGE OSBORNE'S GLITTERING CAREER IN FULL

■ Chancellor of the Exchequer
■ Er
■ Editor of Evening Standard
■ Um
■ Chair of the British Museum
■ Oops

BRITISH MUSEUM ANNOUNCES URGENT STOCKTAKE

We have to find out who took all our stock

BRITAIN'S WORST SERIAL OVERKILLER

DON'T MISS our 94-page special murder supplement, plus 7-hour real-life murder podcast, giving our most prolific criminal writers the chance to revisit all the gory details in a lengthy forensic analysis of how the gruesome events unfolded.

Will the serial overkillers strike again? Yes, tomorrow – in the 940-page exclusive pull-out souvenir issue on "'The killer nurse I never knew."

PLUS, be sure to order your copy of Thursday's paper for the exclusive serialisation of the 9,400-page book *Inside the mind of the serial overkiller*, to find out what compels these people to write again and again and again about such horrific and unspeakable crimes. Are they hoping to make a killing? Perhaps we will never know.

HEARTBREAK FOR ENGLAND FANS

It's a disaster...

...we're still stuck with that Baddiel and Skinner song

Exclusive To All Tabloids
AN APOLOGY

IN RECENT years, we might have inadvertently given the impression that we had no interest in women's football, that it was vastly inferior to the men's game and, let's face it, was a bit of a joke and played by those sporty types who never seemed very interested in getting a boyfriend at school.

We now realise, in light of the England women's team reaching the World Cup final, that nothing could be further from the truth and that the Lionesses represent everything that is good and pure about the beautiful game, and that their skill, athleticism and ability to look pretty and sell newspapers totally outstrips the men's game, which is why we all cheered our glory girls onto very near victory.

We apologise for any confusion caused and any confusion in the future when we change our minds and...*(cont. p94)*

Earps wins golden trophy

by Our Football Staff **Roly Model**

THERE was joy throughout the nation last night as England goalkeeper Mary Earps was awarded the coveted Golden Tongue trophy for the swear of the tournament.

Throughout the Lionesses' World Cup campaign, Earps' swearing had been world-class in a tournament filled with talented swearers from around the globe.

But in the final, she pulled one of the greatest potty-mouthed performances in swearing history, with a magnificent four-letter-word outburst following her saving of the Spanish penalty.

On hearing of her award, a delighted Earps said, "F*** off!!! Hopefully I will inspire a whole generation of little girls to take their swearing to another level. Anything is possible, profanity-wise, if you turn your mouth to it."

Disappointment for Queen of Stops

by OWEN GOAL
Our Political Football Staff

SHE was hailed as the Queen of Stops but, in the final analysis, Suella Braverman came up short.

She had burst onto the scene with a reputation for stopping everything, from small boats to even smaller boats – but her form deserted her when the country needed her most, and she let in an astonishing 375 boats in a week.

"I'm gutted that I've let the country I love down – and that country is Rwanda," she said. "I left everything out there – mostly small boats overloaded with migrants heading towards Britain."

Her dip in form means that her place in Team Rishi could be taken by someone capable of doing the job better... namely, anyone, or failing that, Kemi Badenoch.

Said one pundit, "The so-called Queen of Stops can't even save herself, let alone anything else. No wonder the whole country is as sick as a parrot and under the moon."

What You Missed

That World Cup final commentary in full

"...and another Spanish cheat falls to the ground, clearly play-acting in a deliberate attempt to waste time, knowing they could never match the skills of the brilliant Lionesses, who are running rings around the señoritas who have... oh, they've just scored, but it was gifted to them by a player of far greater ability and class in Lucy Bronze, and once again England are denied their rightful World Cup victory by England..."
(cont. for next 94 years of hurt)

THE EYE SAYS...

HATS OFF TO THE LIARESSES!

AT LAST, Britain's women politicians have proved that they're just as good at lying as the men.

For years, they've had to watch from the sidelines as their male equivalents treated every issue as a political football, happy to kick problems into the long grass and missing open goals at every opportunity.

Now we salute the liaresses, who are coming into their own, proving themselves worthy of the song "Three lies on my shift". (*Yes, we get the idea. Ed.*)

Just think of all the female stars of the national game and try and tell us they're worse than the men. (*You're fired. Ed.*)

SPANISH WORLD CUP FOOTBALL SCANDAL

RUBIALES STILL REFUSING TO RESIGN AS FA PRESIDENT

I won't be forced into doing anything against my will

Er...

RUBIALES' MOTHER ON HUNGER STRIKE

No one's shoving anything down my throat without my consent

NEVER TOO OLD

A new love story by Dame Sylvie Krin, author of *Heir of Sorrows* and *Duchess of Hearts*

THE STORY SO FAR:
The multi-billionaire media mogul has found love yet again and has taken his new flame on a magical cruise on a luxury yacht around the Mediterranean...

AS the sun set over the beautiful Greek island of Yesbos, in the Dododecanese, Rupert put an elderly arm around his elegant Russian companion, Ivana Legova, and his heart fluttered, though not in a bad way.

"Strewth, Ivana. That's one dingo's arse of a view..." Rupert was turning on the charm to try and woo his new sexagenarian sweetheart from the Land of Borscht and Blinis.

As he gazed at the orange sky over the ancient port of Viagra, he mused, "Those clouds look like the fluffy sheep back in the shearing pen on the farm at Digger's Crack."

Yes, he might be in his 93rd year, but he hadn't lost the ability to sweet talk the sheilas.

Ivana squeezed his bony hand and cooed, "I zink, dahlink, zat ze clouds are from ze huge wild fires on ze island."

Blimey, thought the transglobal tycoon, the Russian doll was right. Bloody climate change! He might have to tell his news channels round the world to stop denying it. He shouted at the Captain of the Crispina Odey to change course:

"Witherow! We'll skip Yesbos and we'll head straight for Corfuwatascorcha!"

Witherow jauntily touched his captain's cap in salute and wheeled the elegant yacht round to set a new course, thus avoiding the holidaymakers swimming out to sea for safety.

What a marvellous trip it had been, thought Rupert, with the Mediterranean magic healing his broken heart and banishing thoughts of his former gun-toting evangelical fiancée. Jeez that had been a close call.

And his kids, though in many ways useless, had been right about her and right about affairs of the heart. He shouldn't rush into things. Take it slow. Easy Tiger... "You don't fancy getting married do you, Ivana?"

Fortunately, the glamorous scientist, who had once been the mother-in-law of Chelsea FC's billionaire proprietor, Roman Oligarkovitch, did not hear him,

as the sound of a helicopter dropping water on the burning forests drowned out Rupert's premature proposal.

His children – what were their names again? Oh yes, Lachlan, Shiv, Kendall and the other ones – were bound to approve this time. Ivana was a mere 26 years younger than him, was a wealthy woman in her own right and didn't put her pistol on the coffee table during prayer sessions.

And, even better, Legova was a top microbiologist. Did she perhaps possess the secret of eternal life? Rupert was doing pretty well on his own, but could do with a little help from someone who might know why turtles live to 230 and Giant Sequoias reach a ripe young age of 500 years.

Suddenly, his Big Apple phone rang and revealed that the call was coming from none other than his former wife, the dragon lady herself, Wendi Ding-Dong. In an extraordinary twist, it was the banshee from Beijing who had introduced Rupert to the siren of the Steppes. What on earth could be her motive, thought Rupert, for this act of mature-media-mogul match making?

"Hi, old man. How is it going with Legova? You dead yet, Lupert? Once again, you look like silly old fool! You even more ancient relic than Elgin Marbles – and looks like you lost yours! Ha ha ha ha ha ha ha!"

(To be continued...)

"I need a minute"

A-LEVEL JUMPING BACK TO PRE-PANDEMIC LOW

by Our Education Staff **Dee Deedy**

THE results are in and there's no getting over it, this year was disappointing, as the first pictures appeared in the newspapers showing fruity girls celebrating their A-Level results.

Gone were the days of the artificially high levels of jumping during the pandemic when teachers estimated the height that the girls would be leaping and this was just accepted by the authorities.

Now the jumping is once again being assessed by independent external examiners who are determined to bring the girls down to earth much quicker.

Whereas before, girls could expect to achieve levels as high as 3 feet, now they can expect a more realistic height of 1 foot 6 inches.

Said leading newspaper editor, Sir Daley Telegraph, "These girls are going to find it harder to get into a top newspaper with this kind of jump. We have a clearing system which requires them to get over 2 feet if they want to appear on the front pages. Have you seen how high the Lionesses are jumping these days?!!"

School news

St Cakes

THE Headmaster would like to congratulate all Cakeians for working so hard on their public examinations this year. Unfortunately, the results were extremely disappointing, due to the fact that we could not give them all the Grade As they deserved, as we did last year when the pandemic self-assessment scheme was operating. This year, St Cake's has sadly fallen from third in the school league tables, with 99% of pupils being awarded A* or above by Mr Perkins, to a less impressive 3594th with no A-Levels passes at all by any pupils in any subjects. Although this is something of a set-back, we are confident that we will bounce back next year, as the Chemistry Department, under Mr Wuhan, is working on an exciting new variant of the Covid virus which promises to restore lockdown conditions and, more importantly, realistic self-marking for the deserving A-level pupils of our renowned fee-paying Midlands Independent School (motto: *"Semper Corona, Semper Alpha Astra"*).

"The Hendersons say they've got Covid. Is that still a thing?"

Financial services	Energy companies	Rail companies	Water companies
	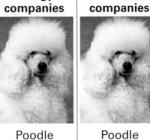		
Poodle	Poodle	Poodle	Shih Tzu

Nursery Times

.... Friday, Once-upon-a-time ....

CROOKED MAN DENIES BEING CROOKED AFTER CROOKED HOUSE BURNS DOWN

by Our Arson Staff **The Little Match Girl**

THE Crooked Man at the centre of the Crooked House Pub Scandal has denied that he and his wife, the Crooked Woman, deliberately set fire to the much-loved hostelry in order to demolish it and then redevelop it.

The Crooked Man had bought the Crooked House for a crooked sixpence, which he claimed to have found on a crooked stile after he had walked a crooked mile. But now he is at the centre of an investigation by PC Plod, since, immediately following the purchase, the Crooked House mysteriously burnt to the ground.

Bob the Builder and Scoop the Digger were actually booked in to demolish the popular pub a week before the fire happened. However, the Crooked Man told reporters, "This is mere coincidence. Sometimes buildings, particularly crooked ones, set themselves on fire for no reason at all..."

He continued, "...like my pants, which have just coincidentally set fire to themselves. Spontaneous combustion is a very common phenomenon."

Fireman Sam was called in to extinguish the pant conflagration, but it was too late and the Crooked Man had already claimed the underpant loss on his insurance with a view to redeveloping his netherware as modern luxury boxer shorts.

Said pub regulars, the Crooked Cat and the Crooked Mouse, "The Crooked House must be rebuilt brick by brick", but restoration expert Mr Humpty Dumpty said, "I personally doubt that, even if they got in all the King's horses and all the King's men, they will be able to put it back together again."

Crooked House *doesn't* burn down

Vlad 'Mad' Putin, Tank No: ZZZZ

Blimey, that Wagner bloke... eh? You know, Prigozhin, my old chef. What a tragic loss. I didn't see that one coming. Honest, guv, I didn't! Sure, he and I had our ups and downs. His last one was a down, obviously, at quite a speed, but I never had anything personal against the guy. We got on like a house on fire. Or a plane on fire, you could say! You what? Me? No, no, nothing to do with me, guv, I'm not that sort of bloke. Ask anyone who knows me. If they're still alive, that is. To me he was just a lovely geezer, full of old war stories – mainly about torture and doing people in with sledgehammers, but he told them with a smile. So, his death, yeah, it really came out of the blue. Literally. Boom!! Where was I when I heard? Sitting in my tank, minding my own business. Well, yeah, the gun barrel may have been pointing slightly upwards, but so what? And I may have been shouting "My compliments to the chef" as I fired the shell into the sky... but what are you implying, mate? No, I'd never do anything like that. All right, so I did catch him recently, driving at me in the wrong direction, but he did a quick U-turn and that was the end of the matter. I never fell out with him. I never fall out with anyone. It's them that do the falling out. From windows, mainly. It's just the way it is, bad luck, pure and simple. Accidents happen. Bang – and you're gone! So, watch what you say, guv, or there might be another accident. Know what I mean? You insured? I'm with Admiral. Well, the late Admiral. He had an accident too. Be lucky. Poor old Prigozhin. Funny he was my chef, last thing he did was give me my favourite dish served cold!!! Ha, ha, ha!

© *A tank driver 2023*

I'll do your lashes

Margaret Atwood serves writ on Taliban

by Our Legal Staff
Gill E. Add

THE novelist Margaret Atwood has begun legal proceedings against the government of Afghanistan, claiming plagiarism from her novel *The Handmaid's Tale*.

The novelist maintains that the Taliban have lifted large sections of her book and rewritten them into their regime's legislation.

Ms Atwood said, "I tried to make my dystopia as unpleasant as possible, but the Taliban have simply used my ideas to create one of the most repressive countries on Earth.

"To be honest, my work was meant to be fiction, but they have ripped it off wholesale and turned it into the grimmest of realities. I mean, the Taliban's decision not to allow women to enter public parks is a straight lift from *The Handmaid's Tale*."

The Taliban has responded to Ms Atwood's complaint, saying "Who cares? She's a woman."

© *Private Underhis-Eye 2023*

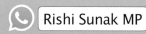
Hey it's crime week. And it's gone very well. Not a single Tory MP has been accused of a crime.

Look at this picture. Here's me with a whole pile of confiscated knives.

Penny Mordaunt
Are you sure that's not taken outside the Cabinet office? 😊

Suella Braverman
I've told the police to investigate crime.

That's brilliant, Suella!

Suella Braverman
And not to commit crime themselves!

Super-brilliant, Suella! That'll revolutionise the police force. This crime week is going super-super-brilliantly!

Nadine Dorries
I'll tell you what crime the police should be looking into. The Assassination of Boris Johnson.

Are you still here? I thought you were resigning.

Nadine Dorries
I am. But first I demand an explanation as to why you, the unelected Prime Minister, are denying me a seat in the House of Lords?

Penny Mordaunt
As an unelected peer, you mean?

Jeremy Hunt
Can you spot the irony, Nadine?

Nadine Dorries
Rishi has behaved disgracefully, with no respect for the rules. Why can't he be more like Boris?

Jeremy Hunt
Can you spot the irony again, Nadine?

Oliver Dowden
It's like that cockney song – "Any old, any old irony!"

Nadine Dorries
Shut up, posh boy.

Oliver Dowden
I went to a state comprehensive in Watford.

Nadine Dorries
You're still posh. Unlike Boris. 🖤

Nadine Dorries has been removed from the group, the party and her constituency, finally.

Jeremy Hunt
Oh dear, I think Nadine might need medical help.

Steve Barclay
Now's not a good time, actually. Maybe in a few years.

Fair point, Steve. I was a little bit disappointed to see that half of the UK deaths last year were people on NHS waiting lists.

Steve Barclay
Disappointed? That means half of them weren't! And the other half shows we're good at identifying people who are really ill. It's win-win!

James Forsyth
Great stats analysis, Steve, but don't say that out loud.

Lee Anderthal
Nothing in this fookin' country works! Except me. I'm working for GB News, telling people every night that nothing in this fookin' country works!

Grant Shapps
I'm working! I've just taken on a new job, as Defence Secretary.

Welcome to the Cabinet, Grant!

Grant Shapps
Actually, I'm already in the Cabinet.

Sorry, Grant, remind me what you were before...

Grant Shapps
Well, I've been Minister without Portfolio, Minister for International Development, Transport Minister, Home Secretary, Business Minister and for the past six months I've been Energy Secretary.

And what have you achieved?

Grant Shapps
Net Zero.

Lee Anderthal
That's right! Fook all.

Come on, guys, it's not Defence week. Can we focus on which week it actually is. That's how we do things now. First we had Boats week, then we had Health week, now we've got Crime week.

Oliver Dowden
Well, the 'weak' bit works! 😊

That's not funny, Oliver, or clever.

Kemi Badenoch
No need to get tetchy.

I AM NOT GETTING TETCHY!!

Daily Mailograph
AN APOLOGY

IN RECENT months and years we may have given the mistaken impression that the radical and destructive actions of protest groups such as 'JUST STOP OIL' were a threat to us all and it was absolutely right for the government to implement a crackdown.

That the firm actions of the police, backed by new legislation, to throw these protestors into the back of a van if they so much as hand out a pamphlet suggesting that not having a monarchy is a good idea, or sit down in a public place to mourn a woman killed by a policeman, is absolutely warranted and correct, and the repression of such disruptive antics is a price well worth paying for living in a civilised society.

We now realise, in the light of the brave and fearless actions of the protest group 'JUST STOP ULEZ' that nothing could be further from the truth and that blocking roads and dismantling cameras is an absolute right in any civilised society. We further accept that JUST STOP ULEZ is a vitally important cause, which addresses the single most vital issue confronting the world today – ie, the impending disaster of a Labour government coming to power.

This change of climate is so severe that we, as a newspaper, must confront reality and place ourselves uncritically 100% behind the JUST STOP ULEZ movement.

We hope that our front page today with the snappy headline; 'Brave Ulez Camera Vandals Are All That Stands In-between Us And Fascist Labour Dictatorship So Let's All Smash The Cameras And Hang Effigies Of Labour Politicians Off The Poles', has clarified our position.

We apologise for any confusion caused, and any confusion in the future, when some bunch of hairy troublemakers organise a march to *(cont. for ever)*

"I'm a recovering melancholic"

Cordell

Family has nice holiday shock

by Our Aviation Staff
Dee Lay and **Kay Oss**

There were scenes of disbelief and anger around the world as news emerged that a British family had had a nice holiday and got home with no trouble at all.

Airlines immediately claimed this was nothing to do with them and they were not responsible in any way for people having "a nice holiday".

Britain's air traffic control also denied any culpability, insisting it had done everything it could to mess things up.

The father of the family told the press, "Yeah, we went to the airport and unbelievably there was our plane, which took off on time and then, on the way back, it did the same.

"We didn't have to stay at the airport for a week or pay extra for a hotel or anything. It was great."

The government has launched an inquiry into how such an unprecedented incident could have occurred.

Said a spokesman, "We can only apologise and reassure the public that we will do everything in our power to make sure this doesn't happen again."

"As a result of the air traffic disruption, many planes are in the wrong place"

NATS to bolster back up system

by Our Airport Correspondent
Oscar Foxtrot

THE head of National Air Traffic Services (NATS), Martin Rolfe, has apologised for the flight chaos which engulfed UK airports on Bank Holiday Monday, after a technical glitch crashed NATS computers. He confirmed that NATS will now look at upgrading its back-up system.

"Whilst the A3 binder and a biro back-up worked incredibly well in what was a highly stressful situation, we're now seriously considering popping down to Rymans and buying another couple of A4 binders and some highlighters," Mr Rolfe told reporters.

"This would supercharge NATS' ability to pass on vital flight information to our air traffic controllers, in the event of another catastrophic computer failure."

LATE NEWS: Britain's favourite staycation destination revealed. It's the Departures Lounge, Terminal 3, Heathrow.

MORTIMER & WHITEHOUSE GONE FISHING (BBC2)

FIRST SEASON

LATEST SEASON

DAILY 🔺 EXCESS

FRIDAY SEPTEMBER 8, 2023

'I WAS MURDERED BY THE FUGGIN' DUKE OF EDINBURGH' SAYS THE LATE MOHAMED AL-FAYED

by Our Pharaoh Tale Staff
Con Spiracy

IN AN exclusive interview with the Daily Express (channelled through the well-known medium and PR man, Michael Cole) the late Mohamed Al-Fugger told this newspaper that he had not, in fact, died peacefully in his bed at a very old age, but had been murdered by Prince Philip acting in collaboration with MI6, the Passport Office, and the entire British establishment.

Mr Fugger confirmed that the husband of the former Queen had personally run him over in a white Fiat Uno in order to prevent him from telling the truth about what really happened to the late Princess Diana.

Mr Fugger said of the Duke, "The fuggin' shirtlifter nazi fuggin fugged me and now I have fugged off for good." *(Not continued age 94)*

Notes&queries

What are the Chiltern Hundreds?

● The Chiltern Hundreds were a group of victims of the worst miscarriage of justice ever to strike the Home Counties. In 1878, 753 middle-class residents of Boring-on-Thames were accused of shoplifting Chiltern cheese (a popular mix of Cheddar and Stilton) from Ye Olde Cheese Shoppe in the village. This was based on the evidence of the store detective, Eric 'Blind' Pugh, so called because he was constantly drunk and who, in the retrial, was found to have a vendetta against the entire community who refused to buy him a drink in the upmarket and somewhat overpriced local hostelry, the Chiltern Firehouse, which later burned down in suspicious circumstances.
M.P. Retiring, Cornwall

● Nonsense! The Chiltern Hundreds is a mechanism to get round the Resolution of the House of 2 March 1624, stipulating that Members of Parliament cannot directly resign their seat. Instead, they are appointed to be Crown Steward and Bailiff of the Chiltern Hundreds. *(I'm sorry, this can't be right. In 2023, this can't be the only way for a mature democracy to get rid of Nadine Dorries? Ed.)*

SCHOOLS BREAKING UP – ALL GOING TO RAAC AND RUIN!

"Hi, kids! This is your new school uniform"

"Any ideas, Education Secretary?"

"Nothing concrete"

"Everything is collapsing and we're not learning any lessons"

"I know how you feel"

"It's crumble for lunch!"

GCSE MATHS EXAM

1 Your school was built in 1982. If the aerated concrete it is made from was designed to last 30 years, what year would it be sensible to take some action to prevent it collapsing?

a 2010

b 2020

c 2023, the day before term starts

2 Do you think that your best course of action now is to:

a Continue with this examination?

b Continue but do so from underneath the desk?

c Leave the building quietly and very quickly?

You have two hours to complete this exam. Or ten minutes. Or five years. There's no way of knowing! Good luck!

Revised school vocabulary

The three Rs
Roofing, Rubble, and Reconstruction.

Assembly
What is required before you start the new school year.

Examinations
What the surveyor should have done years ago in the boarded-up science block.

School run
Short sprint from classroom to outside lesson when ceiling looks dodgy

New term
Term applied to government who won't increase funding, ie ****s!!!

....

STRUCTURAL ENGINEERING QUESTIONS ANSWERED

Q: What is the difference between RAAC and RAAB?

A: One is dense, full of hot air, dangerous and past its expected useful life. The other is a type of concrete.

....

Sarah Vain
Putting the 'me' in mediocre

IS it just me or does nothing in Britain work anymore?

None of our institutions. None of our infrastructure. None of our public services. None of our leading corporations.

From the head of air traffic control to the director of the water company to my over-priced electrician who won't come round to fix my new air frier, even when I urgently need it on a Sunday morning, the stories about this third-rate country of ours are all the same.

Nobody does the job properly. Everyone is lazy and tries to get away with doing the bare minimum *(Is this enough words?)*

(Not quite. Ed – keep going.)

Nothing and nobody works. *(You've already said that. Ed.)*

It's almost as if the government that has been in power for the last 13 years has run the country into the ground. Possibly because it contains my useless ex-husband *(That's enough. Ed.),* who's too busy dancing around nightclubs with young men half his age to do his job properly, whatever that is now. *(I said, that's enough. Ed.)*

What happened to all those people who aren't British who were so good at doing things? Where have they gone? No one knows. No one cares. Nothing works, not even this column. *(I agree. Ed – time for a long lie-down.)*

"Come on... let's do crazy shit"

SENSATIONAL REBRANDING GRIPS ENTIRE WORLD!

Social media commentators were rocked today by the news that leading messaging platform Private Eye has been rebranded as 'Y'.

In a statement, Lord Elon Gnome said, "It made perfect business sense to abandon sixty years of loyalty, experience and goodwill, generated by one of the most recognised logos in the media world. Y is the future state of unlimited interactivity creating a global market place, in which nobody has any idea of what I'm currently talking about.

"All around the world, people will be saying, 'They've rebranded Private Eye,' to which the response will be 'Y?'"

CRASH STREET KIDS

Learning Support Assistant, specialising in Emotuional Literacy
Bracknell Forest Council job listing

A pervert who entered horse stables 'with intent to commit a sexual offence' told police he was in an 'unstable situation'.
Lancashire Telegraph

Response Form – daft new Local Plan Consultation (Regulation 18)
Ealing Council consultation response form

16:00 Last Word Lady Betty Boo... 28 mins
BBC Sounds app

'We're not going away': PM delivers 'straightforward' mess...
Sky News

Minnie Driver: Managing Expectations
This event has been cancelled due to unforeseen circumstances
South Bank Centre website

Boris Johnson arrives at Balmoral to resign as Queen...
Sun Online

Elton John brings down the curtain on Glastonbury with a barnstorming greatest hits set in what could be his last performance in England
MailOnline

Claire Connelly
Chief Financial Officer, Clearly Drinks
BBC News

Millions set for Easter getaway with delays likely
By Oliver Slow
BBC News

CERN, World's largest Physics laboratory uses Linux to power its **hardon collider** ... More than 90% of world supercomputers run on Linux. There...
Linux for beginners

shamima bacon is in the spotlight
GBNews

Map: Which areas of France are worse for house burglaries? | How to pick up free items in France
Connexion French magazine newsletter

Minister faces questions from Laura Kuenssberg after wee...
BBC News

But Labour is already talking about reversing Jeremy Hunt's crapping of the lifetime allowance
The Times

Boris Johnson admits misleading Parliament over Partygate but says it was 'intentional'
City AM (via MSN News)

US shoots down new unidentified object over Canada
4h | US & Canada
BBC

News
Police arrest man outside Buckingham Palace
London World (via Google News)

Two marine flags - the red ensign and the shite ensign
Morphets Auctioneers lot listing

Open day at village graveyard
Bradford Telegraph and Argus

Activity at 'public sex' layby falls by 85% but more action is planned
Eastern Daily Press

UK Conservative lawmaker faces ejection from Parliament for groping strangers at a London club
By Jill Lawless | AP
Washington Post

Everything you need to know about Cambridge's free Strawberry Fair that attacks 30k visitors in a day
Cambridgeshire Live

Tewkesbury Council votes in secret against plans to be more open
BBC News website

Miriam Cates, who represents Penistone and Stocksbridge, will introduce a "sex education transparency" Private Members' Bill today to urge the Govern-
Telegraph

ANUS id card Swipe System Upgrade - IMPORTANT
NHS Lothian staff email regarding new ID card system

Suzy Eddie Izzard
British comedian
Google

Sadiq Khan blocks free public lavatories on the London Underground
Telegraph

We are looking for an euthanistic and self motivated individual
NHS England apprenticeship advertisement in Bristol

Woman arrested on suspicion of possessing fireman after police search Northumberland house
Newcastle Chronicle

Perthshire scientist's premature ejaculation treatment can't come quickly enough
The Courier

Queen's coffin reopens
BBC News

● The following services are not available at the practice any more, contact them for more details: Appointments
GP Surgery update, Manchester